English Language Education Across
Greater China

BILINGUAL EDUCATION & BILINGUALISM
Series Editors: **Nancy H. Hornberger**, *University of Pennsylvania, USA* and **Colin Baker**, *Bangor University, Wales, UK*

Bilingual Education and Bilingualism is an international, multidisciplinary series publishing research on the philosophy, politics, policy, provision and practice of language planning, global English, indigenous and minority language education, multilingualism, multiculturalism, biliteracy, bilingualism and bilingual education. The series aims to mirror current debates and discussions.

Full details of all the books in this series and of all our other publications can be found on http://www.multilingual-matters.com, or by writing to Multilingual Matters, St Nicholas House, 31-34 High Street, Bristol BS1 2AW, UK.

BILINGUAL EDUCATION & BILINGUALISM
Series Editors: Nancy H. Hornberger *(University of Pennsylvania, USA)* and Colin Baker *(Bangor University, Wales, UK)*

English Language Education Across Greater China

Edited by
Anwei Feng

MULTILINGUAL MATTERS
Bristol • Buffalo • Toronto

Library of Congress Cataloging in Publication Data
A catalog record for this book is available from the Library of Congress.
English Language Education Across Greater China/Edited by Anwei Feng.
Bilingual Education & Bilingualism: 80
Includes bibliographical references and index.
1. English language–Study and teaching–China. 2. English language–Study and teaching–Foreign speakers. 3. English language–Social aspects–China. 4. Bilingualism. 5. Language acquisition. I. Feng, Anwei
PE1068.C5E54 2011
428.0071'051–dc22 2011000601

British Library Cataloguing in Publication Data
A catalogue entry for this book is available from the British Library.

ISBN-13: 978-1-84769-350-1 (hbk)
ISBN-13: 978-1-84769-349-5 (pbk)

Multilingual Matters
UK: St Nicholas House, 31–34 High Street, Bristol BS1 2AW, UK.
USA: UTP, 2250 Military Road, Tonawanda, NY 14150, USA.
Canada: UTP, 5201 Dufferin Street, North York, Ontario M3H 5T8, Canada.

Copyright © 2011 Anwei Feng and the authors of individual chapters.

All rights reserved. No part of this work may be reproduced in any form or by any means without permission in writing from the publisher.

The policy of Multilingual Matters/Channel View Publications is to use papers that are natural, renewable and recyclable products, made from wood grown in sustainable forests. In the manufacturing process of our books, and to further support our policy, preference is given to printers that have FSC and PEFC Chain of Custody certification. The FSC and/or PEFC logos will appear on those books where full certification has been granted to the printer concerned.

Typeset by Datapage International Ltd.

Contents

Contributors vii

Foreword
   David Crystal xi

1 Introduction: The Apex of 'the Third Wave' – English Language across Greater China
   Anwei Feng 1

Part 1: Sociolinguistic Profiles of Countries and Regions across Greater China

2 The English Language in Mainland China: A Sociolinguistic Profile
   Jeffrey Gil and Bob Adamson 23

3 English-knowing Bilingualism in Singapore: Economic Pragmatism, Ethnic Relations and Class
   T. Ruanni F. Tupas 46

4 English Language in Taiwan: An Examination of its Use in Society and Education in Schools
   Irene Wen-ling Chen and Jessie Ju-Chen Hsieh 70

5 Improving the Standards and Promoting the Use of English in Hong Kong: Issues, Problems and Prospects
   David C.S. Li 95

6 English Use and Education in Macao
   Ming Yee Carissa Young 114

Part 2: Convergence and Divergence of English Language Use and Education in Different Regions in Mainland China

7 The 'English Curriculum Standards' in China: Rationales and Issues
   Xiaotang Cheng 133

8 Primary School English Language Teaching in
   South China: Past, Present and Future
   Yuefeng Zhang and Jinjun Wang 151
9 English Immersion in Mainland China
   Haiyan Qiang, Xiaodan Huang, Linda Siegel and Barbara Trube ... 169
10 Family Background and English Learning at Compulsory
   Stage in Shanghai
   Weicheng Zou and Shaolin Zhang......................... 189
11 Economic Development and the Growing Importance of
   the English Language in Guangxi
   Binlan Huang... 212
12 Trilingual Education Policy Ideals and Realities for the
   Naxi in Rural Yunnan
   Dongyan Ru Blachford and Marion Jones.................. 228
13 Learning English as a Third Language by Uyghur
   Students in Xinjiang: A Blessing in Disguise?
   Mamtimyn Sunuodula and Anwei Feng.................... 260

Index 284

Contributors

Bob Adamson is a Professor of Curriculum Studies at Hong Kong Institute of Education. He publishes in the fields of language policy, comparative education and curriculum studies. His books include *China's English*; *Comparative Education Research Approaches and Methods* (with Mark Bray and Mark Mason); *Higher Education in Post-Mao China* (with Michael Agelasto); and *Changing the Curriculum* (with Tammy Kwan and Chan Ka Ki).

Dongyan Ru Blachford is Associate Dean (Faculty of Graduate Studies and Research) and Associate Professor in the Department of International Languages, Faculty of Arts, at the University of Regina, Canada. Her research interests include ethnic education and language policy, bilingual and trilingual education, and international education. She has published in book chapters and journals such as *The Pacific Review*, *Journal of Contemporary China*, *Nationalism & Ethnic Politics*, and *World Ethno-National Studies*.

Irene Wen-ling Chen has been teaching English and drama in universities of Taiwan for years. Her major interests include EFL teacher training and the development of English language learning curricula for different levels of schooling. Her recent teaching and research interest focuses on the development of intercultural communication education for EFL learners in the context of Taiwan.

Cheng Xiaotang is currently Dean and Professor at the School of Foreign Languages and Literatures of Beijing Normal University. He holds an MA degree in language teaching and a PhD degree in linguistics. He teaches and researches ELT methodology, language learning theory, syllabus design and materials development, and teacher education. His major publications include *A Course in English Language Teaching*, *English Learning Strategies*, *Evaluating and Designing ELT Materials*, *Task-based Language Teaching* and *A Functional Approach to Discourse Coherence*.

Anwei Feng is Reader in Education at Bangor University, Wales, UK. He teaches, researches and publishes in areas including bilingual education, citizenship education, TESOL and intercultural studies in education. His recent books include *Bilingual Education in China* (2007) and *Becoming Interculturally Competent through Education and Training* (2009, with M. Byram and M. Fleming).

Jeffrey Gil (PhD) is a Lecturer in ESOL/TESOL at Flinders University, Australia, where he is involved in the development, teaching and administration of ESL and TESOL topics. He has also taught at university level in China. His research interests include English as a global language and China's minority languages and cultures.

Jessie Ju-Chen Hsieh has been teaching in technical colleges and universities in Taiwan since 1998 in the areas of public relations, integrated marketing communications and English as an international communicative language. Her recent research interests are concerned with intercultural language education, education for intercultural citizenship and international English. She is currently running two community newspapers in Taipei.

Binlan Huang is Professor of English at the College of Foreign Languages, Guangxi University, China, where she teaches and supervises MA students in linguistics. She earned her doctorate in education at the University of Hull, UK. Her research interests include foreign linguistics and applied linguistics, SLA and intercultural studies. She has undertaken quite a few national and provincial research projects and published books, book chapters and journal articles in all these areas.

Xiaodan Huang is Professor of Education at the Shawnee State University, USA. Her research interests range from teacher education policy, teacher ethics, to multicultural education. Since 2000, she has been actively involved in the English immersion project in China, as the Director of CCUEI on the American side, with regular visits to the immersion schools and developing curricular materials for the project.

Marion Jones is an Associate Professor of Economics at the University of Regina, and was Vice-President of the Chinese Economists' Society 2007–2008. She has conducted research in rural China, particularly Yunnan and Sichuan, since 1991, having fallen in love with China's southwest and its minority peoples while a foreign student at Fudan University. She also works on social welfare for aboriginal peoples and other vulnerable groups in western Canada, and on migrant workers in China.

David C.S. Li obtained his BA in Hong Kong, an MA in France, and a PhD in Germany. His research interests are related to the study of social aspects of language use in multilingual settings. He has published in three main areas: World Englishes and perceptions of 'Hongkong English', code-switching in Hong Kong and Taiwan, and EFL learning difficulties and error-correction strategies.

Haiyan Qiang is Professor of Education at the South China Normal University, China. Her research interests range from comparative education, curriculum and instruction, language education and gender education. She has rich overseas experiences: graduate studies in the University of Massachusetts; visiting academic fellow in the Institute of Education University of London and in OISE of the University of Toronto. She has led several joint international research projects, one of which is CCUEI, the English immersion project in China.

Linda S. Siegel is a Professor in the Department of Educational and Counselling Psychology and Special Education and holds the Dorothy C. Lam Chair in Special Education at the University of British Columbia. She is currently the President Elect of the Division of Learning Disabilities of the Council of Exceptional Children. She was a member of the US National Panel in the literacy development of language minority children and youth.

Mamtimyn Sunuodula has a background in educational psychology. He taught psychology and conducted research in Uyghur education in Xinjiang. He worked for the BBC World Service and the British Library before becoming a specialist in Asian and Middle Eastern information resources at Durham University. He currently teaches research skills to doctoral students and Chinese language and culture at undergraduate level.

Mary Barbara Trube is a teacher educator at Ohio University-Chillicothe, Ohio, USA, with 40 years of experience in programmes for students (P-16) as an instructor and administrator. Dr Trube provides professional development for in-service educators, participates in curriculum design and development, and conducts teacher and site evaluations. Her research topics include English immersion, project approach, multicultural education and programme assessment.

T. Ruanni F. Tupas is Senior Lecturer at the Centre for English Language Communication, NUS, Singapore; Dr Tupas is the 2009 Andrew Gonzales Distinguished Professorial Chair holder (awarded by the Linguistic Society of the Philippines); a 2008 Philippine National Book Award Finalist; and Project Director (with K.C. Lee) of the S$485,000 project on Capability-Building of English Language Curriculum Developers in ASEAN universities (awarded by the Singapore-based Temasek Foundation).

Jinjun Wang is Chairperson of the Institute for Bilingual Education at Qujing Normal University. He is also Chair of the Board of BOESTEDU Ltd. He currently teaches English in the College of Foreign Languages, Qujing Normal University. His focused areas of research include bilingual education, intercultural studies, comparative education and TEFL.

Carissa Young is Associate Professor at Macao Polytechnic Institute. She pursued her doctorate in Language and Linguistics and two master's degrees in English teaching and IT in Education in the UK. Since 1991, she has been teaching and coordinating university English programmes. Her papers on English teaching, learner strategies and Macao education have appeared in international journals and edited books.

Shaolin Zhang is a Professor in Applied Linguistics at the College of Foreign Studies at the Guangxi Normal University, China.

Weicheng Zou is a Professor and Director of the Applied Linguistic Research Center in the Foreign Language School at the East China Normal University in Shanghai, China. He also serves as Editor-in-Chief of *Foreign Language Learning: Theory and Practice*. His major interest is in language education, especially teaching English as a foreign language to Chinese learners.

Yuefeng Zhang is Assistant Professor of School Partnership and Field Experience Office and Department of Curriculum and Instruction at the Hong Kong Institute of Education. Her main research interests include curriculum studies, English language teaching and learning, Learning Study and teacher education. She has publications in these areas.

Foreword

Two questions continually tease students and scholars of global English – especially those interested in the statistics of English use. What on earth is happening in India? What on earth is happening in China? The vast populations of these two countries impact immediately on any estimates we dare to make about the number of people in the world who speak English. We await an up-to-date evaluation of the situation in India. This book provides just such an evaluation for China.

But quantitative data is of far less interest than qualitative. It is not the number of speakers that matter, but their spread, their character and the range of linguistic situations in which they are using English. This sociolinguistic perspective is critical, and it is good to see it present from the opening chapter. A regional perspective is critical too. Generalisations about language use in China often fail to take account of the huge diversity that exists – not only in languages and dialects, but in language policies, planning and pedagogical implementation. It is rewarding to see so many regions of China given separate treatment in this collection – as well, of course, as to see a separate analysis made of the situations in Singapore, Taiwan, Hong Kong and Macao.

Plainly, we can observe a sociolinguistic transition rapidly taking place in China. The timeframes that accompanied such transitions in the past no longer obtain. The internet, in particular, has changed everything, and the rate at which the Chinese have taken to this new technology is bound to have a significant effect on English language awareness, learning and use. The question of fluency remains open: we do not yet know just how well or how often people are using the language, and statistics will remain uncertain until more precise information is available. But, as is pointed out, the increasing presence of competent Chinese English contributions in internet forums is an indication of the speed of progress.

Another indication is the arrival of linguistic creativity. One of the most interesting things I read in this collection was the way a new variety of English – the authors call it China English – is emerging in the literature and the media. Such localised varieties can be predicted for any country that has adopted English as a medium of communication; but hitherto this has been observed chiefly in countries where English is a first or second language. Notions such as American English, Australian English, Caribbean English and Indian English are familiar, not least with reference to the linguistically distinctive literatures they have produced. All countries will develop such literary English varieties in due course, but I imagined that it would take quite some time before we would see such varieties develop in countries where there is no historical tradition of English cultural contact. China is altering that expectation, and cases like Taiwan are providing us with a further affirmation of the fuzziness that exists between the notions of second language and foreign language.

Anwei Feng and his colleagues have done English language scholarship a great service in providing such a wide ranging and detailed account of a linguistic region that is going to play an increasingly important role in the future of English. I saw English in China, hitherto, as through a glass darkly. The image is much brighter now.

David Crystal

Chapter 1
Introduction: The Apex of 'the Third Wave' – English Language across Greater China

ANWEI FENG

This volume, as the title suggests, aims to provide comprehensive coverage of English language use and education across countries and regions in Asia normally defined under the umbrella term, Greater China. The concept of Greater China has been used frequently by economists, political scientists and sociologists to refer to countries and territories including mainland China, Hong Kong, Macao and Taiwan because of the historical ties and the growing economic, cultural and socio-political interactions and activities between them. However, the phrase is also used occasionally in a wider sense to include Singapore and other countries in Southeast Asia, and even other parts of the world, owing to their sizeable Chinese communities (Harding, 1995). In the literature of language education, this term has rarely made an appearance. Recent volumes on English language education, for example, either deal with mainland China exclusively (Adamson, 2004; Feng, 2007; Lam, 2005; Zhou, 2004) or cover many countries in Asia or the Far East that happen to be geographically close (Ho & Wong, 2003; Kachru, 2004; Kirkpatrick, 2002).

As a concept fully laden with socio-political, economic and cultural connotations (Harding, 1995), its potential implications for education in general across the territories and for language education in particular should be appreciated and investigated. This was a major impetus to produce this volume. As the concept is perceived in various ways, to define the scope of the volume and make meaningful comparisons, we do not adopt the concept in its wider sense, but focus on countries and territories that can be seen as the 'core parts' of Greater China. These core parts are geographically close, demographically dominated by ethnic Chinese and culturally, economically and socio-politically interrelated.

More importantly, for a volume on language education, the core parts or territories we choose to study are those that either speak Chinese as their mother tongue or use it as an official language. The rationale behind this selection criterion is that we wish to see how the use of English and English language education impact on Chinese, which is either the mother tongue or an official language in these societies, even though the former is the focus of our study. Hence, mainland China, Hong Kong, Taiwan, Macao and Singapore are chosen in line with this criterion and are examined in turn in this volume. Among these territories, mainland China receives most attention owing to its size and diversity of population.

Another major impetus to compile this volume derived from reviews of the recent literature on the spread of English across cultural and linguistic boundaries. The literature is extensive and well acknowledged. However, there seems to be a lack of agreement on how the historical and current spread of English can be appropriately portrayed. One model often claimed to summarise well the history and current situation of the spread of English and cited widely, including by the authors in this volume, is suggested by Kachru (1985, 1986, 1992b, 2005). With this model, the complex phenomena of the spread of English are graphically conceptualised as three concentric circles: *the inner circle, the outer circle* and *the expanding circle.*

At the centre is the inner circle, traditionally seen as the base of English where the language is used as the native, first or dominant language in public domains, or English as the Native Language (ENL) territories (McArthur, 2001). This circle, to a large extent, reflects the result from what is often termed the first diaspora (Baugh & Cable, 1993; Kachru, 1992b) characterized by the spread of English in the 17th and 18th centuries and involved the migration of significant numbers of English speakers from the British Isles to North America and Australasia. The most noteworthy outcome of this diaspora, juxtaposed with the spread of other languages such as French, Spanish and Portuguese during the same period, is the fact that English was established as the national language of a number of new nation states, including the USA, Canada, Australia and New Zealand (Fishman, 1977). It is commonly suggested that this outcome is a crucial factor in the development of English as a global language.

The outer circle, according to Kachru (1985, 2005), comprises countries such as Singapore, India, Hong Kong, the Philippines, Nigeria, South Africa and Zambia, where English has a long history of institutionalised functions and is used as a second/official language, i.e. English as a Second Language (ESL) territories (McArthur, 2001), usually in formal domains such as education, law, governance and mass media, or the language of the social elite (Crystal, 1997). This circle is often said to be the result of the second diaspora (Kachru, 1992b) that brought about the spread of English in the colonial context. Many authors, such as Crystal (1997) and Kachru et al. (2006), cover in detail the historical development of English into a second and/or official language in regions or countries including South Africa, West Africa, East Africa, South Asia, Southeast Asia and the South Pacific.

The outermost circle is termed the expanding circle, comprising most countries, other than those in the inner and outer circles, including, notably, the world's most populous countries such as China, Russia, Japan and Brazil, where English is taught and learned in most cases as a foreign language, the English as a Foreign Language (EFL) territories (McArthur, 2001). The expanding circle is usually seen as a phenomenon in the post-colonial era when the most rapid spread of English was witnessed all over the world (Bolton, 2006). Statistical data given in Crystal (1997) and McArthur (2001) show that speakers categorised as EFL users in this circle could amount to 1000 million, more than the numbers in the inner and outer circles put together. This global expansion is hugely and increasingly significant for any account of the notion of global English or the spread of English in the 21st century.

It is widely acknowledged that Kachru's three-circle model and his other discussions on varieties of English or world Englishes (notably, Kachru, 1986, 1992a) have contributed substantially to the debates on the spread of English, nativisation of English, English as a global language, world Englishes, etc. These notions themselves suggest the autonomy and plurality or heterogeneity of the English languages in the contemporary world. Kachru's theory is so well-received that it has triggered a sizeable amount of literature on the three concentric circles and on world Englishes. In 1997, a special conference held in Singapore to honour him resulted in a volume by Thumboo (2000) entitled *The Three Circles*. Many authors, such as Melchers and Shaw (2003), use the three-circle framework to structure their work on the history of English or variety of English. In a more recent anthology on world Englishes, Kachru et al. (2006) still make use of the three-circle model as the starting point and indeed the main theme of the massive *Handbook*.

The descriptive model, however, is not without criticism. McArthur (2001: 8) comments that the model 'seems to belong to a tidier world' rather than to the world in the 21st century. It can hardly address issues such as multilingualism, ENL varieties, the 'native speaker' controversies and issues related to changing ENL/ESL/EFL context as a result of mobility and globalisation in the world. In a similar vein, Crystal (1997: 54–60) lists 75 'territories' that may fall into either the inner or outer circle and suggests that the distinction between the outer and expanding circles can also be highly contentious. From a sociolinguistic point of view, Graddol (1997: 10) argues that the seemingly neutral labels, namely, inner, outer and expanding, 'locate the "native speakers" and native speaking countries at the centre of the global use of English, and, by implication, the sources of models of correctness'. This seems to relate the model to Phillipson's (1992: 17) highly political argument about the 'centre-periphery' relations between the dominating rich and dominated countries, a central theme of his theoretical approach to linguistic imperialism. Phillipson describes the relations of the countries as the 'core English-speaking countries' and the 'periphery-English countries' where English is used or learned as either a second language, a foreign language or an international lingua franca.

Although it is not our primary intention to engage in a detailed discussion on the three concentric circles, we are confident that the chapters included in this volume will help shed new light on the issues under debate. The chapters will provide evidence that the categorisation of the countries and regions under our investigation into the three circles may indeed prove over-simplistic because of the changing socio-political and economic contexts in these territories in the last few decades. For example, it may well be more debatable than two or three decades ago to label Singapore as an outer circle country because English is *the* medium of instruction in schools and other formal domains and has become increasingly the most frequently spoken language at home. In the same way, the exceptionally high status of English stipulated in the national curriculum and the popularity of using English as a medium of instruction in many schools and universities in China and Taiwan render the expanding circle label less convincing. As Bolton (2006: 294) argues, the 'exponential spread of English' in the last two decades was so unanticipated that 'a list of the major ten "English-knowing" societies in the world would include not only India but also China'.

In this introduction to the volume, we wish to appropriate a metaphor, the 'third wave', and use it, instead of diaspora or the three circle model, to describe the current surge in the spread of English in the changing contexts of the contemporary world. This metaphor is borrowed from Alvin Toffler[1] (1980), an American sociologist and futurist, who authored the book, *The Third Wave*. Based on the concept of each new wave pushing the older ones aside, Toffler used the term to refer metaphorically to the post-industrial society, which he predicted to be the information age characterised by a knowledge-based economy and an acceleration of changes that are driven by social demands worldwide for greater freedom and cultural diversity. It should be clearly stated here that the three waves conceptualised by Toffler do not correspond either in time or cause to the three 'English waves' we are discussing in this chapter. No one seems to have associated the concept with the spread of English. We appropriate the concept purely because we deem the 'wave' metaphor as more appropriate and effective than diaspora, or any other term, to catch the overall force of the current surge in the spread of English in the world, which pushes the older waves (the historical spread of English in the earlier times as described before) aside and penetrates into every corner of the earth. This new wave is both mightier because of the sheer size of the affected area and population in the world and more unpredictable because of increasing interactions and thus tensions between different cultural, ethnic and social groups in different socio-political, cultural, economic and educational contexts. Therefore, few can forecast how long it will last, what impact it will have on traditional nation states and what fundamental changes it may bring about for mankind, although attempts to forecasts the future of English are sometimes made (e.g. Graddol, 1997, 2006).

The appropriation of the metaphor for use in describing the spread of English is not only due to its capability to catch the power, height and width of the current surge. Its use also suggests that the driving force of the surge is more multifaceted and less traceable than that of previous waves, the first and second diasporas (Kachru, 1986, 1992b, 2005). In each diaspora, with the semantic implication of the term, mass movement of speakers from English-speaking countries to a new territory or colony was the norm and, as mentioned before, this movement usually resulted in a coercive relationship of power between the settlers and the aboriginal people or between the colonisers and the colonised. This largely undisputed cause/effect description helps explain why diaspora is widely accepted as a term to refer to the two historical events. However, very few have used the term to refer to the current phenomenon of the spread of English,[2] even though many agree that the world has witnessed the 'exponential spread of English' in the last two decades or so (Bolton, 2006). The hesitance to label the current spread as diaspora is apparently because the recent surge differs fundamentally from the previous two as it involves much less dispersal of native speakers of English to countries, particularly those in the 'expanding circle' where English is increasingly used for communication and taught in education institutions. The appropriation of the third wave concept is thus necessary for describing the current situation.

The third wave concept we adapt here also suggests that, historically, we see three major surges in the spread of English on a global scale, with the first two corresponding to the two diasporas[3] widely acknowledged in the literature and the third to the recent surge in the last two decades and beyond. In conceptualising the three waves on the basis of the existing literature and models to describe the history of the spread of English, we are able to represent the causes and effects of the three historical surges. The first wave was primarily the result of mass migration of English-speaking peoples. It has been extensively discussed, leading to the formulation of descriptive models such as Quirk's (1988) demographic model. It can be argued that the notion of diaspora is perhaps the most appropriate as far as the first period of the spread of English on a global scale is concerned. The second wave was on an even larger scale. However, as Brutt-Griffler (2002) points out, there was a limit to the migration-based colonialism. This wave was caused by a convergence of 'a transition from colonies as a refuge for Europe's surplus populations to the establishment of political and economic hegemony over entire peoples' and 'England's attainment of domination over the world market' (Brutt-Griffler, 2002: 114). This, for Brutt-Griffler (2002), was a new form of colonial control. In this context, the spread of English to Africa and Asia was prompted by political and economic means, not demographic. Therefore, the terminology used in the literature on the spread of English for this period often includes hegemony, subordination, dominance, imposition, conquest, English for the social elite, centre and periphery, and thus the notion of linguistic imperialism (Phillipson, 1992; Canagarajah, 1999), instead of the seemingly politically neutral term, diaspora, has dominated the discourse on studies of the second wave and further into the post-colonial period. Quirk (1988), however, sees the large-scale acquisition of the English language in this context as an 'econocultural' feature of the language by which the spread of English was for economic and cultural/intellectual reasons.

The third wave is unprecedented and the term, diaspora, is clearly even less relevant. This wave also involves the mobility of people on an unprecedented scale, but, unlike the first, it is a two way, or more precisely multidirectional movement brought about by various forces of globalisation. The language used for communication between internationally mobile people is English in most cases. Out of this context has grown the literature on 'English as an international language (EIL)', 'international English' as a variety, 'English as a lingua franca (ELF)', etc.

It is important to note, however, that in the post-colonial era, one does not need to travel to use or to acquire the language.

The commonplace perception that English is the most important language used globally has prompted governments in the 'outer and expanding circles' throughout the world to make language policies that favour bilingualism or multilingualism, which literally means 'macro-acquisition of English' (Brutt-Griffler, 2002). It has also motivated individuals, particularly ESL or EFL users, to make all efforts to acquire and use English. In analysing the African case, Mazrui and Mazrui (1998: 78) conclude that nowadays more and more people learn English 'simply because it is the most important language globally'. Graddol (2001) believes that of all continents, Europe has been the most affected by the rise of English since World War II. Official statistics prior to 2004 show that more than 90% of all secondary school pupils were learning English. In some countries, mostly Eastern European countries that joined the Union in 2004, most schools have rapidly replaced Russian with English as a school subject (Modiano, 2006). The same is true in South America. Despite suspicion about the implications of the spread of English and some xenophobic legislative attempts by some countries to curb the advance of the language, the continent has witnessed a rapid growth of English as the primary foreign language taught in schools and used in societies. The avid demand for acquiring the language is clearly manifested by the ever-increasing number of private language schools that offer regular or crash courses in English (Rajagopalan, 2006). The exponential growth of the spread of English in Asia has been even more striking. This could be illustrated by the astronomical figure of Japan's US$20 billion investment in 'English conversation' education or of some 300 million people toiling at English lessons in China (Honno, 2006).

To return to the concept of wave, we feel confident to claim that the current exponential growth is perhaps *the* apex of the third wave, and indeed of all waves, as in human history English has never penetrated so widely and deeply into the hearts and minds of individuals and societies, particularly the societies outside the 'inner circle', and it is difficult to imagine that the apex will repeat itself in the future. We believe the chapters included in this volume help justify this claim with sufficient evidence.

The chapters in this volume are divided into two main parts. The first part, comprising five chapters, presents panoramic and penetrating overviews of the sociolinguistic and, in most cases, historical profiles of the countries and regions under investigation. As defined at the outset of this chapter, these territories consist of mainland China, Singapore,

Taiwan, Macao and Hong Kong. This part is intended to allow an easy comparison of the overall situation, policy and practice among the countries and regions under study. The second part consists of seven chapters that 'zoom in' to examine different regions in mainland China, mainly due to its size and diverse population. It starts with a chapter that presents an insider's perspective of key national policy documents on English language education for the new century and moves on to case studies that give detailed accounts of English language use and education in different settings, including economic and political centres such as Shanghai, Pearl River Delta Region and Xi'an, and less-developed regions or areas in Guangxi, Xinjiang and Yunnan. As the introductory notes in the following pages will show, chapters in the second part differ in terms of the approaches to interpreting phenomena as they are unfolded and to examining issues, while keeping the common focus on English language use and English teaching and learning.

Readers do not have to go very far to find the answers to the questions raised earlier: the question of whether the spread of English has reached its apex; the question on the tension between the role of English and politics; and the question on the notion of linguistic imperialism. In Chapter 2, Gil and Adamson provide a panoramic view of the historical and sociolinguistic context of English language use and education in mainland China. On the basis of an analysis of the history of English in China, they conclude that 'the role and status of English in China have reached unprecedented heights, although fundamental cultural and political tensions remain'. The tensions they refer to in the People's Republic of China (PRC) era are illustrated by the sudden shift on a national scale from English to Russian in the early 1950s, the swing back from Russian to English in the early 1960s, the victimisation of English teachers during the Cultural Revolution (1966–1976) and the current 'mania' for English, or in short by the pendulum swings between economic modernisation and politics. Indeed, their historical overview reminds us that the unprecedented popularity and promotion of English in the country can change rapidly as policy making and policy changes are usually driven primarily by the political agenda of the country above anything else. Currently, political stability, economic development and internationalisation appear to be balanced despite some resistance and resentment to the unusually high status given to English. How or, more realistically, how long this balance can be maintained remains to be seen.

The Singapore story as it unfolds in Chapter 3 differs from the PRC story in many ways. Tupas also starts with a historical overview, but he points out that utilitarianism or pragmatism that aims for economic advancement and political stability has remained the ultimate ideology for nation-building and education initiatives. 'English-knowing bilingualism' has played a crucial role in its endeavour to achieve these aims. Given the context in which English, generally perceived as the language of 'pragmatism' and a 'neutral lingua franca', is used in all formal domains and as the medium of instruction in all schools and universities, with the 'mother tongues' of the ethnic groups being taught only as school subjects, not surprisingly English has gradually encroached into more and more homes, resulting in more than 28% of Chinese, Malay and Indian families speaking English at home in 2005 as opposed to 23% in 2000. The reverse trend is true with 'mother tongue' use. For Tupas, this is a 'worrying' situation. Besides this, Tupas lists other issues such as bilingual elitism, subtractive bilingualism, inequality in language access and lack of attention paid to cross-cultural dimensions in bilingual education.

In terms of English language use and education, as Chen and Hsieh reveal, Taiwan has apparently gone very far, to the extent that the government has even made English 'a quasi-official language' on the island. The prestigious status of the language in society, which has led to an exponential increase in its use in many important sectors of society and in many schools as a medium of instruction, coupled with the fact that each year tens of thousands of students go abroad to study in the 'inner circle' countries, has created not only the social and economic elite, but also a huge middle-class population of English-knowing bilinguals. There is at least some indication that Taiwan is moving towards being an 'outer circle' country in linguistic terms. While sufficient evidence is given to the popularity of the language in society and the rigorous responses by the government and local authorities to the demands for English language education, Chen and Hsieh remind us that the current 'national obsession' is creating a linguistic divide that further disadvantages the socially and economically underprivileged and contributes to reproduction of a coercive relationship of power.

The story of Hong Kong is complex in theory and in practice. Because of its economic, political and cultural positioning in the region, Li indicates that Hong Kong has to invest heavily in its 'biliteracy and trilingualism' policy. Despite the popularity of English and the heavy investment in the language, not many learners in Hong Kong are found to be competent in English. Li believes that this is largely due to the immense linguistic distances between English and Chinese and the lack of a favourable environment to use English. Of Li's arguments, two are particularly pertinent to the overview of the literature on ENL/ESL/EFL and world Englishes presented earlier in this chapter. While most scholars with an interest in the linguistic situation of Hong Kong take the metropolis as a society where English is used as a second language (ESL) owing to its long colonial history and common use of English in formal domains, Li holds the view that Hong Kong shows many characteristics of a society where English is used as a foreign language (EFL). His argument is primarily based on the observation that few Hongkongers use the language for intra-ethnic communication. A second argument related to the first is a bold challenge to the notion of 'Hong Kong English'. To Li, some key conditions are yet to be met for the English used in Hong Kong to qualify as a localised variety of English.

Among the territories under discussion in this volume, Macao is unique in that it was formerly a Portuguese colony. However, Young points out that with the recent economic boom fuelled by the gaming industry, English, a non-colonial and non-official language, has surpassed Portuguese to become the most important language for cross-cultural communication. Using Kachru's (1992a) model of linguistic functions for her analysis of the spread of English in Macao, Young presents evidence of the ever-increasing interpersonal, regulative and creative functions of the language in that society. In schools, English has become a compulsory subject from pre-primary level onwards, and is the medium of instruction for most subjects at tertiary level. However, she finds that English curriculum development has been affected by the lack of a long-term English education policy and the diversified educational system. Macao policy makers are clearly facing the dilemma or paradoxical situation that lack of a unified policy has resulted in varied levels of English proficiency, but unification of the system would lead to 'intrusion' on administrative and educational freedom that the current society values.

Part II starts with Cheng's chapter on the English Curriculum Standards (ECS) promulgated by the Ministry of Education in China in 2001. The unique value of this chapter lies in the fact that few can avoid evaluating or at least mentioning the ECS documents when they examine English language education in the country in recent years. Cheng, as a policy maker, presents an insider's account of the context and rationales behind the series of policy documents for both primary and secondary schools. He argues that the 'standards' and the teaching approaches 'advocated' in the ECS, though often criticised as unrealistic, are socially and theoretically sound. Theoretically, as Cheng argues, international research evidence in the bilingualism literature shows that bilinguals have cognitive advantages over monolinguals and the advocated approaches to English language teaching and learning prove effective when they are used appropriately to address contextual factors. Socially, there is a common perception in China that English is the global language and citizens in China should master the language for sustaining economic development as a society and for overall intellectual development and career advancement as individuals. An interesting phenomenon Cheng observes is that despite the flexibility suggested in the ECS with regard to achievement targets for regions less developed economically and less accessible to resources, few regions or provinces show willingness to lower the 'standards'. Positive changes as a result of the new curriculum are already evident and will become even more apparent in time.

Chapter 8 by Zhang and Wang follows Cheng's chapter well. As one of the most developed regions in the country, South China has always taken the lead in economic development and in education. After a brief historical overview, Zhang and Wang describe the unique position of the Pearl River Delta region and its frequent contact with the outside world through hugely profitable economic activities, including the money-spinning China Export Commodities Fair held biannually in Guangzhou. The value of English is apparent and the demand for English-knowing bilinguals is high. In many primary schools, the standards set in the ECS for English language education, which are said to be too demanding for many school elsewhere, do not seem to stay abreast of the increasing need for bilinguals in South China. The schools often offer many more English lessons per week than the periods officially required. Despite issues such as examination-orientated approaches and inequality in English provision, the ECS has had a push effect on professional development, teaching resources, textbook designing and teaching methodology. It is worth noting that, in addition to 'authentic' situations such as interactions in English with business people or tourists from abroad, many opportunities are created by schools and other education authorities to make pupils use English to 'do things'. Examples include conversing in 'English corners' (designated areas in a school compound or in parks or squares where one can go to practise speaking English), celebrating Western festivals such as Christmas in English, competing in English speech contests, etc. All these illustrate the unique status and role of English in schools in prosperous regions.

Qiang, Huang, Siegel and Trube in Chapter 9 describe a partial English immersion model that was developed in Xi'an more than a decade ago and has since spread to other parts of China. The popular model implemented in over 50 kindergartens, primary and secondary schools is a good reminder that, resources permitting, English language provision can be far more rigorous than is stipulated in the ECS. Like Chapter 8, Qiang *et al.* give quite a detailed account of the theoretical ground of the programme and principles in implementing the model. The very existence of this model, which allows 50% of the school time to be immersed in English, not only suggests the popularity and rigour of English provision, but also a high tolerance level by the authorities for the use of English as a medium of instruction and communication despite opposing voices in the bilingual education discourse and in society (see Feng, 2005, 2007; Hu, 2008).

Chapter 10 by Zou and Zhang presents empirical data to show how parents in Shanghai, another major economic and political powerhouse, perceive the importance of English and what measures they take to ensure that their children do not lose out in the 'national movement'. The perceived importance is historically, economically and socially constructed and parents are under enormous pressure to outsource extra-curricular lessons and activities to ensure that their children receive the best English education. By analysing empirical data collected from a relatively large-scale survey, Zou and Zhang conclude that there is indeed a clear correlation between pupils' test results and family background, more so in terms of parents' education background than in terms of their social and economic status. Interestingly, they observe that '[a]lthough Shanghai is not a society (not yet) where English is frequently used in any formal or informal domain, the societal involvement, the numerous English programs accessible to the public as well as to school children, the ever-increasing number of native English speakers and highly proficient non-native speakers have created a *de facto* English as a second language environment'. Both Chapter 9 and Chapter 10 give an account of extensive English language use in schools and in modern societies that challenges the distinction between EFL and ESL and the three-circle model.

Moving on to Chapter 11 by Huang, we read the story of Guangxi. This region (Guangxi Zhuang Autonomous Region in full) is traditionally labelled as one of the most underdeveloped regions in China with the largest population of Zhuang-speaking people. However, its economy has been booming since 2004 when the first China-ASEAN Exposition was held in Nanning, the capital city of the region. The region has gradually become the export-import hub linking China with 10 neighbouring countries. The rapid economic development stimulated by the exposition, together with other economic and cultural initiatives, and ever-increasing investment drawn from foreign companies have drastically pushed up the status of English in the region for the obvious reason that it is used as the lingua franca with business people, investors and tourists from ASEAN countries and beyond. Huang's research in the region suggests that even in Guangxi, traditionally labelled as underdeveloped, English is widely perceived as the key to economic advancement for the region and to individual life prospects. In schools, the ECS promulgated in 2001 by the central authority is being taken seriously, but often at the expense of the mother tongue, Zhuang, in Zhuang-dominated areas.

Blachford and Jones's account of a minority group in Yunnan in Chapter 12 draws from their ethnographic research data collected in a rural village in which the Naxi minority group reside. During their visits to the village, they witnessed the harsh conditions of the village school, the inadequately trained teachers, the actual English teaching classrooms, the lack of resources and the living conditions of pupils and local people. They also observed the sad realities of the largely neglected local written languages, Naxiyu and Dongbawen, and the poorly prepared pupils who, once stepping out of the village school, tend to drop out in highly competitive secondary schools. Despite a largely gloomy picture of English language education in their case study, Blachford and Jones's research findings give clear evidence that the tall order, i.e. the ECS in this case, impacts on even remote corners of the country. The impact seems to be jointly created by the ideological beliefs of policy makers and influential scholars, the local economy and parents' dreams to make their children capable enough to find their own future outside the village. Against all odds, in this village school, there is an English teacher, though trained for another trade, and two periods (1.5 hours) of English were included in the school curriculum, apparently by purging Dongbawen lessons that had originally existed. Again, against all odds, pupils in the school were found to be extremely enthusiastic in learning the foreign language.

In Chapter 13, the last chapter, Sunuodula and Feng also present empirical data collected from a minority region that is thousands of miles away from Yunnan. They conducted ethnographic interviews among a group of tertiary Uyghur students in Xinjiang, the largest minority region in the northwest of the country. In the chapter, they start with an overview of the limited literature and research indicating that Uyghur pupils, particularly those in remote districts, are largely kept out of the system in English language education. Even in situations when minority students are offered English, they are often reported to have lower motivation and greater difficulties than their majority counterparts in learning the language. Many authors state that the national drive to English education is bound to further marginalise them. Sunuodula and Feng's empirical data, however, suggest that despite being disadvantaged in English provision in earlier schooling, the Uyghur students were found to be highly motivated to learn the third language, competitive in the learning process and optimistic about the prospects. Using Bourdieu's (1977) concept of cultural capital, they argue that the current 'English drive' may not inevitably further disadvantage minority groups as they are aware of the importance and are willing to invest in the linguistic capital that the majority Han students equally find difficult to attain. Given equal conditions, minority pupils may have a good chance to become empowered and confident in their own linguistic and cultural identity, and at the same time, they may be better integrated into the mainstream society.

We hope that, after reading these chapters, readers can see as we do that these writings contribute significantly to our understanding of English language use and education in countries and regions across Greater China. In each chapter, we can see how English was perceived and used in each society in the past, in what domains and to what extent it is used today, how policies concerning English language education are formulated, and in what ways they are implemented in schools in each territory investigated. It is apparent that different readers may benefit differently from these chapters. Policy makers, for example, may compare and contrast various dimensions of language planning and policy making across Greater China in Part I to identify similarities and differences in these and the socio-political, cultural and economic consequences of the policies. Through comparison and understanding of language planning policies and consequences, they are more likely to make informed decisions to address issues in their own context. Through reading the chapters in Part II, language teachers in China will gain insights into the rationale of different models and teaching approaches, such as those specified in the ECS, and into societal needs for language use, parents' expectations and other dimensions relevant to language education. With these insights, they can place themselves in a better position to address the issues surrounding English language education.

For theorists and researchers, the chapters offer much food for thought. With the empirical evidence and theoretical argumentation presented in this volume, researchers may wish to revisit concepts or models that are often taken for granted or inadequately debated. For example, as mentioned before, they may look again into the traditional distinction between EFL and ESL territories, in association with the three-circle model. The chapter on Taiwan informs us that English has already been made a 'quasi-official language' on the island. This quasi-official status, together with the exponential increase in English use in society and rigorous promotion of English language in schools have rendered the notion of an EFL territory increasingly problematic, particularly in many formal domains. In Shanghai, Zou and Zhang observe that an ESL situation is evidently in the forming. The popular immersion programme in Xi'an in which students may study up to 50% of their school subjects in English also suggests traditional EFL teaching and learning are a thing of the past in these schools. The Singapore story, in the same way, challenges the distinction between ESL and ENL territories. English is the dominant language in the education system and other formal domains. It is increasingly spoken as the first language in the homes of the three major ethnic groups. Singlish, as it is enthusiastically studied and debated, is evidence that the English language has been nativised in the country.

Another concept that is widely debated in the literature of the spread of English and begs a revisit is the notion of linguistic imperialism as defined by Phillipson (1992). Throughout this volume, there is little evidence to show that the current spread of English across Greater China is imposed by the West, leading to a dominant and subordinate or centre and periphery relationship as characterised in the discourse of linguistic imperialism. As Morrison and Lui (2000) assert, people seek and use English, not because they are unenlightened victims of ideological and cultural hegemony; they do so for various economic, socio-cultural and political reasons. In the post-colonial era, as the last chapter argues, the concept of cultural and linguistic capital (Bourdieu, 1977) appears more relevant to the contexts investigated in this volume.

Emerging from some chapters in Part II on English language in mainland China is the issue of authentic language use. Learners of English in China may use English in the following situations. First, opportunities to use English in naturalistic settings for real life communication have increased dramatically in recent years because of China's frequent contacts with the world, foreign trade, tourism, growing mobility of workforces, telecommunication and so forth. As Chapter 12 shows, even a child from a peasant family in a remote village may have opportunities to talk to foreign visitors. The second setting is the classroom for English learners (either adults or pupils). English lessons as authentic discourse of language use are well debated in the literature (Ellis, 1994; Kramsch, 1993; Widdowson, 1980). Recently, the authenticity of such language use is further enhanced by learners' increasing exposure to native English-speaking teachers, authentic texts and approaches such as Computer Assisted Language Learning (CALL), Content and Language Integrated Learning (CLIL), Task-Based Language Teaching (TBLT) and partial immersion, which all encourage using the language to 'do things' or carry out tasks. Furthermore, in China, many other situations are artificially created purely to improve learners' ability to communicate in English. These situations, as Chapters 2, 8, 11 and 13 show, include the long-lived and ever popular 'English Corners' found in every city or town and even in some school yards; numerous English competitions organised locally or nationally at various levels and for various language skills; various types of tests for people from all walks of life who aspire to climb social ladders; 'English Festivals' organised by schools when every pupil is expected to speak in English, etc. These situations are often only mentioned in passing in the literature in Chinese; few theorists and researchers have discussed or researched into how authentic they are in terms of language use and to what extent they are effective in raising learners' motivation to learn English and in helping acquire the language.

Finally, it is important to note the issues caused by the third wave as revealed in the chapters because these issues pose a challenge to all stakeholders in education, including policy makers, researchers and educators across Greater China and beyond. Among the issues, two are most outstanding and commonplace. The first is the issue of social divisiveness that seems to occur in all societies, particularly salient in affluent societies such as Singapore (Chapter 3) and Shanghai (Chapter 10). As linguistic capital, English is fervently pursued by all people in society. Economically and socio-politically privileged groups have an upper hand because they have access to the resources necessary for amassing this capital and the power to make the rules so that they appear to gain it legitimately. As Bernstein (1973: 202) points out, 'how a society selects, classifies, distributes, transmits and evaluates the educational knowledge [the linguistic capital in our case] it considers to be public reflects both the distribution of power and the principles of social control' (author's interpretation). Thus, theoretically, social divisiveness appears to be an inevitable outcome of the socially constructed value and status of English in these societies. Is it truly inevitable? Can the third wave, as conceptualised in this chapter, have any impact on the existing social order? Chapter 13 discusses the potential effects of the third wave in favour of minority groups, but points out that they remain potential unless key stakeholders such as policy makers and educators have truly engaged themselves to bring about change.

The second is the issue of home or minority language maintenance in this third wave. It is less of an issue in societies such as Hong Kong and most regions of mainland China where the home language is the majority language. As Bisong (1995) asserts, from a Nigerian perspective, a few hours of exposure to English per week, which is the case in public schooling, is unlikely to affect a pupil's home language competence as mother tongue acquisition is a non-stop and ever-present process. Even in cases in which parents send their children to English medium schools, they want their children to become bi/multilingual. However, the issue is clearly more severe in societies and regions such as Singapore, Taiwan, Guangxi and Xinjiang, where the home language is often a dialect or a minority language not used in formal domains. As the chapters show, many Chinese dialects spoken by Singaporeans are clearly dying. Zhuang in Guangxi apparently faces a similar fate, particularly now that the majority of Zhuang pupils follow the same educational system as the majority Han pupils. How dialect speakers and minority language users in these societies can acquire the second (usually the official/national) language and the third language (English) while maintaining their linguistic identity is undoubtedly a huge challenge for all. Existing theories and models in trilingualism and trilingual education offer us only a starting point to explore the issue further by looking into all sociopolitical, economic and cultural factors in each context.

Notes

1. It is worth noting that Toffler's (1980) theory is so popular and influential in China that he is listed as one of the 50 foreigners shaping China's modern development by the official *People's Daily* (Renminwang, 2006). The appropriation of his third wave notion is therefore also motivated by the assumption that this notion impacts on readers from China more than any other possible terms.
2. Despite consistency in the use of the term 'diaspora' in Kachru's earlier discussions (1986, 1992b, 2005) to refer to the two historical periods of the spread of English as described before, strangely, Kachru et al. (2006) organised the first 15 chapters, which present the historical context in their handbook by four diasporas. In this handbook, the first diaspora is said to refer to the forceful replacement of Celtic languages by English in the British Isles because of the extension of English political power. The second refers to the spread of English to North America and Australasia (the first diaspora in Kachru's earlier writings) and the third is said to refer to the period when English was transplanted in the colonial context (roughly the second diaspora). The fourth diaspora is claimed to be the 'world Englishes today' (Kachru *et al.*, 2006: 3), corresponding to the 'third wave' appropriated in this chapter. This organisation of the history of diasporas is inconsistent with Kachru's earlier descriptions.

3. We are aware that some recent discussions (e.g. Brutt-Griffler, 2002; Kachru *et al.*, 2006) draw attention to the early spread of English in the British Isles roughly in the 14th, 15th and 16th centuries (King, 2006). It is of course important to recognise this initial period when the history of English is studied. However, this was a period when English was spreading at a limited local level through conquest (Quirk's (1988) imperial model applies to this case). To maintain a consistent description of the history of the *global* spread of English (the two diasporas discourse), we do not take the initial English conquest as a major wave.

References

Adamson, B. (2004) *China's English: A History of English in Chinese Education* (Asian Englishes Today). Hong Kong: Hong Kong University Press.

Baugh, A.C. and Cable, T. (1993) *A History of the English Language* (4th edn). Englewood Cliffs, NJ: Prentice Hall.

Bernstein, B. (1973) On the classification and framing of educational knowledge. In B. Bernstein (ed.) *Class, Codes and Control: Vol. I* (pp. 202–30). London: Routledge & Kegan Paul.

Bisong, J. (1995) Language choice and cultural imperialism: A Nigerian perspective. *ELT Journal* 49 (2), 122–132.

Bolton, K. (2006) World Englishes today. In B.B. Kachru, Y. Kachru and C.L. Nelson (eds) *The Handbook of World Englishes* (pp. 240–270). Malden, MA: Blackwell.

Brutt-Griffler, J. (2002) *World English: A Study of Its Development*. Clevedon: Multilingual Matters.

Canagarajah, A.S. (1999) *Resisting Linguistic Imperialism in English Teaching*. New York: Oxford University Press.

Crystal, D. (1997) *English as a Global Language*. Cambridge: Cambridge University Press.

Ellis, R. (1994) *The Study of Second Language Acquisition*. Oxford: Oxford University Press.

Feng, A.W. (2005) Bilingualism for the minor or the major? An evaluative analysis of parallel conceptions in China. *International Journal of Bilingual Education and Bilingualism* 8, 529–551.

Feng, A. (ed.) (2007) *Bilingual Education in China: Policies, Practices and Concepts*. Clevedon: Multilingual Matters.

Fishman, J.A. (1977) *The Spread of English: The Sociology of English as an Additional Language*. Rowley, MA: Newbury House.

Graddol, D. (1997) *The Future of English?* London: British Council.

Graddol, D. (2001) The future of English as a European language. *The European Language Messenger* 10 (2), 47–55.

Graddol, D. (2006) *English Next: Why Global English may Mean the End of 'English as a Foreign Language*. London: British Council.

Harding, H. (1995) The concept of 'Greater China': Themes, variations and reservations. In D. Shambaugh (ed.) *Greater China: The Next Superpower?* (pp. 8–34). Oxford: Oxford University Press.

Ho, W.K. and Wong, R.Y.L. (eds) (2003) *English Language Teaching in East Asia Today*. Singapore: Times Academic Press.

Honey, J. (1997) *Language is Power: The Story of Standard English and Its Enemies*. London and Boston: Faber and Faber.

Honna, N. (2006) East Asian Englishes. In B.B. Kachru, Y. Kachru and C.L. Nelson (eds) *The Handbook of World Englishes* (pp. 114–129). Malden, MA and Oxford: Blackwell.

Hu, G. (2008) The misleading academic discourse on Chinese–English bilingual education in China. *Review of Educational Research* 78 (2), 195–231.

Kachru, B.B. (1985) Standards, codification, and sociolinguistic realism: The English language in the outer circle. In R. Quirk and H. Widdowson (eds) *English in the World: Teaching and Learning the Language and Literature* (pp. 11–30). Cambridge: Cambridge University Press.

Kachru, B.B. (1986) *The Alchemy of English: The Spread, Functions and Models of Non-native Englishes*. Oxford: Pergamon Press.

Kachru, B.B. (ed.) (1992a) *The Other Tongue: English across Cultures*. Urbana, IL: University of Illinois Press.

Kachru, B.B. (ed.) (1992b) The second diaspora of English. In T.W. Machan and C.T. Scott (eds) *English in its Social Context: Essays in Historical Sociolinguistics* (pp. 230–252). New York: Oxford University Press.

Kachru, B.B. (2004) *Asian Englishes: Beyond the Canon* (Asian Englishes Today). Hong Kong: Hong Kong University Press.

Kachru, B.B., Kachru, Y. and Nelson, C.L. (2006) *The Handbook of World Englishes*. Malden, MA and Oxford: Blackwell.

King, R.D. (2006) First steps: Wales and Ireland. In B.B. Kachru, Y. Kachru and C.L. Nelson (eds) *The Handbook of World Englishes* (pp. 30–40). Malden, MA: Blackwell.

Kirkpatrick, A. (ed.) (2002) *Englishes in Asia: Communication, Identity, Power and Education*. Melbourne: Language Australia.

Kramsch, C. (1993) *Context and Culture in Language Teaching*. Oxford: Oxford University Press.

Lam, A.S.L. (2005) *Language Education in China: Policy and Experience from 1949*. Hong Kong: Hong Kong University Press.

Mazrui, A.A. and Mazrui, A.M. (1998) *The Power of Babel: Language and Governance in the African Experience*. Chicago: University of Chicago Press.

McArthur, T. (2001) World English and world Englishes: Trends, tensions, varieties and standards. *Language Teaching* 34, 1–20.

Melchers, G. and Shaw, P. (2003) *World Englishes*. New York: Arnold.

Modianno, M. (2006) Euro-Englishes. In B.B. Kachru, Y. Kachru and C.L. Nelson (eds) *The Handbook of World Englishes* (pp. 223–239). Malden, MA and Oxford: Blackwell.

Morrison, K. and Lui, I. (2000) Ideology, linguistic capital and the medium of instruction in Hong Kong. *Journal of Multilingual and Multicultural Development* 21 (6), 471–486.

Pennycook, A. (1994) *The Cultural Politics of English as an International Language*. London: Longman.

Phillipson, R. (1992) *Linguistic Imperialism*. Oxford: Oxford University Press.

Quirk, R. (1988) The question of standards in the international use of English. In P.H. Lowenberg (ed.) *Language Spread and Language Policy: Issues, Implications and Case Studies* (pp. 229–241). Washington, DC: Georgetown University Press.

Rajagopalan, K. (2006) South American Englishes. In B.B. Kachru, Y. Kachru and C.L. Nelson (eds) *The Handbook of World Englishes* (pp. 145–157). Malden, MA; Oxford: Blackwell.

Renminwang [People] (3 August 2006) 50 foreigners shaping China's modern development. On WWW at http://english.people.com.cn/200608/03/eng20060803_289510.html on 02-03-09.

Schneider, E.W. (2003) The dynamics of world Englishes: From identity construction to dialect birth. *Language* 79 (2), 233–281.

Toffler, A. (1980) *The Third Wave*. London: Collins.

Thumboo, E. (ed.) (2000) *The Three Circles of English, Language Specialists Talk about the English Language*. Singapore: Unipress.

Widdowson, H.G. (1978) *Teaching Language as Communication*. Oxford: Oxford University Press.

Zhou, M.L. (ed.) (2004) *Language Policy in the People's Republic of China: Theory and Practice since 1949*. Boston: Kluwer Academic.

Chapter 2
The English Language in Mainland China: A Sociolinguistic Profile

JEFFREY GIL and BOB ADAMSON

> *Conquer English to make China stronger!*
> Slogan, Li Yang Crazy English

Introduction

The phenomenon of English as a global language has impacted on countries all around the world. In Asia, it is having significant and profound effects on the region's language policies, educational systems and patterns of language use (Bolton, 2008; Kirkpatrick, 2008; Nunan, 2003). As Tsui and Tollefson (2007: 18) point out, 'English is perceived by language policymakers in Asian countries as a multinational tool that is essential for achieving national goals and by individuals as an indispensable resource for personal advancement'. Asian countries have therefore promoted the acquisition of English by their citizens, such as by making English an official language, a language of instruction or a working language, increasing resources for English language learning and teaching, and increasing the amount of curriculum time allocated to English. At the same time, however, considerable tensions and concerns over the preservation of cultural identities and languages have resulted from these attempts to respond to the role and status of English as a global language (Nunan, 2003; Tsui & Tollefson, 2007).

This pattern of conflicting views of English reflects mainland China's historical experience. The English language currently enjoys unprecedented importance in the Chinese context, to the extent that it could be argued that its use is now more widespread and has higher status than at any other time in its interaction with mainland China.

> A vast national appetite has elevated English to something more than a language: it is not simply a tool but a defining measure of life's potential. China today is divided by class, opportunity, and power,

but one of its few unifying beliefs—something shared by waiters, politicians, intellectuals, tycoons—is the power of English... English has become an ideology, a force strong enough to remake your résumé, attract a spouse, or catapult you out of a village. (Osnos, 2008)

This is a far cry from earlier contacts between China and the English language in the 18th century, when interpreting was left to *compradores* – Chinese intermediaries who had a smattering of Pidgin English but who suffered for their profession by being shunned by their communities (Feng, 1863, cited in Teng & Fairbank, 1979: 51). The role and status of English has waxed and waned with the political tides, being particularly affected by fluctuations in mainland China's relations with the outside world (Hertling, 1996; Pride & Liu, 1988). Ross (1993) sums up the relationship between foreign language learning and the political climate in mainland China:

> Support for foreign language training is high when sustained participation in the global community is deemed commensurate with China's political and economic interests and low when it is perceived as threatening to internal political and cultural integrity. (Ross, 1993: 42)

Throughout its time in China, English has experienced several drastic changes in its role and status, reflecting long-standing concerns about the cultural impact of learning English on the one hand and a desire to learn English to gain access to the knowledge and opportunities it provides on the other. Adamson (2002) analyses the situation as follows:

> The relationship between the English language and Chinese politics and society has historically been ambivalent. At different times, English has been associated in China with military aggressors, barbarians, and virulent anti-Communists. But English is also a principal language of trade partners, academics, technical experts, advisors, tourists and popular culture. At worst, the language has been perceived as a threat to national integrity. At best, it has been seen as a conduit for strengthening China's position in the world community. These tensions have manifested in policy swings that have far-reaching impacts, most notably for the educational system. (Adamson, 2002: 231)

This chapter is concerned with how the tensions of English in Chinese society have played out from the 17th century to the present day – our main focus. The historical overview, based on eye-witness accounts and second-hand sources, has an explanatory function, bringing out the factors underlying the tensions. The chapter also attempts a portrayal of the current situation regarding the role and status of English in mainland China. This is methodologically challenging, as – to the best of our knowledge – no formal, comprehensive survey or census has been conducted. We argue that, although English has no official status in mainland China, the language is used extensively in science and technology, the media, business, tourism and international connections, and the formal and informal education systems. The evidence to support this argument will be necessarily sketchy and anecdotal in places. Our analytical framework is derived from Kachru (1983) and adopted by linguists such as Nielsen (2003) and Velez-Rendon (2003) to describe the role of English in other countries. This framework consists of four categories of language use: the instrumental function, the interpersonal function, the regulative function and the imaginative/innovative function (Kachru, 1983: 42).

Mainland China is classified as an expanding circle country in which English is used as a foreign language (Kachru, 1985). There are significant differences between the families of English and Chinese languages: for instance, the former are alphabetic and phonetic; the latter are ideographic and tonal. These linguistic differences exacerbate the challenges to Chinese people of learning English – challenges that, as noted above, also have political and cultural dimensions that have influenced official attitudes towards the language at various times in history.

Historical Background: The Impact of English and China's Reaction

In its early dealings with other countries and cultures, the Chinese imperial court maintained a tribute system that required visiting envoys and ambassadors to present themselves to the Emperor as representatives of vassal states. This manifestation of superiority was reflected in initial contacts with the English language. According to Bolton (2002), the first instance occurred in 1637 when four ships under the command of Captain John Weddell arrived in Macao and Guangzhou. This was a short-lived contact, as Weddell and his ships were expelled from China six months after their arrival. The English language arrived more permanently in 1664 when the British established a trading port in Guangzhou, and were restricted to cantonments on Shamian Island

(Pride & Liu, 1988). When knowledge of other languages was needed, the Chinese government traditionally relied on non-Han people or social outcasts to provide translating and interpreting services (Adamson, 2002; Hung, 2002). Business dealings between the British and the *compradores* in Guangzhou gave rise to Pidgin English, which was used for communication (Pride & Liu, 1988).

When the relationship between China and the Western maritime nations turned violent, defeat in the 'Opium Wars' forced the Chinese government to sign a series of treaties giving foreigners privileges such as the opening of ports, extraterritoriality and the right to live in the hinterland (Roberts, 1999). Under these circumstances, the English language began to penetrate mainland China, through the activities of missionaries, customs officials working on behalf of the imperial government and the residents of treaty ports. The latter tended to deal with local merchants and domestic servants through an increasingly elaborate form of Pidgin English (Bolton, 2002; Spence, 1980; Wood, 1998) it was also used on occasion between Chinese speakers whose dialects were mutually unintelligible (Cole, 2007). A utilitarian knowledge of English provided good economic prospects for Chinese people.

However, the foreign presence in mainland China often met violent resistance from peasants backed by members of the aristocracy (Hsü, 1990). In some parts of the country, harassment was a fact of daily life for foreigners and their Chinese associates, whether from organised groups such as the Small Swords triad group in the mid 19th century or randomly on the streets, as Robert Fortune records on his arrival in Fuzhou:

> Quang-yanga, quang-yanga—their term for foreigners—was rung in our ears, and frequently other appellations of much worse signification. Our Chinese servants, who walked by our side, were attacked and reviled for having any connection with us. (Fortune, 1847: 370)

An alternative reaction to foreign intrusion was a determination among some scholars and officials, such as Wei Yuan, Li Hongzhang and Zhang Zhidong, that Western military force had revealed China's inability to protect its territorial integrity, and the solution lay in self-strengthening the nation through technological transfer. One scholar, Feng Guifen, advocated a synthesis of Chinese and Western ideas – as encapsulated in the maxim, *zhong xue wei ti, xi xue wei yong* (Chinese learning for essential principles, Western learning for practical application) – that would allow the preservation of China's traditional culture while building up the nation's power (Pepper, 1996). Feng made the controversial suggestion to set up colleges to study foreign languages with a view to facilitating this process:

> If today we wish to select and use Western knowledge, we should establish official translation offices at Canton and Shanghai. Brilliant students up to fifteen years of age should be selected from those areas to live and study in these schools on double rations. Westerners should be invited to teach them the spoken and written languages of the various nations, and famous Chinese teachers should also be engaged to teach them classics, history, and other subjects. At the same time they should learn mathematics... If we now wish to adopt Western knowledge, naturally we cannot but learn mathematics. (Translated by Teng & Fairbank, 1979: 51)

In this way, Feng believed that China could 'learn the superior techniques of the barbarians to control the same barbarians' ('On the Manufacture of Foreign Weapons', translated by Teng and Fairbank, 1979: 53). In 1862, the first such college, the Tongwen Guan, was established in Beijing as part of the Zongli Yamen or Office of Foreign Affairs. English was the first language to be taught there and later Russian, French, German and Japanese were introduced (Hung, 2002). Similar schools were later set up in Shanghai, Guangzhou and Fuzhou (Pride & Liu, 1988; Roberts, 1999; Ross, 1992).

Following defeat in the Sino-Japanese War (1895) and the disastrous consequences of the Boxer Rebellion (1900), China embarked on comprehensive reforms that embedded Western learning and foreign languages in the school curriculum (Adamson, 2004; Roberts, 1999; Ross, 1993). These official moves boosted the status of English in Chinese society, enhancing interaction in the spheres of science and technology, economics and, in the major cities, popular culture. This effect carried over into the Republican period (1911–1949), which was initially marked by an intellectual revolution, the May Fourth Movement, which rejected the conservatism of Confucian scholars and embraced new ideas, particularly those from the West (Roberts, 1999). Political activists from all sides of politics saw foreign languages as a tool for struggle and personal transformation. Cities such as Shanghai became a melting pot for intellectual debate and multiculturalism, with Western philosophers, literati, jazz musicians and Hollywood film stars gaining popularity (Jones, 2001; Wood, 1998).

However, the Republican period degenerated into economic, social and political instability, with the increasing power of warlords. There was a backlash among some Chinese officials against English, who railed against the cultural erosion attributed to foreign languages and practices (Ross, 1992). During the Anti-Japanese War (1937–1945), however, the pragmatic need to collaborate with allies provoked a brief revival of English, but the situation changed again when the Chinese Communist Party (CCP) took power in 1949. In the early communist period, the CCP turned to the Soviet Union for mentorship. Russian became a prestigious language in mainland China, mainly for technological transfer, while English was officially condemned as the language of the enemy, the USA, who had supported the Nationalists during the Chinese Civil War, and who were ideologically opposed to the Soviet Union (Adamson, 2004). Nonetheless, academics were still encouraged to read journals and books in English in order to access developments in science and technology, and diplomats needed English for their work, including the bid by mainland China to provide leadership to non-aligned nations (Adamson, 2004).

After the breakdown of Sino-Soviet relations in the early 1960s, Russian lost its prestige and popularity, and English once again became the favoured foreign language. Learning English was undertaken for various cultural, educational and economic pursuits, although enthusiasm was tempered by political circumspection arising from the CCP's policy of 'walking on two legs' – economic modernisation (principally industrialisation) paralleled by political transformation of society through class struggle (Pepper 1996). The English language was valuable for the first leg but undesirable for the second, as starkly evidenced by the turbulent decade of the Great Proletarian Cultural Revolution launched by Chairman Mao Zedong in 1966. Broadly speaking, the aim of the Cultural Revolution was to destroy traditions and to purge what was perceived as the pernicious influence of foreign culture from Chinese society, using such methods as public humiliation of people associated with traditional beliefs and practices, the banning and destruction of Chinese art and Western art, the suppression of religious practices and the removal of those deemed to be 'taking the capitalist road' (Mackerras et al., 1998). The revolutionaries associated foreign languages with exploitation of the masses and with the bourgeoisie. Foreign books, films and broadcasts were banned (Cortazzi & Jin, 1996; Yao, 1993), while anyone who could speak a foreign language was considered a 'foreign spy' (Tang, 1983; Zhang, 2000).

Following Mao's death on 9 September 1976, mainland China abandoned the class struggle and resumed the economic modernisation programme, championed by the new paramount leader, Deng Xiaoping (Baum, 1994). The Four Modernisations, targeting agriculture, industry, national defence and science and technology, resulted in mainland China being once again open to the outside world. English learning became 'a mania for the nation' (Tang, 1983: 46), as the language became a requirement for further education, employment, promotion and overseas travel and training (Ross, 1993). The reforms resulted in spectacular economic growth and improvements in the standard of living, especially for people in urban areas.

However, there were limits to how much reform the nation's leaders would allow. Concerns over the impact of reforms on Chinese culture came to the fore in the Anti-Spiritual Pollution campaign in 1983–1984, which resulted in the banning of certain films, pop music and works of art (Adamson, 1998; Mackerras *et al.*, 1998; Spence, 1990). Foreign languages also came under scrutiny. They may have been seen as essential for modernisation, but this did not change the fact that 'foreign languages remained symbols of nonindigenous modernity' (Ross, 1993: 41). Political liberalisation (symbolised in student demonstrations by a statue portraying a Western-looking Goddess of Democracy) was not permitted at the same pace as economic reforms, creating tensions that erupted in the violent suppression of protestors in and around Tiananmen Square in Beijing in the early hours of 4 June 1989.

The 1990s witnessed an acceleration of economic reform and modernisation with spectacular results. In 1992, mainland China's GDP increased by 12% and for the years 1991–1997, GDP grew by an average of 11% (Meisner, 1999). The demand for English language skills intensified. As Jiang (2003) noted, with a hint of caution,

> governments are encouraging their citizens to learn English, parents are persuading, even forcing, their children to speak it and college students are doing English at the expense of their majors. (Jiang 2003: 6)

In the new millennium, English is still seen as vital for modernisation, but it has taken on another role: 'English for international stature' (Lam, 2002: 246–247). The APEC meeting in Shanghai in 2001 and the Beijing Olympic Games in 2008 were preceded by government-sponsored short courses in English and new television and radio programmes aimed at teaching basic English to enable officials and ordinary people to communicate with foreign visitors (*People's Daily Online*, 2000b, 2000c, 2000e; *South China Morning Post*, 2001a). Similar efforts took place in preparation for entry into the WTO (*South China Morning Post*, 2001b) and Shanghai recruited English teachers to help boost English proficiency for the World Expo in 2010 (*South China Morning Post*, 2004).

The Current Use and Status of English in Mainland China

The historical overview suggests that the role and status of English in mainland China have reached unprecedented heights, although fundamental cultural and political tensions remain. We now explore the scale of English penetration. It is difficult to determine how many people use English in the country because of issues such as how a 'user' is defined, and the methods deployed for counting users (Mackey, 2003). Zhao and Campbell (1995) suggest a figure of 200–300 million users of English, based on the number of school and college graduates, because all students study English at some point in their education. (Population growth over the past decade would inflate that figure by some 50 million, resulting in a total that equates to the entire population of the USA.) Obviously, not all these people speak English fluently or even at all: some studies have shown that despite years of study, some school leavers have very little or even no command of English (see e.g. Li, 1996). Nonetheless, the figure is indicative of the significance of the language in Chinese society, and, depending on one's point of view, the size of the potential damage that could accrue to the cultural integrity of that society or of the potential contribution that English could make to the economic development of mainland China.

In this section, we will focus on the role played by English in different spheres of life in mainland China. Our analysis will be structured around a framework that identifies four functions of language use in society. The four functions of language use in this framework are: the instrumental function, the interpersonal function, the regulative function and the imaginative/innovative function (Kachru, 1983: 42). We will then discuss how the tensions underpinning English in mainland China are manifested.

The interpersonal function of English

There are two aspects of the interpersonal function of a language: it acts as a link between speakers of different languages and also symbolises modernity and prestige (Kachru, 1983; Velez-Rendon, 2003). In mainland China, the interpersonal function includes science, technology and research, the media, business and tourism and international connections.

Academic research

Given the historical emphasis in China on technological transfer, and the dominance of English in academic discourse internationally, it is unsurprising that proficiency in the language is increasingly a prerequisite. Prestigious institutions, such as Tsinghua University, publish academic journals in English (Li & Zhang, 2003). English is commonly used in international research conferences in mainland China and in joint projects with foreign academics, while Chinese academics need to be competent in the language to undertake academic exchanges, participate in overseas conferences or publish articles in international journals in order to gain a reputation or a promotion. Institutions are ranked according to the number of such publications, and mainland China's international standing in academic research, based on bibliometric measurement, has increased significantly since the Cultural Revolution, but the need for high competence in English creates a barrier for some academics (Zhong, 1998).

Media

English also has an increasing presence in the media, including daily, weekly and semi-weekly newspapers, periodicals, radio broadcasts, television, wire service and internet sites (Guo & Huang, 2002). Some of the better known examples are: *China Daily, Beijing Review, Shanghai Star, Shanghai Daily, Beijing Weekend, 21st Century English* and *The World of English*, plus English language versions of Chinese publications such as *People's Daily*. Many English language publications are intended for consumption by foreigners living in mainland China or overseas. There is also a Chinese readership, but their reasons for reading English language publications may not be for their information value, as Guo and Huang (2002) describe:

> domestic audience members tend to approach English media with the explicit purpose of improving their English. They view the media content as a product of trained professionals, offering handy English equivalents to prevailing Chinese concepts, a way of describing current events in English, and a collection of simple and straightforward English expressions. (Guo & Huang, 2002: 221)

In addition to print material, there are also various radio and television programmes in English. CCTV 9, mainland China's English language television channel, began broadcasting on 25 September 2000. China Radio International has '290 hours of broadcasting every day in 43 languages' (China Radio International, 2008), with a comprehensive service in English. Many of these media have complementary websites in English.

Indeed, the internet is a major force in the expansion of English in mainland China. By the end of 2008, there were some 2,878,000 websites and over 16 billion web pages in the country, with 298 million 'netizens', whose favourite applications are entertainment (games and music) and instant communications (China Internet Network Information Center, 2009: 12, 27–28). Although statistics are not available regarding the role of English in internet usage among Chinese, there is anecdotal evidence that some Chinese netizens send emails in English or visit foreign websites (Jones, 2006). For instance, online editorials of British newspapers, such as *The Economist*, debating the ill-starred round-the-world torch relay that preceded the Beijing Olympic Games provoked lively contributions from Chinese citizens.

Business

In international business, English is regularly used in joint ventures and business communications between Chinese and foreign companies. Some 40,000 foreign companies are set up in mainland China each year, with an accumulative total of 25 million employees in 2007 (National Bureau of Statistics of China, 2009). A survey by Pang *et al.* (2002) of business people in Zhejiang found that English was used for communication via fax and email and some contracts were written in English. However, in the companies surveyed, only a small number of people were involved in this work, while the majority used English just for filling in forms and reading specialist literature. Many Chinese businesses also have English names for international recognition, i.e. *China Telecom*, *China Mobile*, *Bank of China*, *Agricultural Bank of China* and *Commercial and Industrial Bank of China*.

Tourism

In the first nine months of 2008, 18,352,700 foreign tourists visited mainland China (China Hospitality News, 2008), with their visits facilitated by 1838 tourist agencies that cater for international tour groups (National Tourism Administration of the People's Republic of China, 2008). The use of English in hotels, tour groups and travel agencies is pervasive. Airport announcements are made in Chinese and English, as are on-board announcements. Tourist literature and signs in English are commonplace in sites associated with tourism, such as museums, parks and scenic spots. English also has a 'getting around' function in major cities. Buses, subway trains and light rail vehicles have information and recorded announcements in English. Tourism has also given rise to what has been termed 'peddlers' English' – a variety of English used by street vendors and peddlers across mainland China to attract the attention of and bargain with foreign tourists (Pride & Liu, 1988; Zhao & Campbell, 1995).

International connections

English is used to convey information about and project an image of mainland China to foreign audiences. Figures from the China Bibliographic Library indicate that between 1995 and 2003, 94,400 translated works were published (*People's Daily Online*, 2004b). No exact figures for translations into English were given, but much Chinese literature and the works of important political leaders have been translated into English. According to Hung (2002: 330–331), 'the literary translation work of the Foreign Languages Bureau and Foreign Languages Press have always shown a clear ideological orientation. Writers and work selected for translation all served to reinforce the government's world view, which had no room for those considered antagonistic to the regime'. There is also a trend for English translations of Chinese texts aimed at Chinese audiences – as with other English language media, these translations are primarily used as an aid to learning the language (Hung, 2002).

A growing form of international connection is sport. Overseas basketball and football teams regularly visit mainland China, while there is an annual Formula One motor race in Shanghai and an international tennis tournament in Beijing, to name but a few such events. With English serving as the main language of these events, and Chinese athletes, such as Yao Ming playing professional basketball in the USA and Zheng Jie, who reached the semi-finals of the women's tennis championship at Wimbledon in 2008, demonstrating a high degree of competence in the language, English serves as a conduit for sporting connections.

Instrumental function

The instrumental function of language refers to 'English as a medium of learning at various stages in the educational system of the country' (Kachru, 1983: 42). The formal and informal education systems are the primary places where Chinese learn and come in contact with English.

Formal education

Many recent initiatives promote English language proficiency in the education system. In 2001, the Ministry of Education announced that English classes would begin in grade three of primary school with a view to starting classes from grade one in the future. (In some cities, English learning can start as early as kindergarten, when children learn through songs, games and toys.) Students continue their study of English: in junior secondary school, where it takes up 16% of the curriculum. In senior secondary school, 30% of the time is devoted to Chinese and a foreign language. Over 66 million junior secondary and over 16 million senior secondary students study English (Wang, 2007), with the syllabus envisaging the development of international perspectives and the strengthening of patriotism through the judicious choice of content (Wang, 2007). At the university level, every student has to study a foreign language for at least two years. Foreign language programmes are divided into two strands, one for foreign language majors and the other for non-foreign language majors. The first strand is handled by foreign language institutes and foreign language departments in universities, while programmes for non-majors are handled by language centres in universities (Cortazzi & Jin, 1996; Yao, 1993). The course for non-majors is officially known as College English (Wang, 1999). All students undertaking this course must pass the College English Test 4 (CET-4) to get their degrees, and are encouraged to take CET-6, which offers better job prospects, such as employment in international companies (Lam, 2005; Wang, 1999; Yao, 1993). English majors, on the other hand, are required to pass the Test for English Majors 4 (TEM-4), a more demanding test than the CET, in order to graduate, and are also expected to take the TEM-8, again to improve their employment prospects (Cheng, 2008).

An emergent trend is to teach secondary schools subjects such as mathematics and science through the medium of English. This mode of instruction, known as *shuangyu jiaoyu* (literally 'bilingual education'), has gained so much momentum – although not without controversy – that it is now 'rattling across the country like a juggernaut' (Hu, 2008: 196). In September 2001, the Ministry of Education issued a circular instructing all universities and colleges to use English as the medium of instruction for certain subjects, including information technology, biotechnology, finance, foreign trade, economics and law.

Informal education

In addition to formal education, English language studies can also be pursued through less formal television and radio programmes, community schools and private associations. Even less formal than these options are the 'English corners', such as designated areas in parks and squares where one can go to practise speaking English (Cortazzi & Jin, 1996; Zhao & Campbell, 1995). Informal English learning has become big business: a prime example is Li Yang Crazy English, a company that has developed physical strategies (such as shouting and making exaggerated hand movements) to help overcome Chinese students' shyness in using a foreign language, and has made its eponymous owner a multimillionaire.

Regulative function

The regulative function, the 'use of English in those contexts in which language is used to regulate conduct; for example, the legal system and administration' (Kachru, 1983: 42), does not officially exist as such in mainland China, as English has no status as a language of administration and is not used in domains such as the law courts (Pride & Liu, 1988). The use of English in regard to legal matters bears more resemblance to the interpersonal function. In 2000, judges in Beijing took part in a one-year English course. Gao Xiaoling, the official in charge of education and training for judges, saw English as important because 'with the increase in foreign related cases and international exchanges, we need more judges who know some English' (quoted in *People's Daily Online*, 2000a). What the judges reported that they used English for is similar to the uses described in the section on business. A judge from the No. 1 Intermediate People's Court said 'we often have to deal with business letters, faxes and other material written in English, so improving our English will help us do a better job'. Another judge in the same course wanted to learn English so he could learn about the legal systems of foreign countries (quoted in *People's Daily Online*, 2000a).

Later in the same year, an English language emergency hotline opened in the cities of Nanjing, Wuxi and Suzhou in Jiangsu Province. People in these cities can dial 110 to talk to an English-speaking police officer. The service was established to cater for foreign investors and tourists (*People's Daily Online*, 2000d). Police in Beijing were also trained in basic English, Japanese, Russian and Arabic in the lead-up to the 2008 Olympics. According to the Beijing Public Security Bureau, these languages would be used for public service, traffic control, security checks, crime and accident investigations, interrogations and imposing penalties (*South China Morning Post*, 2001c). Currently, it seems that English is in the initial phase of assuming a regulative function.

Imaginative/innovative function

English is used to express a variety of ideas, concepts and opinions in mainland China. These often differ from the cultural norms of Western societies, or represent a synthesis. Kachru and Nelson (2001: 17) refer to this phenomenon as 'bilingual creativity'. There is already a considerable amount of fictional and autobiographical literature written in English by Chinese writers that documents Chinese experiences (Zhang, 2002). A more recent trend is song writing in English, with heavy rock groups such as Tang Dynasty or punk groups such as Brain Failure synthesising

Western genres with Chinese musical traditions, including the use of the pentatonic scale (Cheng, 2006).

Gil (2005) identifies a number of other ways in which Chinese people use English creatively, drawn from his time living and working in mainland China. One example is questioning the authority of native speakers (in a debate about grammar, for instance). Another is 'talking back', whereby English is used to tease and make fun of native speakers and inner circle countries. Gil cites a description of himself written by a student:

> He is the tallest in our class. His hair is quite short and a little curly. He has many beards but he has shaved them off. He wears sports jumper and trousers which look quite active. Sometimes I think he is a little shy maybe because there are so many beauties in our class. I most like to hear him say "OK let's have a break". (Cited in Gil, 2005: 131)

Indeed, Gil reports that joking in English was commonly used to relieve tension during times of stress, such as the SARS epidemic in 2003. Classes were reduced, students were confined to the university campus and identification checks were carried out at the entrance to the university. This resulted in a generally dreary and, at times, fearful mood among the students and teachers. However, some students lightened the mood by writing various interpretations of the acronym SARS on a blackboard in the lobby of the foreign languages building:

> SARS means Smile and Remain Smile
> Start Abort Reboot Start
> Sorry And Repeat Sorry (advice for those who were in trouble with their girlfriends) (Cited in Gil, 2005: 137)

China English

So far, this chapter has discussed the impact of English on mainland China and provided a snapshot of its current use and status. Another aspect of mainland China's interaction with English that deserves attention is how mainland China has shaped the English language.

As English spreads around the world, it is influenced and altered by the new environments to which it spreads. As Trudgill and Hannah (2002: 124) observe, 'English has become or is becoming *indigenized*' in many parts of the world (italics original). To say that English *is* indigenised in mainland China would be an overstatement, as McArthur (2006) points out, but the *process* of indigenisation has been, and still is, occurring in mainland China. One result of this is mainland China's own variety of English, known as China English. Although there are some differences among scholars on the precise definition of the term, China English is generally defined as the variety of English used by people with a linguistically and culturally Chinese background, which exhibits Chinese features (Jiang, 2003; Liu, 2008; Pan, 2005). It is important to distinguish China English from Chinglish, another term often used to describe the English used in mainland China. Chinglish is heavily influenced by Chinese turns of phrase – Liu (2008: 30) offers the following examples of Chinglish: 'My stomach is hungry', 'His age is very young', 'His brain is clever'. At its extreme, Chinglish may even be unintelligible to other English speakers (Jiang, 1995; Kirkpatrick & Xu, 2002).

China English, on the other hand, is a variety of English based on Standard English but with uniquely Chinese features in pronunciation, vocabulary, syntax and discourse patterns. By way of example, speakers of China English tend to pronounce the sounds /θ/ (the first sound in 'thin') and /ð/ (the first sound in 'this') as /s/ and /z/ because these sounds do not exist in Chinese (Li, 1995). In terms of vocabulary, there are many words to describe Chinese objects, concepts and ideas, some of them transliterations of Chinese, such as *taichi*, *fengshui* and *kowtow*, while others are translations, such as four modernisations, open door policy and iron rice bowl (Kirkpatrick & Xu, 2002; Wei & Fei, 2003). China English also tends to omit subjects, making phrases such as 'very glad to write to you again' common features at the level of syntax (Kirkpatrick & Xu, 2002: 271). The discourse patterns of China English include explaining the reasons why one holds an opinion before stating the opinion and, similarly, when making a request, speakers of China English often give reasons for the request before stating the request itself (Kirkpatrick & Xu, 2002; Wei & Fei, 2003). China English is currently receiving much attention from both Chinese and Western scholars and its features are increasingly well documented (see, e.g. Jiang, 1995, 2003; Kirkpatrick & Xu, 2002; Li, 1995; Wei & Fei, 2003). However, most scholars agree that China English is still in the early stages of development. In a survey of 1251 students at Three Gorges University for example, Hu (2004) found that only 15.5% of students had heard of China English and only a slightly higher portion (22.6%) thought China English and Chinglish were different. This suggests that the Chinese population may still be largely unaware of this emerging variety of English.

According to Hu (2005: 38), the next step towards the indigenisation of English in mainland China will be 'when a literature starts to emerge (poems, songs, novels), and we reach a point when Chinese people take a pride in what will have become their second national language'. Although the current state of affairs may indeed be 'a long way from this target' (Hu, 2005: 38), there are examples of English used in this sense, as demonstrated by this chapter's discussion of the imaginative/innovative function.

The information on mainland China's interaction with English presented here suggests that the English language is becoming increasingly connected and entwined with Chinese society. However, as the next section shows, there are many factors that could significantly influence the ongoing use, status and development of English in mainland China.

New Concerns in the New Millennium

From the early days, when the language was quarantined on an island in Guangzhou, to its prestigious role and status in contemporary mainland China, English has been closely interlinked with the opening of the nation to the outside world and mainland China's acceptance of industrialisation as a key to regaining her political power on the international stage.

Yet, as Zhao and Campbell (1995) point out, despite mainland China's acknowledgement of the importance of English and the concerted effort to learn it, it would be inaccurate to assume that 'the Chinese government holds a positive or favourable attitude toward English, let alone its native speakers'. As noted earlier, opposition to the language has, at times, been virulent and violent, resulting in the death of some who were associated with it, while new concerns have also arisen, such as the opposition to the 'juggernaut' of bilingual education noted above. Official support for the language has traditionally been grudging and circumspect, although stimulated by the perceived benefits to the nation. While the current penetration of English suggests a softening of resistance, it would be inaccurate to say that the language is welcomed unreservedly in the various domains in which it is most prevalent. This section explores some of the prominent contemporary concerns.

English as a judge of talent and value

There is growing resistance to the tendency for competence in English to be used to judge a person's talent and value:

> At present, people who cannot speak English are considered second-class talents; people who cannot write in English are third-class

talents; and those who know nothing about English are not talents at all. (*People's Daily Online*, 2003)

Some young people, who might be expected to embrace language learning opportunities because of their status as 'netizens', seem to have reservations about English, as exemplified in the following letter to the editor of the *China Daily* (28 September 2000):

> Editor: Please allow me to present an example at the beginning of this letter. There is a junior middle school student, who proves himself the best student in the maths course in his class, but he is poor at English. The maths teacher appreciates him most, and expects him to do something special in mathematics in the future. But this student was not admitted into senior middle school just because of his poor English score which made him fail the national college entrance examinations. He has no other way to continue studying his favourite course. Maybe a future mathematician has been strangled. It's true that not every student is doing well at all subjects set by the national educational department. There are some students who are excellent in some subjects but fail in others, even though they are considered important by the educational authorities. Should these students be turned down by higher learning institutions?
> These students with special capabilities should be given opportunities to continue their study by improving educational system [sic] and not forcing them to be proficient in particular subjects.

English as a gatekeeper

Similar concerns have been raised over foreign language tests for scientists and other professionals wanting a promotion. The importance of this test is such that 'failing in this test, even a Nobel Prize winner will be rejected for promotion to professor, senior researcher, chief physician, or even class-I teacher in a school' (Jiang, 2003: 4). According to a report in the *People's Daily Online* (2004a), some Chinese intellectuals refuse to take part in such tests on the grounds that they are unfair because lack of foreign language ability does not indicate lack of ability in other disciplines.

Inequity of access to English

At the same time, inequity of access to English has become an issue of social justice. The vast differences between mainland China's rich coastal provinces and poor inland provinces, as well as urban and rural areas, are well known and these differences determine both the opportunities to learn English and the quality of the learning experience (Cortazzi & Jin, 1996a; Nunan, 2003). In addition, there is evidence to suggest a strong desire among members of mainland China's ethnic minorities to learn English (Dreyer, 2003; Gil, 2006), yet studies of language policies in ethnic minority areas show that provision of English in formal education is patchy at best (Adamson & Feng, 2009; Huang, 2007), which disadvantages minority students in accessing university education and well-paid jobs.

Conclusion

It is unpalatable to a nation that, historically, has a proud sinocentric worldview, to acknowledge the political and economic hegemony that English is perceived to represent, and accept that mastery of this language is necessary for mainland China to restore its self-esteem and prestige. The philosophy and approach of Li Yang Crazy English serve as an eloquent metaphor for attitudes towards the language over the past two centuries. Li Yang Crazy English is not premised on the notion of fostering a love for English and a sympathetic understanding of English-speaking cultures. Instead, its philosophy asserts that studying the language can help mainland China to develop as an economic superpower. In this regard, it has echoes of the self-strengtheners. Meanwhile, some of the practices, such as getting large rallies of students to hold their textbooks aloft and to yell in unison, are (at least for critics of Li Yang) uncomfortable reminders of the mass political mobilisations of the Cultural Revolution (Osnos, 2008). While associating Li Yang Crazy English with extreme politics is an overrepresentation, there have been times when there have been powerful and violent reactions against the English language and those associated with it. The goal of mainland China's officials has been to appropriate English while withstanding the forces of linguistic and cultural imperialism. The inability to preserve traditional culture and national integrity provoked backlashes against English, such as the patriotic education movement in the 1930s, the victimisation of English teachers during the Cultural Revolution and the repudiation of Western cultural artefacts in the Anti-Spiritual Pollution campaign of 1984.

However, given that the process of *zhongxue wei ti xixue wei yong* explicitly involves a synthesis of Western and Chinese ideas, and that culture is not a static, monolithic entity, it was inevitable that Chinese society would transform – often in ways that those with an interest in preserving the status quo did not relish. Mainland China's relationship with the English language is a symbol of her relationships with the outside world – most notably, the powerful economic nations that often pursued antithetical political lines – and the role and status of the language represents, as Ross (1992: 251) notes, a barometer of the nation's modernisation. As the economic modernisation of mainland China continues, whether the road is smooth or rocky, the tension between the appropriation of English and the language's capacity to bring about social and cultural transformation will be played out on an increasingly larger scale. Pye (1985: 182) has described mainland China's experience with modernisation as 'one of history's great balancing acts, whose outcome is still far from certain' and this certainly applies to mainland China's interaction with the English language.

References

Adamson, B. (1998) Modernizing English language teacher education. In M. Agelasto and B. Adamson (eds) *Higher Education in Post-Mao China* (pp. 141–164). Hong Kong: Hong Kong University Press.

Adamson, B. (2002) Barbarian as a foreign language: English in China's schools. *World Englishes* 21 (2), 231–243.

Adamson, B. (2004) *China's English: A History of English in Chinese Education.* Hong Kong: Hong Kong University Press.

Adamson, B. and Feng, A. (2009) A comparison of trilingual education policies for ethnic minorities in China. *Compare* 39 (3), 321–333.

Baum, R. (1994) *Burying Mao: Chinese Politics in the Age of Deng Xiaoping.* Princeton, NJ: Princeton University Press.

Bolton, K. (2002) Chinese Englishes: From Canton jargon to global English. *World Englishes* 21 (2), 181–199.

Bolton, K. (2008) English in Asia, Asian Englishes, and the issues of proficiency. *English Today* 24 (2), 3–12.

Cheng, L. (2008) The key to success: English language testing in China. *Language Testing* 25 (1), 15–37.

Cheng, W. (2006) Beijing's underground rock scene. [Electronic version.] *Theme* magazine, Issue 5, Spring.

China Daily (2000) Letter to the Editor: Special talents should be given chance. 28 September 2000.

China Hospitality News (2008) CNTA: China's inbound tourist numbers continued to decrease in October. On WWW at http://www.chinahospitality news.com. Accessed 5.12.08.

China Internet Network Information Center (2009) *Statistical Survey Report on the Internet Development in China* (January). Beijing: China Internet Network Information Center.

China Radio International (2008) Brief introduction: About us. On WWW at www.crienglish.com/about/intro.htm. Accessed 22.12.08.

Cole, S. (2007) The functionalist account of English in China: A sociolinguistic history. University of Toronto Website. On WWW at http://www.chass.utoronto.ca/ ~ cpercy/courses/eng6365-cole.htm. Accessed 22.12.08.
Cortazzi, M. and Jin, L. (1996) English teaching in China. *Language Teaching* 29, 61–80.
Dreyer, J.T. (2003) The evolution of language policies in China. In M.E. Brown and S. Ganguly (eds) *Fighting Words: Language Policy and Ethnic Relations in Asia* (pp. 353–384). Cambridge, MA: MIT Press.
Gil, J. (2005) English in China: The impact of the global language on China's language situation. Unpublished PhD dissertation, Griffith University, Australia.
Gil, J. (2006) English in minority areas of China: Some findings and directions for further research. *International Education Journal* 7 (4), 455–465.
Guo, Z. and Huang, Y. (2002) Hybridized discourse: Social openness and functions of English media in post-Mao China. *World Englishes* 21 (2), 218–230.
Hertling, J. (1996) China embraces the English language. *The Chronicle of Higher Education* 5 January, A49–A50.
Hsü, I.C.Y. (1990) *The Rise of Modern China*. Oxford: Oxford University Press.
Hu, G. (2008) The misleading academic discourse on Chinese–English bilingual education in China. *Review of Educational Research* 78 (2), 195–231.
Hu, X. (2004) Why China English should stand alongside British, American and the other 'World Englishes'. *English Today* 20 (2), 26–33.
Hu, X. (2005) China English, at home and in the world. *English Today* 21 (3), 27–38.
Huang, B. (2007) Teachers' perceptions of Chinese-English bilingual teaching in Guangxi. In A. Feng (ed.) *Bilingual Education in China: Practices, Policies and Concepts* (pp. 219–239). Clevedon: Multilingual Matters.
Hung, E. (2002) Translation and English in twentieth-Century China. *World Englishes* 21 (2), 326–335.
Jiang, Y. (1995) Chinglish and China English. *English Today* 11 (1), 51–53.
Jiang, Y. (2003) English as a Chinese language. *English Today* 19 (2), 3–8.
Jones, A. (2001) *Yellow Music*. Durham, NC: Duke University Press.
Jones, A. (2006) The great educational technology wall: The benefits and difficulties of using the internet as part of a foreign language teaching methodology in China. In W. Dai (ed.) *FLT in China: Looking Back, In and Ahead – Collection of Papers of the First International Conference on Foreign Language Teaching Methodology in China* (pp. 159–165). Shanghai: Shanghai Foreign Language Education Press.
Kachru, B.B. (1983) Models for non-native Englishes. In B. Kachru (ed.) *The Other Tongue: English across Cultures* (pp. 31–57). Oxford: Pergamon Press.
Kachru, B.B. (1985) Standards, codification and sociolinguistic realism: The English language in the outer circle. In R. Quirk and H. Widdowson (eds) *English in the World: Teaching and Learning the Language and Literatures* (pp. 11–30). Cambridge: Cambridge University Press.
Kachru, B. and Nelson, C.L. (2001) World Englishes. In A. Burns and C. Coffin (eds) *Analysing English in a Global Context: A Reader* (pp. 9–25). London and New York: Routledge.
Kirkpatrick, A. (2008) English as the official working language of the Association of Southeast Asian Nations (ASEAN): Features and strategies. *English Today* 24 (2), 27–34.

Kirkpatrick, A. and Xu, Z. (2002) Chinese pragmatic norms and 'China English'. *World Englishes* 21 (2), 269–279.
Lam, A. (2002) English in education in China: Policy changes and learners' experiences. *World Englishes* 21 (2), 245–256.
Lam, A.S.L. (2005) *Language Education in China: Policy and Experience from 1949*. Hong Kong: Hong Kong University Press.
Li, D. (1995) English in China. *English Today* 11 (1), 53–56.
Li, L. and Zhang, F. (2003) Developing English-language academic journals of China. *Scientometrics* 57 (1), 119–125.
Li, X. (1996) How much English do our school-leaving students have? – Report of a study. In G. Xu (ed.) *ELT in China 1992: Papers from Tianjin Conference* (pp. 657–674). Beijing: Foreign Language Teaching and Research Press.
Liu, J. (2008) China English and its linguistic features. *International Journal of Language, Society and Culture* 25, 27–36.
Mackerras, C., Taneja, P. and Young, G. (1998) *China since 1978: Reform, Modernisation and 'Socialism with Chinese Characteristics'* (2nd edn). Melbourne: Longman.
Mackey, W.F. (2003) Forecasting the fate of languages. In J. Maurais and M.A. Morris (eds) *Languages in a Globalising World* (pp. 64–81). Cambridge: Cambridge University Press.
McArthur, T. (2006) China syndrome? *English Today* 22 (2), 2.
Meisner, M. (1999) *Mao's China and after: A History of the People's Republic* (3rd edn). New York: The Free Press.
National Bureau of Statistics of China (2009) Statistical bulletin. (In Chinese) On WWW at http://www.stats.gov.cn/tjgb/. Accessed 5.1.09.
National Tourism Administration of the People's Republic of China (2008) Announcement No. 13. On WWW at http://www.cnta.gov.cn/html/2008-10/2008-10-31-14-54-78263.html. Accessed 31.12.08.
Nielsen, P.M. (2003) English in Argentina: A sociolinguistic profile. *World Englishes* 22 (2), 199–209.
Nunan, D. (2003) The impact of English as a global language on educational policies and practices in the Asia-Pacific Region. *TESOL Quarterly* 37 (4), 589–613.
Osnos, E. (2008) Crazy English: The national scramble to learn a new language before the Olympics. *New Yorker*, 28 April. On WWW at http://www.newyorker.com/reporting/2008/04/28/080428fa_fact_osnos. Accessed 22.12.08.
Pan, Z. (2005) *Linguistic and Cultural Identities in Chinese Varieties of English*. Beijing: Peking University Press.
Pang, J., Zhou, X. and Zheng, F. (2002) English for international trade: China enters the WTO. *World Englishes* 21 (2), 201–216.
People's Daily Online (2000a) Beijing judges learning English. On WWW at http://english.peopledaily.com.cn/. Accessed 20.4.2000.
People's Daily Online (2000b) Shanghai people learn English for APEC meeting. On WWW at http://english.peopledaily.com.cn/. Accessed 25.4.2000.
People's Daily Online (2000c) Beijing popularizes English for Olympic bid. On WWW at http://english.peopledaily.com.cn/. Accessed 30.5.2000.
People's Daily Online (2000d) English-language police hotline opens in Nanjing. On WWW at http://english.peopledaily.com.cn/. Accessed 5.7.2000.

People's Daily Online (2000e) Beijingers enthusiastic about learning English. On WWW at http://english.peopledaily.com.cn/. Accessed 5.12.2000.
People's Daily Online (2003) Is English invading Chinese culture? On WWW at http://english.peopledaily.com.cn/. Accessed 2.11.2000.
People's Daily Online (2004a) Chinese intellectuals rebel against foreign language tests. On WWW at http://english.peopledaily.com.cn/. Accessed 12.4.04.
People's Daily Online (2004b) China's translation industry, big but not strong: experts. On WWW at http://english.peopledaily.com.cn/. Accessed 10.11.04.
Pepper, S. (1996) *Radicalism and Education Reform in 20th-Century China*. Cambridge: Cambridge University Press.
Pride, J.B. and Liu, R.S. (1988) Some aspects of the spread of English in China since 1949. *International Journal of the Sociology of Language* 74, 41–70.
Pye, L.W. (1985) *Asian Power and Politics: The Cultural Dimensions of Authority*. Cambridge: The Belknap Press of Harvard University Press.
Roberts, J.A.G. (1999) *A History of China*. Houndmills: Macmillan Press.
Ross, H.A. (1992) Foreign language education as a barometer of modernization. In R. Hayhoe (ed.) *Education and Modernization: The Chinese Experience* (pp. 239–254). Oxford: Pergamon Press.
Ross, H.A. (1993) *China Learns English: Language Teaching and Social Change in the People's Republic*. New Haven, CT: Yale University Press.
South China Morning Post (2001a) Beijing brushes up on English for Olympics. July 28.
South China Morning Post (2001b) Beijing recognises need for English as WTO entry looms. October 27.
South China Morning Post (2001c) Police to breach language barrier. November 24.
South China Morning Post (2004) Shanghai to recruit English teachers. April 17.
Spence, J. (1980) *To Change China: Western Advisers in China 1620–1960*. London: Penguin.
Spence, J.D. (1990) *The Search for Modern China*. London: Hutchinson.
Tang, L. (1983) *TEFL in China: Methods and Techniques*. Shanghai: Shanghai Foreign Languages Press.
Teng, S.Y. and Fairbank, J.K. (1979) *China's Response to the West: A Documentary Survey, 1839–1923*. Cambridge, MA: Harvard University Press.
Trudgill, P. and Hannah, J. (2002) *International English: A Guide to the Varieties of Standard English* (4th edn). London: Arnold.
Tsui, A.B.M. and Tollefson, J.W. (2007) Language policy and the construction of national cultural identity. In A.B.M. Tsui and J.W. Tollefson (eds) *Language Policy, Culture, and Identity in Asian Contexts* (pp. 1–24). Mahwah, NJ: Lawrence Erlbaum.
Velez-Rendon, G. (2003) English in Columbia: A sociolinguistic profile. *World Englishes* 22 (2), 185–198.
Wang, G.T. (1999) *China's Population: Problems, Thoughts and Policies*. Aldershot: Brookfield.
Wang, Q. (2007) The National Curriculum changes and their effects on English language teaching in the People's Republic of China. In J. Cummins and C. Davison (eds) *International Handbook of English Language Teaching* (pp. 87–105). Dordrecht: Springer.
Wei, Y. and Fei, J. (2003) Using English in China. *English Today* 19 (4), 42–47.

Wood, F. (1998) *No Dogs and Not Many Chinese: Treaty Port Life in China 1843–1943*. London: John Murray.
Yao, X. (1993) Foreign languages in China's higher education. *Language Learning Journal* 7, 74–77.
Zhang, A. (2000) Language switches among Chinese/English bilinguals. *English Today* 16 (1), 53–56.
Zhang, H. (2002) Bilingual creativity in Chinese English: Ha Jin's *In the Pond*. *World Englishes* 21 (2), 305–315.
Zhao, Y. and Campbell, K.P. (1995) English in China. *World Englishes* 14 (3), 377–390.
Zhong, W. (1998) Chinese scholars and the world community. In M. Agelasto and B. Adamson (eds) *Higher Education in post-Mao China* (pp. 59–77). Hong Kong: HKU Press.

Chapter 3

English-knowing Bilingualism in Singapore: Economic Pragmatism, Ethnic Relations and Class

T. RUANNI F. TUPAS

Singapore is a multiethnic country. It has a relatively stable ethnic configuration composed mainly of Chinese (75%), Malays (13.7%) and Indians (8.7%), with an estimated resident population of around 3.6 million (Department of Statistics, 2008). The total population including those with non-resident status is around 4.6 million. But while the country is a Chinese-dominant society, it is also an English-speaking society. English is the language of inter-ethnic communication, of education, government and commerce. On the other hand, Singapore is also one of the most developed and globally connected countries in the world, second only to the USA as the most competitive economy (*World Competitiveness Yearbook*, 2007). What is the role of English in Singapore's story of economic success and political stability?

In this chapter, the role of English in Singapore education and society will be explored. More specifically, the chapter will discuss the role of education within which the use of English as the medium of instruction is a centrepiece policy that has had a massive impact on the transformation of Singapore from a poor, ethnically divided society in the 1950s to a highly developed cosmopolitan country today.

There are three main sections. The first section broadly sketches the historical context of Singapore's education system, while the second section discusses in more detail the key features of the country's bilingual education. The final section explores some problems in the Singaporean brand of bilingualism (referring mainly to the use of English and another mother tongue, which is the officially preferred socio-linguistic configuration despite the reality of multilingualism), noting in particular some 'unintended' effects of the policy, such as the dominant presence of English in Singaporean homes, the reductionist deployment of the concept of bilingualism in policy implementation and the clustering of class-based issues around the use of English. The purpose of the chapter is to introduce readers to the unique nature of Singaporean bilingualism while raising critical issues surrounding English, which may also be of concern in many parts of the world.

Historicising Singapore's Education System

Singapore's 'astonishing transformation' 25 years after its separation from Malaysia in 1966 reveals the pivotal role of education in nation-building and economic development (Yip *et al.*, 1994: 2). Today, education continues to be a fundamental tool in effecting socioeconomic change and cultural reaffirmation in the country in the midst of recent global upheavals and changes (Tan *et al.*, 2001; Ho, 2006; Lo Bianco, 2006). This section discusses in broad terms the changing concerns of Singapore's education system by locating it within the country's political and economic history.

Early postcolonial education in Singapore was concerned with the provision of education for all, while education in the 1980s and 1990s concentrated on quality teaching and learning. Education today, on the other hand, is said to focus on critical and creative ways to teach and learn, purportedly to keep the population highly competitive in the midst of international competition. However, there is still a common thread that cuts across different periods of education reform in Singapore: the system has been consistently framed within a utilitarian or pragmatist ideology.

Early postcolonial education: Focus on quantity through universal education

In the 1950s and 1960s, Singapore was a struggling nation plagued with unemployment, economic stagnation and ethnic divisiveness:

> The core concern then was to reduce inter-ethnic divisions, promote a national identity and promote economic growth via education and training to provide the desired language competencies and skills. (Gopinathan *et al.*, 2004: 232)

The challenge for education was to bring more children into schools and develop a national curriculum across all four streams of the education system, each stream characterised by its language of instruction. In other words, the education system then had four types of schooling based on language of instruction, but these four types of schools had no one common curriculum that could potentially help address economic decay and inter-ethnic animosity. Thus, when a national curriculum was put in place in the late 1960s against a political backdrop of instability and vulnerability mainly caused by the country's independence from Malaysia, the focus was on the capacity of education both to help make the shift from an economy dependent on import substitution to one that was export driven, and to discipline a society with core national values needed to establish cohesion among the different ethnic groups (Yip *et al.*, 1990).

Consequently, through much of the 1970s, educational infrastructures were utilised to produce human resources needed to industrialise the state. The curriculum veered away from a focus on academic content and shifted to the teaching of technical skills to supply human resources to multinational companies that would establish plants and factories in the country and help strengthen the economy. This focus on the supply side of education would lead Singapore's brand of bilingual education – to be discussed in more detail in the next section – to be prominently positioned to steer the country forward through industrialisation.

Education in the 1980s and 1990s: Focus on streaming for quality and efficiency

In the early 1980s, the focus was on streamlining education through a careful rationalisation of its intrinsic values for Singaporean children. This focus was mainly influenced by the Goh Kweng Swee Report of 1979, which exposed inefficiencies and inadequacies in bilingual education that pushed out many students at the end of Primary 6 and produced insufficiently bilingual secondary school leavers (Gopinathan, 2001: 8). Whereas in the earlier decade the concern was to educate Singaporeans for the needs of industry without a broad vision of what education means to each child that went to school, the early years of the 1980s saw education being consolidated within a principled view of schooling. The focused question was:

> (H)ow do you educate children in a universal education system where everybody comes in, with a wide range of abilities: how do you deal with them, how do you cater for them? (Tay, 1990: 8)

This would be accomplished primarily through a system of ability-based streaming, a highly efficient but controversial process of segregating children from Primary 3 onwards based on the assumption that different capacities of learning would require different paces of learning. Such an elaborate streaming process was intended to address the problem of wastage in education because each child would be slotted into a type of schooling that she/he was deemed fit to attend. In official state discourse, the 'ends of general education' (Tay, 1990: 4) would be to bring out the 'greatest potential' of a child to make them a 'good' and 'useful' citizen of Singapore.

Singapore, however, was rattled by the global recession of 1985, which led to a report by the Economic Committee in 1986 recommending several key measures to make Singapore globally competitive (Yip et al., 1990). These measures, which included raising Singaporeans' education level in general and retraining the entire workforce, brought forth the intensification of the competitiveness discourse that further entrenched the education system within a utilitarian framework, but now with a broader notion of the individual's fullest potential to include creative, critical and innovative abilities.

This expanded utilitarian ideology was to saturate the content of the highly significant education report, *Improving Primary School Education* (1991), and power an efficiency-driven education system in the 1990s, characterised by rising enrolments especially in the primary level and more choices for teachers in the curriculum (Ang, 2000). The general assessment of the education system in the early years of the 1990s was that Singapore's economic fundamentals were strong, but the educated local workforce was still not adequate to address the needs of the new service and knowledge-orientated industries (Gopinathan, 2001: 10).

Education today: Focus on critical and creative thinking for economic competitiveness

In June 1997, the then prime minister, Goh Chok Tong, announced further fundamental changes to the education system through a framework collectively called Thinking Schools, Learning Nation (TSLN), which sealed the 1990s as the 'big bang in Singapore's education reforms' (Gopinathan, 2001: 11). The announcement was made amidst the increasing role of cyber technology in the free flow of information, the further intensification of global free trade and the rising economic and political power of many developing countries, such as China and India.

This new framework envisions the role of 'National Education' as harnessing the nation's intellectual assets, not just technical know-how, which will compete with, even out-perform, economic rivals in the future. In this paradigm, the education system is tasked to produce independent-thinking and creative individuals through school work that privileges quality over quantity, experiential learning over rote learning and memorisation, and quality of interaction among teachers and pupils over highly individualised work.

The current system continues to work within this broad paradigm of teaching and learning, with syllabuses, school policies and classroom strategies spelling out ways to produce so-called 'thinking, independent and innovative young Singaporeans' through whom the nation's future wealth will be assured (see Table 3.1).

Table 3.1 A selection of recent initiatives in education in Singapore

The school system	The curriculum	Teachers
• Clustering of schools	• Class size reduction	• New career tracks
• Improving learning spaces	• Teaching thinking skills	• New recognition structure
• Singapore Excellence Model	• IT Masterplans I & II	• Enhanced Performance Management System
• Education made compulsory	• National education	• Work Attachment Scheme
• Refinements to primary streaming	• Changed junior college/upper secondary school landscape	• About 3000 more teachers for schools by 2010
• School ranking refinement	• Refinements to mother tongue language policy	
• A sports school and an arts school		
Post-secondary Education		
Institute of Technical Education	The polytechnics	The universities
• The first ITE Regional College was set up in 2005. The other two are ITE College Central and ITE College West.	• A new polytechnic, Republic Polytechnic, was set up in 2002, with its first batch of students admitted in 2003	• Singapore Management University was established in 2000

Table 3.1 (*Continued*)

	• This new polytechnic will offer, in addition, diplomas in sports and exercise science and leisure and events management	• The National Institute of Education moved to a new campus within the Nanyang Technological University (NTU)
	• From 2006, the five polytechnics, which traditionally began their courses in June, will start their academic year in April, saving students a month of waiting	• The National University of Singapore and NTU have started to allow gifted junior college and secondary school students to take undergraduate courses while still in school
		• UniSIM was established in 2005, with the first batch of 1275 students starting their degree courses in January 2006

Source: Adapted from Ho (2006: 20).

However, this brief historical survey of Singapore's education system reveals what has been consistently asserted in much local and international literature: education reforms and initiatives have always worked within a utilitarian ideology, or what Tan (2006: 181) refers to as the state's 'perennial, almost obsessive, concern with economic relevance'. Indeed, the (qualitative) success of TSLN depends largely on how it is able to reconcile the seeming irony of developing a 'creative, thinking, and learning population' and 'developing new technologies to enhance corporate profits' (Spring, 1998: 83):

> Creative, thinking and learning people might reject the authoritarian structures of government and corporations. Heaven forbid, they might even reject the basic premise of current capitalism – that the quality of society depends on the efforts to maximize profits. (Spring, 1998: 83–84)

Contextualising English-knowing Bilingualism

Singapore's brand of bilingualism is described as 'English-knowing' because of the primacy of the English language in the definition of what it means to be a bilingual person (Pakir, 1991, 1993). One is bilingual if he or she speaks English *and* Chinese, Malay or Tamil, the three official mother tongues taught in schools. Education reforms and the sociopolitical and economic contexts within which such reforms were initiated and implemented as discussed above, are crucial in understanding the character of Singaporean bilingualism and bilingual education.

This section will discuss how an English-knowing bilingualism has emerged from the changing sociopolitical and economic landscape of Singapore since its early postcolonial years. In particular, the section discusses the roots of Singaporean bilingualism in the context of early postcolonial need to manage ethnic relations, which developed into an English-dominant bilingualism in the 1970s when economic pragmatism and efficiency became the guiding principle in state-led social development. Today's Singaporean bilingualism, as initially discussed in the earlier section, is officially framed within a 'critical' discourse that promotes creative and innovative thinking among learners capable of independent work and informed risk-taking decisions. Of course, the development of the essential character of English-knowing bilingualism in Singapore has been consistently utilitarian as well.

Managing ethnic diversity through languages of education

Before and immediately after the British ceded power to local authorities in 1959, Singapore was a society fragmented along the lines of ethnic and linguistic differences. Such fragmentation was reinforced by a segmented, 'very divisive' education system (Tay, 1990: 5), which had four media of instruction (English, Chinese, Malay and Tamil), and was generally characterised by deep resentment from those who were non-English educated (Gopinathan, 2001: 7). The resentment was generally fed by the common perception that the British did not do enough to support the teaching of languages other than English, with the Chinese-educated especially feeling betrayed and marginalised by the colonial government's official support of English-medium schools while the Chinese-medium schools were left in the care of the Chinese themselves. Even the limited jobs available in the private sector required some proficiency in English, which certainly disadvantaged Chinese-medium graduates.

Thus, non-English streams would look elsewhere for curricular frameworks, with different groups 'clinging on' to their own ethnic practices and ideologies, with Chinese textbooks heavily influenced by communist China and Malay resources heavily saturated with local ideological and cultural content (Ho, 2006: 16). Meanwhile, the traditional literacy practices that undergirded non-English classrooms were radically different from those of English-dominant, British-influenced classrooms, and this resulted in an even greater cultural, political and ideological chasm between these groups (compare current streaming practices in English and Chinese in Hong Kong in Li, this volume).

Thus, the *Report of the All-Party Committee of the Singapore Legislative Assembly on Chinese Education* (Singapore, 1956) has been credited by many as a key point in the country's educational transformation as it called for parity of treatment among the languages of education through a nationally orientated curriculum and Singapore-centred textbooks (Yip *et al.*, 1994: 5; Ho, 2006: 16). This call led to the integration of the four systems of education through the use of a common syllabus for the teaching of school subjects (although using different media of instruction) starting in 1961, and to the introduction of a compulsory bilingual policy in 1966, which required secondary students from any language-medium stream to take a second language. Ultimately, such integration transformed into a unified national system of 'bilingual' education for all, starting in 1987 when English became the 'first language' of education (the medium of instruction in all subjects except mother tongue education and moral education) and the three mother tongues were relegated to the position of 'second languages'.

Therefore, from the 1960s onwards it has been clear that whatever the specific shape of the education system, a multiculturalist perspective was to frame it to help manage ethnic diversity (Gopinathan, 2001: 7), such that as early as 1965 when Singapore achieved full independence from Malaysia, a universal primary education had been put in place through education reforms that 'muted' protests from Chinese, Malay and Tamil communities (Yip *et al.*, 1994: 8). In the words of Ganguly (2003: 239), Singapore in 1965 pursued 'a vision of civic nationalism' that was committed ideologically to creating and maintaining a multiracial, multilingual society.

Economic pragmatism in early bilingual education

However, Singapore's early postcolonial dismal economic condition also presented a socioeconomic context within which such a multiculturalist framework of education was to be put in place. In other words, Singapore's educational postcolonial transformation can be understood in light of both its history of ethnic relations and its pursuit of capital to jump-start and sustain economic development. How was ethnic diversity going to be managed as Singapore developed into an economically stable state? The racial/ethnic riots of 1969, for example, occurred against the backdrop of Singapore gearing its economy towards export-driven industries and making sure that its economic fundamentals were put in place to encourage foreign investors to come in.

Thus, it was inevitable that economic pragmatism would shape the contours of a multiculturalist education; in Chua's terms (1995), the ideology of pragmatism or survival would override all other concerns because any form of social control (e.g. to manage ethnic relations) would qualify as pragmatic for as long as it helped the economy improve. This ideological posturing resulted in a highly unique kind of education where English and the three mother tongues would take on mutually exclusive roles in official discourses, curriculum development and classroom management. English, as the language of 'pragmatism' and a 'neutral' language, would serve as a bridge between the different ethnic groups, an ironic but convenient twist since English was primarily cast 'as having value in the economic but not cultural sphere' (Gopinathan *et al.*, 2004: 234). The three mother tongues would only serve as conduits through which local ethnicities, cultures and histories would be affirmed and celebrated. In the words of Tay (1990), Singapore's brand of bilingual education:

> meets aspirations and desires of the different language communities we have in Singapore, without causing any one group to lose out, but at the same time giving all the advantages of an economic role in this open society of ours that has to deal with countries all over the world. (Tay, 1990: 6)

The consolidating power of English in the era of efficiency-driven education

In the 1970s, however, there was a marked drift in enrolment from non-English language schools to English-medium schools. While this could be attributed to free choice given to parents to send their children to any preferred school, such free choice was conditioned within the context of the consolidating symbolic power of English in the economic market. While only close to half of the student population went to English-medium schools in 1959, around 90% of the cohort went to similar schools in 1978. This led to the establishment of Special Assistance Plan (SAP) schools whose main task was to teach English and Chinese at the first language level, and the Supplementary English Language Programme (SELP) for non-English stream students to attend additional immersion English language classes.

While the 1960s and 1970s could be defined as two decades of survival-driven education (Ho, 2006) mainly because the major concerns were to address fundamental sociopolitical, cultural, ethnic and economic problems, 1979 through the Goh Report mentioned above could be said to have ushered in an efficiency-driven education that would minimise wastage and maximise educational resources in the service of the developing economy. The streaming process introduced in 1980 through the New Education System framework highlighted even more the role of languages in education. Not only did language learning occupy 50% of the curriculum in the early primary years, but such learning could also be seen as primarily the learning of English because of its role as the medium of instruction in content subjects like Mathematics and Science.

More importantly, bilingual competence (in English and another official language) would take on an even more discriminatory function through the streaming system. At the end of Primary 3, students would be channelled into three different systems of upper primary education: the Normal Bilingual course ('N' course), for students who passed the Primary 3 examination; the Extended Bilingual course ('E' course), for those who failed Primary 3 but passed the Primary 2 examination; and the Monolingual course ('M' course), for those who failed both examinations (Yip et al., 1994: 16).

The implication for language learning would be that a child 'not meant for academic endeavours' (Yip et al., 1994) would be required to learn English, Mathematics and the oral skills of a second language, as opposed to the child in the 'N' and 'E' courses who would be assessed in English, Mathematics, Science and both oral and written skills of a second language. The monolingual stream would make certain assumptions about children's learning capabilities: that they would be incapable of learning two languages effectively, that this inability would translate to inability to cope with content subjects taught in English, and that this inability would ultimately mean intellectual weakness. Therefore, a stratifying efficiency-driven education to serve the country's developmentalist agenda was evident in the reification of not just one but different layers of English-knowing bilingualism with clear roles to play in society. The monoliterate English-knowing bilinguals would later constitute the country's technical manual workforce, while the most capable English-knowing bilinguals would later become the country's intellectual assets. What is worth pointing out here is that the 'pragmatist' multiculturalist character of Singaporean bilingualism shaped in the earlier decades remained essentially the same, but this time it was to serve not a struggling Singapore, but one poised to become one of Asia's economic tigers. This could be compared with similar pragmatist assumptions in the privileging of English in other Chinese-dominant societies, such as China (Gil & Adamson, this volume), Taiwan (Chen & Hsieh, this volume), Hong Kong (Li, this volume) and Macao (Young, this volume).

Bilingualism today: The 'critical' way

When a new 'paradigm' of education was introduced in 1997 through TSLN, the essence of bilingual education remained unchanged: English (as a medium of instruction and a separate subject) for global competitiveness, and Chinese, Malay and Tamil as mother tongues for cultural rootedness, that is, as '"impractical languages" in relation to the supposedly pragmatic but actually ideological demands of economic modernity' (Wee, 2007: 252). The economic imperative that shaped the formulation, establishment and continuation of bilingual education policies and initiatives in the past has also remained the core guiding principle in recent and current educational initiatives. However, a new feature in TSLN is the greater and centralising emphasis on the promotion of critical and creative thinking to further enhance Singapore's competitiveness in the global market. More importantly, lifelong learning, pursuit of innovation, independent decision-making skills and flexible attitudes towards differing ideas are some of the important values to be inculcated in learners through a broadened curriculum in order to steer the country towards a knowledge-based economy where intellectual assets, not just technical skills, are fundamental ingredients for success (Retna, 2007).

These could be accomplished through various initiatives and programmes, such as 'National Education' and the 'Masterplan for IT in Education (IT Masterplan)' both launched in 1997, which together would help introduce into the English-medium curriculum a broad array of literacy skills (critical and creative skills, as well as IT skills) needed to confront the new global economy. Content reduction was initiated to make education more relevant to the students, and in order for literacy learning, not simply language learning, to take place (Cheah, 2004: 371). Quality of interaction between teachers and students, and among students themselves, is given prominence through multidisciplinary project-based work and other learner-orientated approaches. Drilling and rote learning have been de-emphasised, especially in the lower grades (Silver, 2002: 147).

In language instruction, content reduction has been stark: a reduction in the number of characters to be learned in Chinese, a reduction of grammar items in Malay, and less language items, poems and proverbs in Tamil (Silver, 2002). In English language teaching, a similar content reduction has not taken place because it has been essentially skills-based from the start. However, what is noteworthy is the *English Language Syllabus 2001* (Curriculum Planning and Development Division, 2001), which uses text types as its main structuring principle as opposed to themes, which were used in the communicative 1991 syllabus. The focus is on language use – mainly for information, for social interaction and literary response and expression – determined by purpose, audience, context and culture, and within which grammar will be explicitly taught.

If one looks to international literature, text types are derived from 'world-wide trends in language learning' (Cheah, 2004: 365), especially that the syllabus explicitly states the meaning-making nature of language as one of its philosophical foundations. However, their use in the 2001 syllabus is also framed within the new national thrust of helping 'pupils become independent lifelong learners, creative thinkers and problem solvers who can communicate effectively in English' (Curriculum Planning and Development Division, 2001: 2).

Indeed, while a broader philosophy of literacy learning through the meaning-making nature of language underpins the overt discourse of *the English Language Syllabus 2001*, 'contradictory discourses of materials like the grammar course and textbook packages intended to aid the syllabus's implementation (are) taken-for-granted understandings of earlier times, when stability of social and linguistic forms could be assumed' (Kramer-Dahl, 2007: 66). The same can be said about earlier national English Language syllabuses, especially the 1991 syllabus in which the successful inclusion of 'culture' was not fully developed because cultural literacy did not work well with the dominant concern with 'technical literacy, i.e., language learning as a linguistic tool for economic purposes only' (Cheah, 2004: 358; see also Sripathy, 2007).

In sum, what can be concluded from our discussion of the historical and politico-economic contexts of Singapore's education system and, more specifically, bilingual education, is the belief that:

> the educational system offers the best medium for social engineering through the teaching of values, eradication of prejudices and

misconceptions and to imbibe the respect for pluralism and diversity (Tan, E., 2004: 68).

In the contexts of the official languages of education, this has meant the use of English as the medium of instruction because it is a 'neutral lingua franca' and the teaching of the mother tongues to keep local cultures and histories alive (Tan, E., 2004). The economic imperative of social engineering is crucial in this regard because of Singapore's precarious early postcolonial independent years and strong yet continually vulnerable economy today, which is consistently restructured to respond to global changes and trends. Singapore's bilingual education, in other words, has undergone massive transformations in response to the needs of specific postcolonial political and socioeconomic milieus, but the pragmatic or economic imperative in state discourse on the languages of education has remained essentially the same. Even literacy ideology, which underpins much of recent educational work in Singapore (TSLN, text types and English Language Syllabus 2001, etc.), 'has always been based on economic arguments' (Sripathy, 2007: 90). In other words, the education system in general 'is still in the grip of a mechanistic account of the nature of thought, thinking and learning' (Nathan, 2001: 37).

Problematising English-knowing Bilingualism

Much has been said about the debilitating effects of the dominance of English on education and society (see Pakir, 1993; Silver, 2002), but responses to these sociolinguistic phenomena have not dealt squarely with the fundamental question of whether or not Singaporean bilingualism is sociolinguistically, ideologically and politically sound in the first place. In this context, it makes sense to say that that there has been much 'rethinking of language policies albeit within the framework of current language policy' (Kassim, 2008: 50) because, while much has been and is currently being done to address the problems accruing to English-dominant bilingualism, the essence of such bilingualism has remained untouched. Singapore's undisputed economic achievements, accomplished primarily through education, have led many analysts to 'pay less attention to the ways in which the Singapore state has managed the issues rising from an ethnically and linguistically diverse population' (Gopinathan *et al.*, 2004: 229).

This last section highlights some key problems associated with English-knowing bilingualism. The first problem concerns the role of such bilingualism in the big shift in home languages, where English has replaced (and continues to do so) the mother tongues and other Chinese 'dialects' as the dominant home language. The second problem concerns the reductionist nature of Singaporean bilingualism, which does not reflect the realities on the ground where uses of languages are mixed, conflictual and dynamic. The third problem deals with the issue of social class in English-knowing bilingualism, a much ignored element in the study of the sociolinguistics of Singaporean education. It will be argued below that the changing landscape of home language use in the country has an undeniably class-based character: Singaporean homes shifting to English are generally more economically advanced, while such shifts make possible a hierarchy of English varieties where those families that speak the standard variety usually come from more well-to-do backgrounds as well. In short, Singaporean bilingual education promotes a less-than-ideal meritocratic reality (see Tan, 2008).

Home language use: The great shift towards English

For almost three decades now, but more so in recent years, the most highly discussed impact of Singaporean bilingualism is in the area of language shifts and maintenance, notably the home language shift towards English from Mandarin, Malay, Tamil and other Chinese 'dialects' (e.g. Xu & Li, 2002; Zhao & Liu, 2007; Kassim, 2008). For example, because of the phenomenon of English-knowing bilingualism, Pakir (1993: 74) had already noted that the language environment in Singapore 'has been so dramatically altered that individuals within the population could be said to have changed their verbal repertoires'. Recently, concerns with language shifts in Singaporean homes have led to major revamps in mother tongue curricula, as proposed separately in the *Report of the Chinese Language Curriculum and Pedagogy Review Committee* (2004), *Report of the Malay Language Curriculum and Pedagogy Review Committee* (2005) and *Report of the Tamil Language Curriculum and Pedagogy Review Committee* (2005). Customisation of courses in the primary level and a greater focus on reading and oral communication have been recommended to help keep interest in mother tongues among students whose main language at home has shifted to English.

Recent statistics confirm this trend (*Yearbook of Statistics*, 2008), with English as the most frequently spoken language at home, observed in more Singaporean homes in 2005 than in 2000, while the opposite trend was true with other languages (see Table 3.2). Moreover, among the Chinese, Malay and Indian groups between 2000 and 2005, English as the main home language exhibited increasing dominance as levels of education in the household also increased, while the mother tongues,

Table 3.2 Language most frequently spoken at home (aged 5 years and over)

	Total		Chinese		Malays		Indians		Others	
	2000	2005	2000	2005	2000	2005	2000	2005	2000	2005
	100.0	100.0	100.0	100.0	100.0	100.0	100.0	100.0	100.0	100.0
English (%)	23.0	28.1	23.9	28.7	7.9	13.0	15.6	39.0	68.4	65.8
Mandarin (%)	35.0	36.0	45.1	47.2	0.1	0.1	0.1	0.1	4.4	4.4
Chinese dialect (%)	23.8	18.2	30.7	23.9	0.1	0.1	0.1	0.1	3.2	1.5
Malay (%)	14.1	13.2	0.2	0.2	91.6	86.8	11.6	10.6	15.6	12.2
Tamil (%)	3.2	3.1	–	–	0.1	–	42.9	38.8	0.2	0.4
Others (%)	0.9	1.4	0.1	0.1	0.3	0.1	9.7	11.4	8.2	15.7

including Chinese 'dialects', were spoken less and less as students moved up the educational ladder (see Table 3.3). According to Gopinathan *et al.* (2004: 237), this 'changed linguistic environment has brought about greater linguistic heterogeneity in terms of student background and less intensive exposure to the mother tongue in the community'.

Despite this trend, however, the bilingual policy that has resulted in home language shifts is generally spared from criticism. There has been a flurry of state initiatives to counter the negative effects of English on different facets of Singaporean society, dating back to the late 1970s when the 'Speak Mandarin' campaign was launched precisely to counter the dominance of English (Wee, 2003), and the 'Asianisation' or 'Shared Values' discourse was officially introduced in the early 1990s as part of the national ideology to resist the infusion of so-called individualist, decadent practices of the West through the English language (Chua, 1998). The response to recent educational directives to help reverse the trend of language shifts has put the onus of change on mother tongue curricula, which need to realign themselves with the present-day concerns of Singaporean youth. This means less reliance on written language, especially rote learning of characters and grammar, and more focus on reading and oral communication because it is through these that mother tongues can remain relevant to the students. Moreover, innovative teaching techniques and lesson plans have been put forward by all

Table 3.3 Resident students aged 5 years and over by language most frequently spoken at home and level of education attending

Ethnic group/ language	Primary		Secondary		Post-secondary		University	
	2000	2005	2000	2005	2000	2005	2000	2005
Chinese (%)	100	100	100	100	100	100	100	100
English	36.5	44.9	27.5	38.5	25.1	35.9	29.9	39.2
Mandarin	59.3	52.8	63.8	57.8	60.5	58.4	53.1	52.9
Chinese dialect	3.9	2.0	8.2	3.3	14.1	5.5	16.9	7.6
Others	0.3	0.3	0.4	0.2	0.3	0.2	0.1	0.3
Malays (%)	100	100	100	100	100	100	100	100
English	9.2	17.6	8.4	14.1	12.2	17.6	26.4	32.8
Malay	90.3	82.3	91.0	85.7	87.3	82.1	73.1	67.2
Others	0.5	0.1	0.6	0.1	0.6	0.2	0.5	–
Indians (%)	100	100	100	100	100	100	100	100
English	43.5	47.8	41.4	46.7	46.2	51.9	56.7	64.2
Malay	13.2	9.4	14.7	14.4	11.9	11.9	6.1	4.9
Tamil	35.9	32.8	38.0	33.5	33.9	29.6	26.9	26.7
Others	7.4	10.0	5.9	5.5	8.0	6.6	10.2	4.2

levels of the education system to incorporate critical and creative thinking, which, as earlier discussed, constitutes the core principle of the TSLN framework of education.

All this means that postcolonial education in Singapore has relied heavily on its unique bilingual policy, successfully bringing about desired results according to state ideologies of multiculturalism and economic developmentalism through highly centralised education reforms and initiatives. However, recent changes have not transformed the essence of bilingualism and bilingual education in Singapore. English as the medium of instruction is rationalised through economic pragmatism needed to compete in the global market, while the mother tongues as second languages of education are justified as carriers of local cultures and histories needed to keep the country's 'Asian values' alive in the midst of the so-called decadent values of the West creeping in through English. The many sacred cows of bilingual education, according to one of the foremost education specialists in Singapore, have escaped criticism because some of them 'are just too sacred to review' (Gopinathan, 2002: 87).

Reductionist bilingual education

According to Gopinathan *et al.* (2004), Singapore's bilingual education can be best described as reductionist. The bilingual framework is one that does not provide a full or adequate picture of the multilingual landscape of Singapore. There are officially (still) four 'races' in Singapore – Chinese, Malays, Indians and Others – which reduce the complex language situation of the country to one national language (Malay) and four official languages (English, Chinese, Malay and Tamil) (see also Lai, 2004).

Consequently, the realities on the ground are not fully understood. For example, there is cultural border crossing in the classrooms where different literacy and cultural practices are brought into the classroom by both teachers and students belonging to different ethnic groups. However, the classroom rarely acts as a space for substantial intercultural discussions among students who speak different 'mother tongues'. Gopinathan *et al.* (2004) provide several reasons for this inability of the classroom to transcend linguistic and cultural boundaries. First, that the bilingual framework artificially treats English and the official mother tongues as conceptually separate, thereby implying that they should be treated as distinct entities in the classroom as well. Second, the economic imperative of the education system in general focuses on the mastery of language skills, not negotiation of literacy practices where different languages are used for different purposes in different contexts or are used simultaneously through codeswitching and codemixing practices.

The neutrality of English, which is assumed in the bilingual policy, is problematic in this regard because the focus on skills prevents the language from being used as an inter-ethnic bridge that helps create social cohesion and harmony. On the other hand, the pedagogic focus on skills training also renders problematic the assumption that mother tongues are cultural ballasts. A multiculturalist perspective on language education, in other words, does not necessarily mean a deep understanding of the realities of multiculturalism in the classroom:

> The mere availability of languages in the school curriculum is insufficient for language to play a powerful role in fostering

inter-cultural competence essential to strengthening ethnic harmony. Many of the efforts in the past decade in addressing language learning issues have tended to focus on skills and acquisition issues, with less attention paid to needed outcomes such as the complex communicative competencies needed for crossing cultural borders. (Gopinathan *et al.*, 2004: 237)

Similarly, bilingual education is reductionist in the sense of creating the home language shifts discussed above. While bilingual education is officially rationalised as part of the efforts to maintain and sustain the mother tongues (the official ones at least), what is happening in Singaporean homes seems to be the reverse because of the 'encroachment' of English (Zhao & Liu, 2007). The terms that can better describe what is happening are 'subtractive bilingualism' (Gopinathan *et al.*, 2004: 240) or 'bilingual elitism' (Silver, 2005: 62). It does not help that the official state discourse casts other Chinese 'dialects' as negative and inferior since they are perceived to get in the way of learning Mandarin efficiently and effectively, even though these 'dialects' in the 2005 census still constitute 18.2% of all Singaporean home language varieties (*Yearbook of Statistics*, 2008).

The problem of social class

An even less discussed aspect of bilingual education in Singapore is the problem of social class that the education system engenders. Of course, the use of 'social class' here is not unproblematic, but as Bourdieu (1989, 1991) argues, it is a powerful concept because it actually involves the coupling of material and symbolic elements and dispositions that define groups of people in a society. It is not reducible to one element only, thus it is difficult to pin down, but education, socioeconomic status and home background usually cluster together to form a particular social class. 'Socioeconomic status' may be a safer alternative because it can be quantified or scientifically demonstrated, but it rarely exists on its own and, in reality, is ideologically and politically imbued with relations of power to do with, among many, language use, educational attainment and even ownership of types of housing. Indeed, while social class is a slippery concept, it does point to interests and practices – *habitus* in Bourdieu's sense – in Singapore that both sustain and are sustained by its brand of bilingual education.

Because of the primacy of ethnicity in the 'neat' official discourse of bilingualism in the country (Lo Bianco, 2006), how class complicates the socioethnic picture has scarcely been part of policy-making discourse. As noted several times in this chapter, English has always been couched as an ethnic-free language in Singapore, but even if this is a generally accepted proposition (especially if one rationalises the choice of English over other competing ethnic/indigenous languages as the medium of instruction), English is 'certainly not a class-neutral language' because it was already a common language among the local elite during the British colonial period and the early language of use among political elders who then had access to British university education (Chua, 2005: 12):

> The adoption of English as the primary language in all public life obviously accentuated this class dimension. The political utility of the ideological illusion or intentional camouflage of "neutrality" enables the state to use English to delineate discursive spaces, to articulate its own interests distinctly, away from the interests of all racial groups. (Chua, 2005)

Nevertheless, while scholarly articulations of class-based issues in Singapore (although language use is usually not taken up as a crucial variable) appear in sociological studies (e.g. Tan, E.S., 2004), they are rare in educational and language policy-orientated research. Even in recent papers on language, ethnicity and education in Singapore, references to class are made but not followed through, for example when Lai (2004) contends in two sentences that present-day intensification of economic competition 'is emerging and threatens to assume a class-race overlap' where the economically dominant class is the Chinese population and the economically weaker ones are the Malays and Indians (11). Gopinathan *et al.* (2004) also briefly remark on social inequalities in Singapore, especially among the Malays, which undermine inter-ethnic social relations especially because they overlap with ethnic identity. However, other than the sentence where it appears, there is no further discussion of how language education and class/socioeconomic status are intertwined (Gopinathan *et al.*, 2004: 233).

Like most studies on home language shifts and maintenance in Singapore, Zhao and Liu (2007) note that the mother tongues, especially Chinese which is the focus of their research, are gradually being pushed out of the homes to give way to English. However, unlike others, they view such transformation through the lens of class, specifically the correlations between home language use and socioeconomic variables, such as housing conditions, occupation, educational qualification of parents and type of kindergarten of children. The results show 'neat' and 'obvious' (Zhao & Liu, 2007: 117) parallels between language use and social stratification. First, the more expensive and exclusive the housing conditions are, the more likely that English is spoken rather than Chinese; the reverse is true in less expensive housing units. Second, parents in dominantly English-speaking homes are more formally educated than their counterparts in dominantly Chinese-speaking homes. Third, children from the economic elite and more affluent homes are more likely to attend private kindergartens (where the teaching of so-called Standard English is strong) than children who come from lower-income homes. The latter are more likely to attend less expensive public kindergartens where the more colloquial type of English is taught, thus already disadvantaging them before they start formal schooling, even if the language to be learned is supposed to be English. And fourth, parents' choice is overwhelmingly to speak English to their children at home, even parents who believe that their English is 'not very good'. This means that in low-income homes where the desire to use English is also very strong, there is a high probability that the variety used is the colloquial one, which could hamper the children's acquisition of the more standard variety that carries more symbolic power and prestige.

According to Lo Bianco (2006: 2), outcomes are 'sometimes, possibly often, quite different from what planners intend or forecast', and this is especially true with the bilingual policy concerning the 'maintenance' of the mother tongues in education. The reality on the ground is radically different from the idealised discourses of bilingual education: one of the consequences of English-knowing bilingualism is not the mere shift of home language use from the mother tongues and other 'dialects' to English, but the association of the Chinese language or dialects of Chinese (the most dominant mother tongue) 'with poverty and marginalisation' (Zhao & Liu, 2007: 121). Similarly, in lower-income Chinese-dominant homes where English gradually becomes the language of choice of parents allegedly to help their children learn the language of pragmatism and social mobility, socioeconomic disadvantage is actually perpetuated because of the use of Singlish, the so-called 'uneducated' variety of English.

In other words, whether low-income Chinese-speaking homes keep Chinese as the dominant home language or shift towards English for pragmatic reasons, class is still a factor in the choice. English is not a monolithic language, and Zhao and Liu (2007) allude to the fact that different homes and families stratified according to socioeconomic status move towards different varieties of English. Perhaps, low-income groups are shifting towards only one variety of English – Singlish – thus, ironically, perpetuating their low socioeconomic status even as, in the first place, they make the shift from mother tongues to English supposedly to pluck themselves out of their low class conditions. The great shift towards English in Singaporean homes must not only be addressed by doing something more with mother tongue education, as is the case in recent government initiatives through curricular changes. This shift is related to socioeconomic status at the very least, and not ethnic-free at all, so attention must be drawn towards the fundamental assumptions of Singaporean bilingual education.

Conclusion

This chapter has provided a snapshot of Singapore's brand of bilingualism. As far as achievement of professed goals is concerned, the educational and sociolinguistic literature is almost unanimous in saying that the country's education system is a story of great success. Through education, the Singapore government has transformed the country into one of the world's most prosperous states, certainly a remarkable feat considering the fact that when Singapore was expelled from Malaysia in 1965, it practically had no natural resources to depend on. It can therefore be rightly argued that English-knowing bilingualism, the consequence of privileging English in the education system, constituted part of the core of Singapore's political and economic power, as it was through this unique sociolinguistic configuration that ethnic relations were effectively managed, human resources efficiently harnessed and national wealth greatly accumulated.

But, as discussed in the latter part of the chapter, there are also emerging issues to do with English-knowing bilingualism. In particular, the relationship of bilingualism to social class has been largely ignored in earlier literature, but this and other issues are gradually animating recent debates in education and sociolinguistics. There is wisdom in articulating these problems in the open because not doing so could mean that, in the words of Tan (2008: 8), 'the problem of securing equality of opportunity and a reasonably level playing field will be severely underestimated'. There may come a time when these 'hidden' problems in Singaporean bilingualism and bilingual education may unravel themselves more rapidly, 'which the government will, of course, continue to try to manage ideologically, but with much greater difficulty' (Tan, 2008: 24).

References

Ang, M.Y (2000) Development in the English language curriculum in Singapore. *TELL* 16 (2), 3–8.
Bourdieu, P. (1989) *Distinction: A Social Critique of the Judgment of Taste*. Cambridge, MA: Harvard University Press.

Bourdieu, P. (1991) Language and Symbolic Power. Cambridge, MA: Polity Press.
Cheah, Y.M. (2004) English language teaching in Singapore today. In W.K. Ho. and R.Y.L. Wong (eds) *English Language Teaching in East Asia Today* (pp. 353–374). Singapore: Eastern University Press.
Chua, B.H. (1995) *Communitarian Ideology and Democracy in Singapore*. London and New York: Routledge.
Chua, B.H. (1998) Racial Singaporeans: Absence after the hyphen. In J.S. Kahn (ed.) *Southeast Asian Identities: Culture and the Politics of Representation in Indonesia, Malaysia, Singapore, and Thailand* (pp. 28–50). London and New York: I.B. Tauris.
Chua, B.H. (2005) Taking group rights seriously: Multiracialism in Singapore. *Working Paper No. 124*. Australia: Asia Research Centre, Murdoch University. On WWW at http://wwwarc.murdoch.edu.au/wp/wp124.pdf. Accessed 20.7.08.
Curriculum Planning and Development Division (2001) *English Language Syllabus 2001 for Primary and Secondary Schools*. Singapore: Ministry of Education. On WWW at http://www1.moe.edu.sg/syllabuses.
Department of Statistics (2008) *Yearbook of Statistics Singapore*. Singapore: Department of Statistics.
Ganguly, Š. (2003) The politics of language in Malaysia and Singapore. In M.E. Brown and Š Ganguly (eds) *Fighting Words: Language Policy and Ethnic Relations in Asia* (pp. 239–261). Cambridge and London: MIT Press.
Gopinathan, S. (2002) The challenge of globalization: Implications for education in Singapore. *Commentary* 18, 83–90.
Gopinathan, S., Ho, W.K. and Saravanan, V. (2004) Ethnicity management and language education policy: Towards a modified model of language education in Singapore. In A.E. Lai (ed.) *Beyond Rituals and Riots – Ethnic Pluralism and Social Cohesion in Singapore* (pp. 228–257). Singapore, Eastern University Press.
Ho, W.K. (2006) *Education in Singapore: Focusing on Quality and Choice in Learning. A Country Report*. Singapore: Singapore Teachers' Union.
Kassim, A.Md. (2008) Malay language as a foreign language and the Singapore's education system. *GEMA Online Journal of Language Studies* 8 (1), 47–56.
Kramel-Dahl, A. (2007) Teaching English language in Singapore after 2001: A case study of change in progress. In V. Vaish, S. Gopinathan and Y. Liu (eds) *Critical Studies of Language and Education in Singapore* (pp. 47–72). Rotterdam/Taipei: Sense Publishers.
Lai, A.E. (2004) Introduction: Beyond rituals and riots. In A.E. Lai (ed.) *Beyond Rituals and Riots – Ethnic Pluralism and Social Cohesion in Singapore* (pp. 1–40). Singapore: Eastern University Press.
Lee, C.J.W.-L. (2007) Afterword: Language, capitalist development, cultural change. In V. Vaish, S. Gopinathan and Y. Liu (eds) *Critical Studies of Language and Education in Singapore* (pp. 249–258). Rotterdam/Taipei: Sense Publishers.
Lo Bianco, J. (2006) Advantage + identity: Neat discourse, loose connection. Singapore's medium of instruction policy. In V. Vaish, Y. Liu and S. Gopinathan (eds) *Language, Capital Culture* (pp. 5–21). Rotterdam: Sense Publishers.
Nathan, J.M. (2001) Making 'Thinking Schools' meaningful: Creating thinking cultures. In J. Tan, S. Gopinathan and W.K. Ho (eds) *Challenges Facing the Singapore Education System Today* (pp. 35–49). Singapore: Prentice Hall.

Pakir, A. (1991) The range of depth of English-knowing bilinguals in Singapore. *World Englishes* 10 (2), 167–179.
Pakir, A. (1993) Two tongue tied: Bilingualism in Singapore. *Journal of Multilingual and Multicultural Development* 14 (1 & 2), 73–90.
Report of the Chinese Language Curriculum and Pedagogy Review Committee (2004) Singapore: Ministry of Education.
Report of the Chinese Language Curriculum and Pedagogy Review Committee (2005) Singapore: Ministry of Education.
Report of the Malay Language Curriculum and Pedagogy Review Committee (2005) Singapore: Ministry of Education.
Retna, K.S. (2007) The learning organisation: A school's journey towards critical and creative thinking. *The Asia-Pacific Education Researcher* 16 (2), 127–142.
Silver, E.S. (2002) Policies on English language education and economic development. In R.E. Silver, G. Hu and M. Iino (eds) *English Language Education in China, Japan, and Singapore* (pp. 100–169). Singapore: Graduate Programmes and Research Office, National Institute of Education, Nanyang Technological University.
Silver, E.S. (2005) The discourse of linguistic capital: Language and economic policy planning in Singapore. *Language Policy* 4, 47–66.
Singapore (1956) All-party committee on Chinese Education. *Report of the All-Party Committee of the Singapore Legislative Assembly on Chinese Education*. Singapore: Government Printer.
Spring, J. (1998) *Education and the Rise of the Global Economy*. Mahwah, NJ: Lawrence Erlbaum Associates.
Sripathy, M. (2007) Cultural scripts and literacy pedagogy. In V. Vaish, S. Gopinathan and Y. Liu (eds) *Critical Studies of Language and Education in Singapore* (pp. 73–102). Rotterdam/Taipei: Sense Publishers.
Tan, E. (2004) "We, the Citizens of Singapore...": Multiethnicity, its evolutions and its aberrations. In A.E. Lai (ed.) *Beyond Rituals and Riots: Ethnic Pluralism and Social Cohesion in Singapore* (pp. 65–97). Singapore: Eastern University Press.
Tan, E.S. (2004) *Does Class Matter? Social Stratification and Orientations in Singapore*. Singapore: World Scientific.
Tan, J. (2006) Singapore. *Higher Education in Southeast Asia*. Bangkok: UNESCO Asia and Pacific Regional Bureau for Education.
Tan, J., Gopinathan, S. and Ho, W.K. (2001) *Challenges Facing the Singapore Education System Today*. Singapore: Prentice Hall.
Tan, K.P. (2008) Meritocracy and elitism in a global city: Ideological shifts in Singapore. *International Political Science Review* 29 (1), 7–27.
Tay, E.S. (1990) The ends and means of education. *Commentary* 8, 4–12.
Wee, L. (2003) Linguistic instrumentalism in Singapore. *Journal of Multilingual and Multicultural Development* 24, 211–224.
World Competitiveness Yearbook (2007) Lausanne, Switzerland: International Institute for Management Development.
Xu, D. and Li, W. (2002) Managing multilingualism in Singapore. In W. Li, J-M. Dewaele and A. Housen (eds) *Opportunities and Challenges of Bilingualism* (pp. 275–296). Berlin: Mouton de Gruyter.
Yearbook of Statistics, Singapore (2008) Singapore: Department of Statistics.

Yip, J.S.K., Eng, S.P. and Yap, J.Y.C. (1994) 25 years of educational reform. In J.S.K. Yip and W.K. Sim (eds) *Evolution of Educational Excellence – 25 Years of Education in the Republic of Singapore* (pp. 1–32). Singapore: Longman.

Zhao, S. and Liu, Y. (2007) Home language shift and its implications for language planning in Singapore: From the perspective of prestige planning. *The Asia-Pacific Education Researcher* 16 (2), 111–126.

Chapter 4

English Language in Taiwan: An Examination of its Use in Society and Education in Schools

IRENE WEN-LING CHEN and JESSIE JU-CHEN HSIEH

Introduction

The call to meet the challenge of internationalisation and globalisation has become the undertone of almost every political, economic and educational statement of the Taiwan government, and proficiency in English in particular seems to be the passport that connects the islanders to the outside world. English has gained a prestigious status in every aspect of Taiwanese society as the 'linguistic software' (Tonkin, 2001, cited in Crawford, 2003: 1) for economic growth and competitiveness. Interestingly, though, as Taiwan is a multicultural society,[1] a contested battleground has developed between different ethnic groups striving for recognition of their identities through national language planning and policy, it is English, a language from a foreign land, that has won due to its overwhelming popularity over all other languages (Tsao, 2001). Price (2005: 1) observes that Taiwan seems to be tolerating the dominance of a foreign language in society, while advocating a 'supra-ethnic Taiwanese identity' within the country and to the outside world. This paradoxical attitude towards language spread and language policy, Price argues further, leads to tensions between the global influences and the local approaches to educational policies and practices. Recognising the opposing perspectives of indigenisation and internationalisation, Taiwanese society finds herself obsessed with the English language while striving for a balance between national identity and competitiveness.

English Fever in Taiwan

'English is not everything!' This is a stern statement made by the CommonWealth Magazine (CWM), one of Taiwan's leading news and finance magazines. At the end of 2004, CWM devoted a special issue to looking at the problems of Taiwan education. On the basis of an in-depth investigation and carefully conducted surveys (Chou, 2004), the issue concludes that there is 'English fever' in Taiwan. It warns Taiwanese society that the passion of English acquisition has become a serious problem.

Overwhelming enthusiasm in learning English

According to the CWM survey (Chou, 2004), over 60% of interviewed parents perceive that their level of English proficiency determines their life, as it does for their children. Nearly 80% of them believe English proficiency is very important to their children's future. As a result, parents in Taiwan are very keen on sending their children to cram schools, purchasing English learning materials and/or, if possible, trying to speak English with their children at home.

Because of Taiwan parents' enthusiasm for their children to learn English, the English language teaching (ELT) industry has expanded dramatically since the late 1990s. According to an estimation provided by the Ministry of Education in 2004, the output value of the ELT industry accounts for an outstanding 20–25 billion New Taiwan Dollars (US$590–738 million) each year, excluding the revenue share from the US$90 million e-learning industry (Market Intelligence Center, 2004). Studying English has become a 'national obsession' (Liu, 2002: cover page) or, in other words, the 'whole-nation movement in the 21st century' (Chern, 2004: 437).

English use in Taiwan

In contrast with their enthusiasm to learn English, Taiwanese have not yet used English as a major means for communication. However, given that there are more and more formal and informal opportunities, such as frequent contact with foreigners at work or access to English-spoken Hollywood entertainment, the use of English is increasing, especially for the generation aged 19–29 (Chen, 2003: 198) and beyond. Nowadays, English is increasingly used by Taiwanese in two aspects of life: study and work.

The use of English as an academic language

The importance of English as an academic language is a commonplace observation. For academic promotion in higher education, for example, the MOE has made it a directive that only articles published in the three English language academic indexes, the Science Citation Index

(SCI), Social Sciences Citation Index (SSCI) and Engineering Index (EI), are to be accredited as academic contributions in assessing academic achievement (Liu, 2004: 26). As a result, Taiwanese academics have to master English as an academic skill in order to survive academic competition.

The second example is the fact that English is also used by Taiwanese as the main language for advanced overseas study. According to government statistics, since 2000, each year more than 30,000 Taiwanese students apply for overseas student visas (Bureau of International Cultural and Educational Relations, 2009). Among all the study abroad destinations, the USA has always been the nation that grants the most student visas to Taiwanese. Other top destinations for the years 1996–2007 were the UK, Australia, Canada and Japan (*The Republic of China Yearbook*, 2008). It is apparent that, except Japan, all the destinations in the students' top list for studying abroad are English-speaking countries, in other words, the 'inner circle countries' (Kachru, 1986). In 2008 alone, about 88% of students studying abroad went to the inner circle countries (see Table 4.1). It should be noted that this table does not include the number of students enrolled in international study programmes, which take place in non-inner circle countries, such as Germany or Singapore, but offer courses in English.

Table 4.1 Number of students studying in the inner circle countries in 2004–2008

	2008	2007	2006	2005	2004
USA	19,402	14,916	16,451	15,525	14,054
Canada	3,266	3,984	1,997	2,140	2,149
UK	5,885	7,132	9,653	9,248	9,207
Australia	2,370	2,570	2,862	2,679	2,246
New Zealand	596	618	538	498	534
(a) Total of students studying in inner circle countries	31,519	29,220	31,501	30,090	28,190
(b) Grand total of students studying abroad	35,698	34,991	37,171	34,058	32,525

Source: Adapted from Bureau of International Cultural and Educational Relations (2009).

The use of English as a work language

According to a survey conducted by 104 Job Bank in 2004, the largest human resources company in Taiwan, 53% of its total job vacancies require the applicants to have foreign language skills; and 95% of these jobs ask specifically for proficiency in English (104 Job Bank Report, 2004a). Interestingly, these vacancies are mostly created by local Taiwanese corporations as they wish to employ people with English competence to meet their needs to develop or serve the global market.

Take the tourism industry for example. In 2008 alone, 3.8 million foreigners visited Taiwan either for pleasure or business (National Immigration Agency, 2009). In order to better serve foreign visitors in Taiwan, the government has also begun to sponsor English courses to help service workers, such as taxi drivers and tourism industry employees, improve their English (Chern, 2004; *China Times*, 2006).

In addition, more and more foreigners take up jobs in Taiwan. Up to February 2009, the Bureau of Employment and Vocational Training (2009) has accepted and issued about 370,000 working permits for foreign professionals, not including foreign labourers from East Asian countries. About 100,000 of these foreign professionals work in the education sector; most others work in industries such as information and technology, commerce and trading, and finance. Among them, the professionals from inner circle countries make up one third of the total population of these foreign professionals.

As Sommers (2008) indicates, the use of English among Taiwan's workforce is a fact; it is only a matter of whether it is intensive English use, elective use or assessment-based use.

The Pragmatic View of the English Language in Taiwan

In sum, it is obvious that Taiwanese take the learning and use of the English language from a very pragmatic perspective. This perspective not only suggests a natural causal relationship between English proficiency and economic success, but also a perception of English as a 'neutral' language. Interestingly, this view is apparently shared in other Greater China regions (see Gil & Adamson; Tupas; Li; and Young, this volume).

However, is pragmatism the only cause of English fever? In the following section, we will closely examine the English language through a historical overview in the context of Taiwan in order to gain a better understanding.

English as a Foreign Language in Taiwan: A Historical Overview

Practices before the 1950s

In the late 19th century, before Taiwan officially became a part of China, George Leslie Mackay, a missionary and dentist from British Columbia, set up a modern school in Tamsui, the largest harbour city in Taiwan at that time, with donations from his own town people in Canada. The school was called Oxford College (牛津學堂), and was dedicated to the teaching of theology, geography, physics, medicine, etc. – knowledge that belonged to the western culture – to the Taiwanese people (Aletheia University, 2005). In an effort to modernise Taiwanese education, Dr Mackay approached the local society from a unique perspective in that, rather than transforming the local culture to meet his own call, he became extremely fluent in the local language and contributed greatly to the preservation of indigenous culture. Although a few subjects were still taught in English (Sung, 2003), the teaching and learning of English was not the main purpose of the institution, since an overall antagonistic attitude towards foreigners and their cultures was still the pervading mindset of the time. Yet, Dr Mackay and his institution successfully helped to modernise the local educational landscape through the introduction of western knowledge in many ways, particularly in the fields of women's education and medical practice (Aletheia University, 2005).

In 1887, in the wake of other cities in China that underwent increasing exposure to foreign interactions, Taiwan witnessed the establishment of the first official foreign (English) language teaching and learning institution in Taipei (Rhythms, 2006). The institution was set up by Liu Ming-chuan, the first viceroy of Taiwan, under the name Hsi-hsueh-tang (西學堂), which literally means 'Western Educational Institution'. Unlike its counterpart in the capital city in mainland China, this western-style educational institution opened its doors to local commoners – albeit commoners with outstanding intellectual abilities.

However, when Taiwan became a colony of the Japanese after China's defeat in the first Sino-Japanese War in 1895, the new government suspended all English teaching and learning practices. As learning Japanese, the colonist language, became the major task of all levels of schooling, English was only taught in teachers' schools, either as a compulsory or an elective course (Tseng, 2007: 223). During this stage of development, the English curriculum in Taiwan, if any, followed the prescription of the Japanese Ministry of Education for ELT models developed by Harold Palmer, a British scholar commissioned by the Japanese government to renovate teaching pedagogy and revise textbooks and dictionaries for English teachers and learners (Howatt, 1984; cited in Tseng, 2007: 223). The focus of English language education, nevertheless, was mostly on grammar acquisition (Tseng, 2007: 231).

The post-war period: American aid and English as a foreign language education

Following Japan's defeat in World War II and the subsequent return of Taiwan to China, in 1949 the Nationalist government retreated to Taiwan and started to solidify its dominance over the island. Tsao (1999) states that the language policy of the Taiwan government during this stage was dictated by two factors: one was nationalism and national unification, and the other was modernisation and economic growth (Tsao, 1999: 350). The new political power in Taiwan stipulated a strict language policy that boosted Mandarin as the national language and marginalised all other mother tongues in formal education. It was not surprising that, with this badge of nationalism, English language learning was attributed a considerably minor significance even in secondary school curricula, with as little as two teaching hours a week.

Yet, for the ethnic Chinese in general, the call for national identity and unification is always embedded with complicated sentiments resulting from unavoidable confrontations with the western world. In Chapter 2 of this volume, Gil and Adamson make this complexity very clear when they state, 'the role and status of English has waxed and waned with the political tides, being affected by fluctuations in China's relations with the outside world'. As such, notwithstanding that significant efforts were made to solidify the status of the national language, Taiwan was also moving into a stage in which 'modernisation and economic growth' (Tsao, 1999: 350) became the two major drives for society, and proficiency in the English language was clearly defined as the major means to economic prosperity. Thus, the second social reform under the influence of western culture[2] began – only this time, the Taiwanese people willingly, but ambivalently, adopted many perspectives that represent western ideology.

Primarily, the overall tone of English learning and teaching in Taiwan after World War II was particularly shaded with significant influence from the Americans (Hsu, 1981; cited in Tseng, 2007: 233). Having been defeated in the civil war and given up the continent to the Communists, the KMT government in Taiwan secured the position of a member of the

Sino-American Mutual Defense Treaty (Wikipedia, 2009) and became a significant ally of the USA. At this stage, learning the English language won tremendous popularity under the deliberate influence of the American government (Chao, 2001). In 1951, the first US assignment of a Military Assistance Advisory Group (MAAG) established a station in Taiwan. During the Vietnam War, Taiwan became the retreat and supply centre for American troops. When the Americans sent armed forces to defend Taiwan against China, according to the abovementioned treaty in 1954, the influence of American culture flourished on the island, ranging from songs to movies and magazines, which became important resources for language learning (Chao, 2001).

Moreover, from 1951 to 1965, during and after the Korean War, the Taiwan Strait Crisis and the Vietnamese War, Taiwan accepted significant US aid that helped in the country's major economic development (Chao, 1985; Wen, 1989). Wang Chao-ming, the former minister of economics and one of the key persons in Taiwan's economic development in the post-war period, remarked that American aid played a significant role in setting up the bedrock for the modernisation of Taiwanese society; without American aid, Taiwan could never have achieved the economic miracles (Chao, 1985).

Actually, the aid from the USA did more than just provide financial stimulus to the island country. Taiwan has subsequently opened its door to English – American English, to be exact – both in terms of the culture and ideological impact of the language, and this overwhelming popularity of a foreign language in Taiwan certainly grew out of a mixture of ambivalent sentiments. Chen (2005: 9) states that the key to the success of 'American neo-colonialism' in Taiwan was due to the approach of the US government to cultural penetration into Taiwanese society. This approach aimed to achieve 'deliberate cultivation of pro-American, anti-communist, conservative elite class' (Chao, 2001: 93), and played a significant role in the reform of the social system. The measures taken included support for various institutions and project funding, endeavours for students to study abroad, governmental exchange programmes and various research projects with American universities and institutions (Chao, 2001). Like their predecessors at the beginning of the 20th century, students and scholars supported by such projects have in turn brought back tremendous American influences into Taiwanese society in the last few decades. The fast-track development of Taiwan in the last half of the 20th century is often seen as the result of the effort of these socio-economic and political elites who were educated in the USA. It is estimated that, in the last two decades or so, more than 60% of the cabinet members have been educated in the USA (Chao, 2001), including the former president Li Teng-hui, the former vice presidents Lien Chen and Lu Hsiou-lien, and the current president Ma Ying-jeou.

Aid from the USA also played a significant role in the development of an English education system and language training centre in Taiwan. In 1951, funded by American aid, the English Language Centre (ELC) was established. It offered English language training courses to people preparing to go to the USA under government funding. The centre also offered courses in other foreign languages, such as French and Spanish. Aid from the USA was minimised after 1954, and the management of the ELC was then shifted to the National Taiwan University, providing services mostly to government-sponsored personnel (LTTC, 2010a). After 1963, owing to the significant boom in the popularity of English language courses, the centre became financially independent of American funding, changing its name in 1979 to the Language Training and Testing Centre (LTTC), and was then commissioned by the Taiwan government to develop language teaching and learning guidelines and assessment projects for the national curriculum. The development of the General English Proficiency Test (GEPT), which has been the dominant nationwide language testing system of the country since 2001, is one of the projects of this centre.

English as a foreign language and educational reform in the post-martial law era

Education policy, particularly that of English language education, moved into a new phase of development when 40 years of political restraint from martial law was officially lifted in 1987. Economic prosperity and internationalisation stood firm as the urgent calls of the nation, and have been evident in educational policy statements since 1995, as shown in Table 4.2.

It is clear that in almost every major policy statement since 1995, English language education has been prescribed as a key element of economic growth and internationalisation. As a consequence of such an educational perspective, English language courses, of all other subjects in schools, are regarded as the primary means to economic prosperity, and the acquisition of linguistic competence in English is believed to facilitate exposure to the outside world and lead to business opportunities in the global village (LTTC, 2010a).

The Educational Reform Procession, which echoed this urge for internationalisation at all levels of education, was called into action on

Table 4.2 Government policy statements and major claims relating to English education since 1995

Government policy statements	Major claims for English education
The Republic of China Educational Report, Ministry of Education (1995)	Multicultural education Freedom in education Internationalisation Diversification of foreign languages education International exchange educational programmes
Advisory Proposal for Educational Reform and the Consultants' Concluding Report on Education Reform, Education Reform Advisory Committee, Executive Yuan, Republic of China (1996)	Democratisation, modernisation and internationalisation of education De-regulation of elementary and junior high schools, curriculum reform, introduction of English to primary school students
Master Plan for Educational Reform, Ministry of Education (1997)	Internationalisation Diversification of foreign languages education International exchange educational programmes
Educational Reform Action Plan, Ministry of Education (1998)	Internationalisation Diversification of foreign languages education
Challenge 2008: the Six-year National Development Plan, Executive Yuan (2002a)	For universities and graduate schools: 　To offer professional English education courses; 　To enroll international students and sending students abroad; 　To increase of overseas travel and information exchange. The ultimate goal: to shape Taiwan into a suitable centre for cultural exchange of resources of all kinds with foreign countries
Action Project for Building an English Living Environment, Executive Yuan, Republic of China (2002b)	Reinforcement of integrated establishment and integration of a bilingual environment Training in English talents to relevant competency levels Reinforcement of the publicity campaigns, advertisements, and websites in English and Mandarin

Sources: MOE (1995, 1997, 1998); Education Reform Advisory Committee, Executive Yuan, Republic of China (1996, 2002a, 2002b).

10 April 1994 by over 50,000 teachers and educators in the country, seeking modernisation of educational policy and practices. Issues such as policy, curricula, teachers' education, teaching pedagogy and teaching materials were raised and scrutinised in numerous research studies, forums, hearings and discussions in all sectors of society. In response, between 1996 and 1998, the MOE reformed directives and guidelines for all levels of education (MOE, 1998, 1999). In 1999, the MOE finalised the plan for the implementation of a crucial educational change: the Grade 1-9 Curriculum, which revolutionised the existing nine-year national compulsory educational system, was put into practice in 2001. The call for and efforts towards reforms encompass many aspects of education, among which several changes in the process of facilitation of English courses in the curriculum are pertinent to this discussion.

English had been taught in secondary schools prior to the 1990s, as discussed in the previous section. Due to the educational reform, the Taiwan government proposed to officially extend the provision of ELT to primary schools. In 1993, the Taiwan government began to allow primary schools to provide English teaching during the extra-curricular activity hours (Shih, 1998). In the years that followed, in attempting to follow the advice of the Educational Reform Committee, the MOE conducted feasibility studies, proposed training programmes and formulated guidelines for the reform plan. English language education was envisaged not only as a subject taught at all levels of schooling, but also a movement of change in all sectors of society. Table 4.3 summarises this development chronologically.

The notion of 'Every citizen to learn English' highlighted the determination of the government to promote ELT in every corner of society, while the move to extend English provision to fifth and sixth graders in primary schools in 2001 aimed to initiate a significant change in educational practice. However, the final guidelines of the Grade 1-9 Curriculum for English/Language Arts provided only a short, brief structure for the implementation of the curriculum and left out far too many details regarding actual practice (Tsao, 2008). Little planning or renovation was forthcoming from policy makers in terms of objectives, pedagogy, teachers' training or subject assessment. The Taipei City government progressed through five stages of development of the implementation of English teaching in the primary schools from 1984 to 1999 (Chern, 2002). This demonstrated the city government's caution in finalising the details of a dramatic change in education. However, the policy to extend ELT to primary school level was still strongly criticised by many scholars and teachers as blunt and abrupt (issues arising from

Table 4.3 Development of the EFL policy in the 1990s and 2000s

Year	Programmes/ proposals	Significant details	Initiation
1993	Educational Policy	Primary schools are allowed to facilitate English classes in extra-curricular activity hours	MOE
1996	Advisory Proposal for Educational Reform	Proposition of: (1) the inclusion of the reading and writing knowledge of the 26 letters as official requirement for K12 students (2) the extension of English language education to primary schools	Educational Reform Committee, Executive Yuan
1998	Training for Primary School English Teachers	Proposing training of English teachers for primary schools	MOE
1998	Feasibility Study and Proposal for English Curricula for Primary School Students	Report of the feasibility study team on the facilitation of English courses in primary schools, which proposed the objectives, implementation process, resources, teacher training necessary to administer the curriculum	MOE-commissioned project
1998	Education Reform Action Plan	'Every citizen to learn English' becomes one of the main goals of the 1999–2003 educational policy	MOE
1998	General guidelines for English Language Arts of Grade 1-9 Curriculum	Specified that, from 2001, English will be taught to fifth and sixth graders in primary schools	MOE
2001	General guidelines for English/ Language Arts of Grade 1-9 Curriculum	English begins to be taught to fifth and sixth graders in primary school	MOE

Table 4.3 (*Continued*)

Year	Programmes/ proposals	Significant details	Initiation
2003	The Grade 1-9 Curriculum: Phase 3 for English language education	English education is planned to be extended to grade three pupils in 2005	MOE

Sources: MOE (1995, 1997, 2001, 2003)

the implementation of ELT programmes in the primary schools will be taken up later in more details).

It should be noted that, in practice, the move of the MOE fell far behind those of city governments in terms of implementation of starting ELT programmes at primary schools. Although the MOE's prescription that ELT be provided to fifth graders was to start in 2001, many cities had been allowing such practice in primary schools long before the enforcement of the policy. From 1993, several city governments had begun to 'experiment' with such programmes before the MOE gave its official blessing. In 1997, of the 2561 primary schools nationwide, 50% had already started to teach English on a regular basis (Dai, 1998). Kaohsiung City, for instance, which is a highly industrialised harbour city in the south with a population of over 2 million, began allowing the teaching of English to fifth and sixth graders in 1997, and the practice extended to third and fourth graders in 1998 (Dai, 1999; Lin, 2003). Taipei, the capital city, started the provision of English teaching to fifth and sixth graders in 1993, and extended it to third and fourth graders in 2001 (Dai, 1999), and then to all primary school children in 2002. Although the provision of English teaching from the third grade on was officially implemented in 2005, by 2003 eight major cities of the island had already opened the door to English teaching to all, with six others joining them after (Lin, 2003). A survey conducted by the National Teachers' Association in 2003 further confirmed that almost 90% of the cities nationwide had already started teaching English in primary schools, among which 10 had extended the practice from first graders onwards.

Furthermore, according to a survey conducted in 2000 (Chang *et al.*, 2002), as many as 97.2% of private kindergartens and one third of public kindergartens were teaching English to children; nearly 63% of the parents surveyed sent their children to kindergartens that offered English programmes, and 77% of parents would want the government to enforce the inclusion of English learning in the kindergarten curriculum (Chang et al., 2002). Moreover, for most parents, two hours study in English every week in school is not sufficient in terms of language exposure. Pupils are also sent to after-school supplementary classes, or 'cram schools' (*bu-xi-ban*), for more intensive learning in English. In an MOE survey of 28,804 pupils in 2002, 53.87% of primary school children attended after-school classes, and more than one third of these cram schools were dedicated to English teaching (MOE, 2002).

Another survey by the League for Children's Welfare in 2002 showed that 60% of pupils in the metropolitan Taipei city area had already started to learn English before entering primary schools (Child Welfare Leaguer Foundation, 2002). In 2005, there were significant increases in the number of fifth and sixth graders attending after-school English classes, up to 84% (Cheng, 2005), or 72% with all graders counted (104 Tutor's Net, 2005). In actual practice, children from socially and economically privileged families do not only start early, generally at the age of 4, which is eight years earlier than was the norm 15 years ago, but the time they spend on English is also longer. Around one-tenth of pupils have attended immersion programmes in English since kindergarten, and continue to study English in cram schools for over eight hours a week in addition to the normal school hours.

Among the major reasons for sending children to cram schools, the top two are: (1) the fear of lagging behind other children (73%); and (2) the belief that English language skills are better acquired at an early age (60%) (Child Welfare Leaguer Foundation, 2002). This has created a situation where some pupils may have acquired English as their first or second language before they enter the junior high schools, as compared with the two-hours-per-week language experience of those students who have never had cram school experience.

Discrepancies between policy and practice

Actual practice in terms of the allocation of class hours and levels of instruction in the primary schools give clear evidence of the discrepancy between government policy and implementation. Since its launch in 2001, the Grade 1-9 Curriculum for primary and junior high schools has thus triggered more debates and confusion than its predecessor, the unified compulsory system (Shih, 2001; Chern 2002; Chan & Wu, 2004; Lee, 2007). Most of the discussions challenge some of the major issues described below.

Lack of clear guidelines to develop core competences

Although it is intended that the curriculum provides more freedom for teachers and schools regarding pedagogies and evaluation, only very rough guidelines for core competence are included (MOE, 2003), with no clear specifications as to the target language proficiency level for each grade. Moreover, the guidelines and core competencies fail to recognise the differences in objectives and approaches for ELT between primary and secondary sectors. While the primary schools follow what can be generally called a communicative approach, the junior high schools adopt a grammar centred, rote-learning approach and aim for teach-to-test in preparation for the Achievement Test for entry into senior high schools. Disparity in teaching and learning approaches between primary and junior high schools thus become key concerns of the educators.

Textbook selection and teaching resources

By allowing teachers tremendous flexibility in choosing teaching materials, the 2001 Curriculum assumes that teachers have received sufficient training. Teachers are not always capable of developing their own materials and syllabi, owing to the long history of state-controlled and prescribed curricula for teacher training. Moreover, with a heavy workload of 25 teaching hours per week on average, even competent teachers do not usually have sufficient time to develop their own teaching materials. The opening-up of textbook selection puts even more pressure on teachers and school administration. As there are more than 15 domestic textbook publishers in the market, it can be too challenging for teachers to select the most suitable materials themselves. As a result, in material selection, teachers usually give priority to those textbooks with supplementary teaching materials and test banks in order to ease their burden, rather than to the overall suitability of textbook material for quality language education.

For junior high school teachers, the burden and stress of selecting textbooks is greatest because they need to prepare students for the Achievement Test. While only general guidelines are provided by the curriculum, junior high school teachers usually need to develop mock tests based on every textbook available in the market.

Teacher training and recruitment

To meet the demand of all primary schools nationwide, around 3000 extra specialised English teachers were needed for the new century. In 1999, the Taiwan MOE recruited over 1900 trainees into a two-year intensive teacher training programme, yet fewer than 10% completed the course and stayed in the profession (Scott & Liu-Chen, 2004; cited in

Tsao, 2008: 11). In recent years, as many teachers universities and colleges have begun to offer degree programmes to meet the demand, the shortage of teachers has now eased, yet the supply of qualified English teachers still remains a pressing issue for primary schools in remote areas and communities.

Disparity in students' proficiency levels

Perhaps the most urgent issue confronting school teachers is the vast differences in the proficiency levels of the students. As discussed in the previous sections, different cities have their own interpretation and implementation strategies regarding the starting grade for ELT. Moreover, as only one or two hours of English teaching per week is provided in primary schools, parents with better financial resources are usually capable of sending their children to after-school institutions for more English education, while the students from less privileged families remain less proficient in the class. Such disparity in students' proficiency levels is referred to as the 'twin-peak phenomenon' and is perhaps the most noteworthy issue in the Taiwan ELT landscape.

This phenomenon has had a significant impact on teachers and pupils. Teachers may be forced to ignore the more proficient students to attend to the needs of less proficient ones, or vice versa. In junior high schools, students may be most diverse in terms of English education and the disparity in students' proficiency levels poses a great challenge for teachers (Crawford, 2001; Su, 2001; Wang *et al.*, 2004).

Research has shown high anxiety in those pupils who are less proficient in using English in school contexts and there is a negative correlation between foreign language anxiety and English learning achievement (Liao, 1999; Chan & Wu, 2000). From a large-scale survey of 601 fifth graders from 205 elementary schools in Taipei and interviews with nine English teachers, Chan and Wu confirm this correlation and further identify several causes of language anxiety, including low proficiency, fear of negative evaluation and pressure from students themselves and their parents (Chan & Wu, 2004). Anxiety helps to explain why low-proficient pupils tend to give up on learning English altogether.

While these studies all conclude with a similar call for raising more awareness on the part of the teachers and encouraging maintenance of balance between high and low achievers of English proficiency, it is crucial to examine the socio-cultural factors that contribute to this twin-peak situation. In the following sections, we will turn to the social milieu to identify possible sources and impacts for the above-mentioned education development.

English proficiency = competitiveness? English as a foreign language in Taiwan: A national obsession

As mentioned before, this nationwide indulgence in the learning of English is appropriately described as an 'English fever' (Krashen, 2003) and a 'national obsession' (Liu, 2003). It originated from an urge to speed up westernisation before the 1950s, and to connect with the 'American dream' after the 1950s. The promotion of English is now even more widely advocated owing to the perception of globalisation and internationalisation commonly held by policy makers and the general public. In 2002, the Taiwan government initiated a six-year plan: 'Challenge 2008: National Development Plan' (Executive Yuan, 2002a), which aimed specifically to strengthen the nation's competitiveness in the global village through grand-scale projects and programmes. Emphasised in this plan are statements on the quality of English language education and the construction of an English-friendly living environment.

In recognising that '(t)he first step to facing future challenges requires a high adaptability to globalization, as well as an environment for fostering such abilities' (Executive Yuan, 2002b), the government states that 'English in particular has become essential to global connection, and accordingly the government made English a quasi-official language six years ago to boost the range of English application in everyday life'. Moreover, to improve the English proficiency level of the people and to attract more attention from the outside world, the government proposed to 'cultivate an English-friendly living environment', which will 'efficiently bilingualize public signs, modernize regional service facilities and remedy the general lack of English information' (Executive Yuan, 2002b).

The status of English in Taiwan has thus been formally verbalised by the government as the 'passport to the world' (Hsieh, 2009: 3). Hsieh (2009) observes that English is not only viewed by the Taiwanese people as a language to be used for economic growth and a subject to be taught in schools, but also as a global lingua franca, the ultimate foreign language and, in particular, a trendy language for the social elite. As such, one could argue that Taiwanese society confers on this language a prestigious status and pays disproportionate attention to proficiency in English, as demonstrated in the dominant interests in using GEPT scores as English proficiency indicators in many facets of society, including college graduation threshold, job application and recruitment for public service officers.

As mentioned before, over 50% of the current job listings required a certain level of English proficiency, which is mostly defined by GEPT assessment scores (104 Job Bank, 2004b). In its policy statement in 2002, the Executive Yuan of Taiwan asserted that 50% of government employees, 50% of university students and 100% of future primary and secondary school teachers should be able to pass the intermediate level of the GEPT by 2007 (Executive Yuan, 2002b). The GEPT office estimated a total of over 3,800,000 test participants since the launch of the system in 2000 (LTTC, 2010b). Be it in the public or private sectors, from 2000 onwards, the GEPT score has become an indicator of competence in English for people of all ages and social groups, ranging from ages 5 to 80 (LTTC, 2010b). Proficiency in English has become not just one of the determinants of academic achievement, but also a threshold for higher education and social attainment (Lin, 2003). It was not surprising when the former president Chen Shui-bien announced his wish to include English as the lingua franca by 2008 (Lin, 2002). Though it was countervoiced and eventually vetoed by the opposition party leaders and cabinet members as not applicable to the current situation, Chen's intention was still echoed in the 2008 reform plan prescribed by the Executive Yuan in that year (Executive Yuan, 2002a).

In her discussion of the spread and status of English in Taiwan, Chen (1996) observes that English has been attributed values that transcend the pragmatic role of the language. As a symbol of social status, the acquisition of English proficiency helps secure job opportunities and thus economic competitiveness; as a symbol of intellectual sophistication, the language guarantees its users a window to the knowledge and information on the outside world, and thus is equivalent to academic achievement; and finally, as a symbol of professionalism, it signifies a high educational level, thereby demonstrating a working competence in the job market (Chen, 1996: 328). To highlight the significance of this situation in Taiwanese society, let us take a look at a newly emerging ELT practice.

The Bilingual English Programme: A new trend in English language teaching

It is not surprising that the Bilingual English Programme (BEP), a strong form of ELT programmes developed on the basis of the principles of ESL and immersion education, became popular in the education landscape at the turn of the century. The BEP is a form of intensive ELT programmes, which aims to serve the need of parents and students who, under the pressure of competitive college admission and the job market, prefer an alternative that can guarantee a well-developed English learning experience conducted in an 'official'[3] bilingual environment. It has gained popularity in the last decade especially when the Taiwan government started to loosen its restrictions on the curricula of the secondary and primary schools (Educational Reform Advisory Committee, 1996). Up to March 2009, in Taipei city alone, over 10 well-known secondary schools have offered such programmes under the MOE classification of 'programmes for the gifted and talented students', and more state-funded schools that are seen as highly competitive for college entrance admission are joining the market (Taipei Resource Centre for the Gifted and Talented, 2009).

As the Taiwan government would only tolerate the inclusion of a maximum of 35% of courses in English in primary and high schools, be it private or public (MOE, 2004), the BEP won popularity as a marketing solution that circumvented such government restrictions. In these BEP schools, in addition to the legally permitted number of English teaching hours, the hours of the 'secondary courses' (subjects not included in the high school or college entrance examinations, such as arts, music and PE) could be conducted in English and taught by foreign teachers. In this way, the school could claim that 50–60% of courses in the curricula are all-English.

BEPs are usually taught by certified foreign EFL (English as a foreign language) teachers (i.e. native English speakers). Though they may not be qualified to teach other subjects in schools, they are often asked to do so. School subjects, such as social studies, science, history, geography, and arts, when taught by foreign teachers, focus heavily on the teaching of language skills rather than on content. In this kind of immersion language education conducted in English for an average of almost 16 hours a week, as compared with 4–5 hours in a regular programme (see Table 4.4 for a comparison of class hours between BEPs and ordinary school programmes), students receive little 'content-based' education in these 'extra' language classes. It also implies that the amount of time spent on subjects taught in Mandarin, the mother tongue, is drastically reduced.

Sociological Perspectives and Concerns

As mentioned before, the BEP is designed especially for pupils from socio-economically privileged families who expect more exposure to English and foreign teachers from kindergarten level onwards. It is

Table 4.4 A comparison of the number of hours of classes taught in English on BEPs versus regular programmes

	Ages	Regular schools (hour/week)	Bilingual/intensive English programmes (hour/week)
Primary schools	7–12	2	4–10 (after school)
Junior high schools	13–15	4–5	14–16
Senior high schools	16–18	4–5	14–16

Sources: MOE (2003); Nieh (2004); Sagor Bilingual School (2009).

therefore only the social elite with financial prestige and social influence who can afford the high tuition fees and accompanying expenses that are incurred owing to extra payment required for the foreign teachers, imported books, library fees, uniforms, transportation expenses (as these schools are usually located away from the students' neighbourhoods), costumes for parties and talent shows, luxury field trips to places offering American flamboyance, etc. As parents, rather than the students themselves, make the final decision over the selection of school programmes, most schools open their doors for the parents to be involved to some degree in the design and implementation of the programmes. This strategy is especially effective when there is strong competition in the market. Students with influential parents would attract students from similar social backgrounds and also those students with parents who wish to advance their social status by entering such bilingual programmes.

It is not surprising to find that ELT in this sense is taken as one form of cultural capital in society. Throughout human history, education has long been treated as one of the means for social reproduction, creating possibilities as well as inequalities for different social groups in society. Borman *et al.* (2000: 239) argue that, in this process, persistent inequality is created and results in 'gaps in academic achievement between groups of students'. When educational policy prescribes a clear system that, in every aspect of its practice and reception, actively surrenders to the power of socio-economic class, such inequality is too obvious when classes with fewer social and economic advantages do not have access to that kind of education. In the long run, the education system that, as an institution that secures the acquisition of 'educational qualification and appropriate attitudes and values' (Demaine, 2003: 126), inevitably becomes a process for remaking and reproducing the coercive relationship of power.

Research into the sociology of education has been particularly concerned with the process of socialisation involved in such a reproduction system. Bourdieu (1986: 246) alerts us that when language, or the language of an elite class, is taken as a form of cultural capital, the 'symbolic efficacy of such cultural capital... lies in the logic of its transmission'. It is the schooling process, as the major actor in executing the transmission, that 'generates practices by which the class is renewed, integrated, and reconstituted in the face of changes, in its own composition and in the general social circumstances in which it tries to survive and prosper' (Borman *et al.*, 2000: 310).

Several studies of ELT in Taiwan testify to this sociological concern for the popularity of EFL by indicating a close relationship between family backgrounds and language learning. Su (2002) observes that attainment through education is a significant factor of occupational success in his study of social mobility in Taiwan. He also finds that the more advantaged social group even use the privilege to obtain better educational opportunities (Su, 2002). Using several scales to measure the socio-economic status of over 3000 primary school pupils, Nieh (2004) also demonstrates a high correlation between educational attainment and family incomes in Taiwanese society, and that parents with more financial privileges had been able to send their children to private institutions to learn English long before the government made the move.

Conclusion

This chapter presents a critical overview of the 'national obsession' with English as evident in Taiwanese society and the current practice of English language education in its schools. With regard to the latter, we can see that academic research, discussions and document analyses reveal many issues concerning English pedagogy, education outcomes, policy making and policy implementation, and above all, inequality in education. Indeed, how Taiwan will address these issues and resolve tensions caused by the various forces of globalisation, social stratification and national identity still remains a huge question for all, particularly for key stakeholders in education, including policy makers, parents, teachers and the pupils themselves.

Notes

1. There are four major ethnic groups in Taiwan: the Taiwanese or Minnanren (referring to people who have immigrated to Taiwan before 1949), Mainlanders (referring to people who came to Taiwan from mainland China with the KMT retreat to the island mostly in 1949), Hakka and the Austro-Polynesian

Aboriginals. Taiwanese, Mandarin, Hakka and aboriginal languages are their mother tongues, respectively. Huang (1991) provides an estimate of the percentages of population as follows: Minannren: 73.7%, Mainlanders: 13%, Hakka: 12%, and Austro-Polynesians: 1.7% (Huang, 1991, quoted in Tsao, 1999: 329).
2. The first social reform in China with western influence refers to the reformation that was initiated with the May Fourth Movement in 1919, which was a clear manifestation of the magnitude of influence from the west. Probably one of the most significant reform efforts in Chinese history towards democratisation and modernisation, the movement was initiated by elites and scholars who had studied abroad, mostly in the USA. It called for a fighting back against foreign invasion, from the Japanese in particular, for national pride and identity, and demanded a more open policy for knowledge from the west, democracy and science in particular. This social reform resulted in a gradual revolution of the knowledge system, culture, and education of society.
3. Before the emergence of the BEP, all public and private schools had few options in curriculum designs but to follow the national curricula, in which the hours for teaching English are stratified. That means that if students aspired for more English teaching hours and exposure, they had to go to private after-school institutions. The idea of the BEP helped the schools to find a way out of these restrictions; since 1996, schools have been allowed to try out programmes like the BEP under two kinds of existing categorisation: the experimental programme and the gifted students programme. Originally, these two categories were not designed to suit the purpose of intensive language programmes, but were later adopted by interested schools to suit the regulation, which suggests that the BEP does not totally follow the 'official' prescription, but rather flourishes as a 'tolerated' compromise between policy and practice. Up to March 2009, legally the 'all-English' programmes in primary and secondary schools could only be set up for students holding non-Taiwanese passports (MOE, 2009). Alternative titles for the BEP include 'intensive English programmes', 'experimental bilingual programmes' and 'programmes for the gifted and talented students'.

References

104 Job Bank (2004a) 104 Job Bank Report. (In Chinese) On WWW at http://www.104.com.tw. Accessed 6.6.06.

104 Job Bank (2004b) Foreign language proficiency required for job applications. (In Chinese) On WWW at www.104.com.tw/cfdocs/2000/pressroom/104news931008.htm. Accessed 8.11.10.

104 Tutor's Net (2005) Survey of after-school education of primary and junior high school students. (In Chinese) On WWW at http://www.104.com.tw/cfdocs/2000/pressroom/104news940817_a.htm. Accessed 8.11.10.

Aletheia University (2005) Dr. George Mackay and Oxford College: Digital Archives Program. On WWW at http://www.au.edu.tw/ox_view/mackay/3index.htm. Accessed 20.1.09.

Borman, K.M., Fox, A. and Levinson, B.A. (2000) Cultural production and reproduction in contemporary schools. In B.A. Levinson, K.M. Borman,

M. Eisenhart, M. Foster, A. Fox and M. Sutton (eds) *Schooling the Symbolic Animal: Social and Cultural Dimensions of Education* (pp. 239–247). Oxford: Rowman & Littlefield.

Bourdieu, P. (1986) The forms of capital. In J. Richardson (ed.) *Handbook of Theory and Research for the Sociology of Education* (pp. 241–258). New York: Greenwood.

Bureau of Employment and Vocational Training (BEVT) (2009) Foreign professionals in Taiwan-categorised by job and work address. Taipei: Bureau of Employment and Vocational Training. (In Chinese) On WWW at http://www.evta.gov.tw/files/60/719037.csv. Accessed 25.3.09.

Bureau of Employment and Vocational Training (BEVT) (2009) Foreign professionals in Taiwan-categorised by sex, education, and nationality. Taipei: Bureau of Employment and Vocational Training. (In Chinese) On WWW at http://www.evta.gov.tw/files/58/718030.csv. Accessed 25.3.09.

Bureau of International Cultural and Educational Relations (2009) Number of Taiwanese students studying abroad, 1998–2008. Taipei: MOE. (In Chinese) On WWW at http://www.edu.tw/files/site_content/B0003/1998-2008visa.pdf. Accessed 25.3.09.

Chan, D.Y.C. and Wu, G.C. (2000) A study of foreign language anxiety of elementary school EFL learners in Taiwan. In Graduate School of Mathematics Education, National Taipei Teachers College (ed.) *The Proceedings of the 2000 Conference of Education and Academic Research on "New Vision of Education in 21st Century: Theory and Practice"* (pp. 85–100). Taipei: National Taipei Teachers College.

Chan, D.Y.C. and Wu, G.C. (2004) A study of foreign language anxiety of EFL elementary school students in Taipei County. *Journal of National Taipei Teachers College* 17 (2), 287–320. (In Chinese)

Chao, E. (2001) Educational and cultural exchange activities of American government in Taiwan: 1951–1970. *EurAmerica (Academia Sinica)* 31 (1), 79–127. (In Chinese)

Chao, J.C. (1985) *American Aid in Taiwan*. Taipei: Linking Books. (In Chinese)

Chen, K.H. (2005) Academic production in the age of neo-liberalism globalisation In Reflective Forum Team (ed.) *Globalization and Knowledge Production: Critical Reflection on the Practices of Academic Evaluations* (pp. 3–30). Taipei: Tang Shan. (In Chinese)

Chen, S.C. (1996) The spread of English in Taiwan: A sociolinguistic study. In M.C. Yang et al. (eds) *The Proceedings of the 13th Conference on English Teaching and Learning* (pp. 321–330). Taipei: Crane.

Chen, S.C. (2003) *The Spread of English in Taiwan: Changing User and Shifting Attitudes*. Taipei: Crane.

Cheng, H.M. (2005, 18 April) 88% primary school pupils suffer from English learning. *The China Times* (In Chinese)

Chern, C.L. (2002) English language teaching in Taiwan today. *Asia Pacific Journal of Education* 22 (2), 97–105.

Chern, C.L. (2004) English language teaching in Taiwan today. In W.K. Ho and R.Y.L. Wong (eds) *English Language Teaching in East Asia Today: Changing Policies and Practices* (pp. 427–437). Singapore: Eastern University Press.

Child Welfare League Foundation ROC (2002) Survey of pre-school children's experience in English language learning. (In Chinese) On WWW at http://www.children.org.tw/database_report.php?id=169&typeid=4&offset=45. Accessed 30.1.09.

China Times (2006, 7 March) Tourist taxi drivers have to speak English. (In Chinese) On WWW at http://news.chinatimes.com/Chinatimes/newslist/newslist-content/0,3546,1105060/1+112006030700261,00.html. Accessed 15.10.06.

Chou, H.J. (2004, 15 November) How internationalized Taiwanese people are? *CommonWealth Magazine* 311, 80–85. (In Chinese)

Crawford, J. (2001) Teacher perceptions of the primary English language program in Taiwan: From the outside looking in. Paper presented at the Applied Linguistic Association of Australia Annual Conference, Canberra University, Australia. On WWW at http://eprints.qut.edu.au/archive/00000510/01/crawford_teacher.PDF. Accessed 1.11.08.

Dai, W.Y. (1998) A study of the current English language education in primary schools. In Department of English, National Kao-hsiung Normal University (ed.) *The Proceedings of the Fifteenth Conference on English Teaching and Learning in the Republic of China, Taipei* (pp. 223–242). Taipei: Crane. (In Chinese)

Demaine, J. (2003) Social reproduction and education policy. *International Studies in Sociology of Education* 13 (2), 125–140.

Education Reform Advisory Committee, Executive Yuan, Republic of China (1996) Advisory Proposal for Educational Reform. (In Chinese) On WWW at http://www.sinica.edu.tw/info/edu-reform/. Accessed 5.10.08.

Executive Yuan, ROC (2002a) Challenge 2008: The Six-Year National Development Plan. On WWW at http://english.moe.gov.tw/fp.asp?xItem=7043&ctNode=784&mp=1. Accessed 5.10.08.

Executive Yuan, ROC (2002b) Action Project for Building an English Living Environment. (In Chinese) On WWW at http://www.i-taiwan.nat.gov.tw/ct/filemgr/rdec/c1-2w05.pdf. Accessed 20.10.08.

Hsieh, J.J. (2009) Reconceptualising English teaching in Taiwan: Action research with technical college students. Unpublished EdD thesis, Durham University.

Kachru, B.B. (1986) *The Alchemy of English: The Spread, Functions, and Models of Non-native Englishes*. Oxford: Pergamon Institute of English.

Krashen, S. (2003) Dealing with English fever. In Y. Chen and Y. Leung (eds) *Selected Papers from the Twelfth International Symposium on English Teaching* (pp. 100–108). Taipei: Crane. On WWW at http://sdkrashen.com/articles/fever/fever.pdf. Accessed 12.6.10.

King Car Education Foundation (2003) A survey of EFL teachers in elementary schools. (In Chinese) On WWW at http://www.kingcar.org.tw/about.asp?ID=16. Accessed 1.4.07.

Language Training & Testing Center (LTTC) (2010a) Overview of LTTC. On WWW at http://www.lttc.ntu.edu.tw/LTTC_history/history.htm. Accessed 15.7.10.

Language Training & Testing Center (LTTC) (2010b) LTTC Annual Report 2009. On WWW at http://www.lttc.ntu.edu.tw/Annualreportfiles/2009annualreport.pdf. Accessed 15.7.10.

Lee, B.W.R. (2007) A first investigation into Taiwan's English education – its current situation and dilemma. *Language, Literary Studies and International Studies: An International Journal* 4, 95–107. (In Chinese)

Liao, Y.F. (1999) The effects of anxiety on Taiwanese EFL learners. In J. Katchen and Y. Leung (eds) *The Proceedings of the Eighth International Symposium on English Teaching* (pp. 453–464). Taipei: Crane.

Lin, C. (2003) English Language Teaching (ELT) in Taiwan during the Period of Globalization: A critical perspective. Electronic paper. (In Chinese) On WWW at http://ccs.nccu.edu.tw/UPLOAD_FILES/HISTORY_PAPER_FILES/255_1.pdf. Accessed 2.1.08.

Liu, L. (2002, 8 November) Studying English: A national obsession. On WWW at http://publish.gio.gov.tw/FCJ/past/02122071.html. Accessed 12.12.05.

Lin, M.J. (2002, 2 April) Controversy brewing over English. *Taipei Times*. On WWW at http://taiwanauj.nat.gov.tw/ct.asp?xItem=19773&CtNode=122. Accessed 12.5.08.

Market Intelligence Center (2004) *Market Intelligence Center Report*. Taipei: Market Intelligence Center.

Ministry of Education (MOE) (1995) The Republic of China Educational Report. (In Chinese) On WWW at http://192.192.169.230/edu_paper/data_image/e0000004/0n0/19950300/p0000001.pdf. Accessed 11.10.08.

Ministry of Education (MOE) (1997) Master Plan for Educational Reform. (In Chinese) On WWW at http://www.edu.tw/content.aspx?site_content_sn=5431. Accessed 10.10.08.

Ministry of Education (MOE) (1998) Education Reform Action Plan. (In Chinese) On WWW at http://www.edu.tw/content.aspx?site_content_sn=1388. Accessed 10.10.08.

Ministry of Education (MOE) (2001) The General Guidelines for English Language Arts of Grade 1-9 Curriculum. (In Chinese) On WWW at http://teach.eje.edu.tw/9CC/index_new.php. Accessed 10.10.08.

Ministry of Education (MOE) (2003) Evaluation Report of the Implementation of the Grade 1-9 Curriculum. (In Chinese) On WWW at http://www.edu.tw/content.aspx?site_content_sn=948. Accessed 15.10.08.

Ministry of Education (MOE) (2009) Regulations for the Establishment of Private Elementary and Secondary Schools' International Curriculum Programs. (In Chinese) On WWW at http://www.edu.tw/files/site_content/EDU01/18-2.pdf. Accessed 25.3.09.

National Teachers' Association & CitiSuccess Fund (2003) Survey of English Teaching & Learning Status in Primary Schools. Taipei: National Teachers' Association. (In Chinese) On WWW at http://forum.nta.org.tw/v362/epaper/17/17-10.htm. Accessed 20.9.08.

National Immigration Agency (NIA) (2009) Visitor Arrivals by Residence, 2008. Taipei: National Immigration Agency. (In Chinese) On WWW at http://admin.taiwan.net.tw/statistics/File/200812/table02_2008.pdf. Accessed 25.3.09.

Nieh, P.L. (2004) Elementary graduates' EFL proficiency in Taiwan: A factorial analysis. Unpublished PhD thesis. National Kao-hsiung Normal University.

Price, G. (2005) The language barrier? Analysing English education in Taiwan. Paper presented at the Second Conference of the European Association of Taiwan Studies. Bochum: Ruhr-University Bochum.

Rhythms Editorial Group (ed.) (2006) *Four Hundred Years of Education in Taiwan*. Taipei: Rhythms Books. (In Chinese)

Sagor Bilingual School (2009) Bilingual programme. On WWW at http://www.sagor.hc.edu.tw/index.php?page=admissions/admissions-middle.php. Accessed 5.2.09.

Scott, M. and Liu Chen, P. (2004) English in elementary schools in Taiwan. In P. Lee and H. Azman (eds) *Global English and Primary Schools: Challenges for Elementary Education* (pp. 51–71). Melbourne: CAE Press.

Shih, Y.H. (1998) Recommendations for the directions of English language teaching in elementary schools. *Bimonthly Journal of Educational Resources & Research* 23, 1–5. (In Chinese)

Shih, Y.H. (2001) Evaluation of the MOE primary school English teacher training program. *English Teaching & Learning* 26 (1), 86–108. (In Chinese)

Sommers, S. (2008) The English needs of workers in corporate Taiwan: Toward an understanding of what graduating students will need on the job. Paper presented at 2008 International Conference and Workshop on TEFL and Applied Linguistics. Ming Chuan University, Gwai Shan, Taiwan.

Su, J.H. (2002) Family background and educational attainment. *E-Soc Journal* 23. (In Chinese) On WWW at http://mail.nhu.edu.tw/~ society/e-j/23/15.htm. Accessed 20.5.08.

Su, S.F. (2001) A survey study of instructional innovation: Focusing on English teaching in junior high schools in Taiwan. *English Teaching & Learning* 26 (13), 28–48. (In Chinese)

Sung, C.H. (2003) Taiwanese people learning English. (In Chinese) On WWW at http://mypaper.pchome.com.tw/news/peggylin/3/3358619/20030712062312/. Accessed 5.2.09.

Tsao, F.F. (1999) The language planning situation in Taiwan. *Journal of Multilingual and Multicultural Development* 20 (4&5), 328–376.

Tsao, F.F. (2001) Teaching English from elementary school in an Asian context: A language-planning perspective. *The Language Teacher Online* 30.06.01. On WWW at http://www.jalt-publications.org/tlt/articles/2001/06/tsao. Accessed 12.6.10.

Tsao, F.F. (2008) The language planning situation in Taiwan: An update. In R.B. Kaplan and R.B. Baldauf, Jr. (eds) *Language Planning & Policy in Asia* (pp. 285–300). Clevedon: Multilingual Matters.

Tseng, D.S.D. (2007) ELT in Taiwan before and after Restoration. In D.S.D. Tseng (ed.) *Foundation and Heritage of ELT: In Memory of Prof. Yang Jing-Mai* (pp. 217–244). Taipei: English Language Centre, English Department, National Taiwan Normal University. (In Chinese)

Wang, H.Z., Li, H.C., Lu, Z.Y., Yin, T.Y., Shen, P.L. and Zhang, J.(2005) Strategies and suggestions for the continuity of English curricula between elementary and junior high schools in Taipei City. (In Chinese) On WWW at http://www.edunet.taipei.gov.tw/public/pub2_content.asp?SEQ=112. Accessed 14.7.07.

Wen, H.Y. (1989) *Behind the Economical Miracle*. Taipei: IDN Books. (In Chinese)

Wikipedia (2009) Sino-American Mutual Defense Treaty. On WWW at http://en.wikipedia.org/wiki/Sino-American_Mutual_Defense_Treaty. Accessed 17.11.09.

Chapter 5
Improving the Standards and Promoting the Use of English in Hong Kong: Issues, Problems and Prospects

DAVID C.S. LI

Introduction

With over 7 million people in an area of about 1100 km^2, Hong Kong is one of the most densely populated cities in the world. Being a former colony of Britain for over 150 years, Hong Kong's sovereignty was returned to China and it became a Special Administrative Region (SAR) on 1 July 1997. Around 95% of the population are ethnic Chinese; the overwhelming majority (about 90%) have Cantonese as their 'usual' language (Li, 2006). The non-Chinese population have rarely exceeded 5%, with Filipinos and Indonesians being the largest groups (1.7 and 1.6%, respectively; *Hong Kong 2006 Population by-census Main Report Volume I*, 2007: 39).

The success story of Hong Kong under British rule, notably its rise from a barren rock to an international metropolis rivalling London, Tokyo and New York, has inspired a sizeable body of literature on Hong Kong studies, particularly around the time of the handover (e.g. Lau, 1997; Tsang, 1997). Natural resources being negligible, international trade and commerce have always been a main source of revenue and the lifeline for a significant percentage of Hongkongers. For about two decades after the early 1960s, the 'Pearl of the Orient' made a name and won international acclaim through its sundry price-worthy manufactured goods bearing the etiquette 'Made in Hong Kong'. Following the move of the manufacturing sector to the Pearl River Delta in the last two decades, however, the principal economic activities gradually shifted from manufacturing to those that are service and knowledge based. Among the most vibrant sectors today are banking, investment and finance, imports/exports, telecommunications, transport and logistics, tourism, hotels, restaurants, insurance, retail trade and real estate services. Bustling economic activities since the early 1960s have fuelled an impressive economic growth, making it possible for the Hong Kong SAR government under first Chief Executive, Mr Tung Chee-hwa, to reposition the former British colony as 'Asia's World City'.

From an international perspective, probably no other sector commands as much international attention as investment and finance, where the Hang Seng Index (HSI) is a highly visible index for traders of stocks and shares worldwide. How successful and important the Hong Kong Stock Exchange has been may be gauged by the increasingly popular abbreviation 'Nylonkong' – abbreviation for 'New York, London and Hong Kong' – in the discourses of international investment and global finance. More recently, in the face of a global financial tsunami that struck in October 2008, financial services was named by the Task Force on Economic Challenges headed by Mr Donald Tsang, the Chief Executive, as the most affected economic pillar in need of government support (the other three pillars, now turned problem areas, are 'trade and logistics', 'tourism and consumption-related services' and 'real estate and construction', in that order). One of the ten appointees of the Task Force, then Standard Chartered Bank Chairman, Mr Mervyn Davies, was quoted as saying that 'this market correction gives Hong Kong as a regional financial center a huge opportunity to stand side by side with New York and London' (Lo, 2008: 10).

'Biliteracy and Trilingualism': Hong Kong SAR Government's Language Policy Goal

The socioeconomic realities of a service- and knowledge-based economy outlined above have significant implications for Hong Kong's language policy and the language needs of the local workforce. Cantonese is no doubt a viable regional lingua franca in the Pearl River Delta area. To do business with people elsewhere in Greater China, however, a working knowledge of Putonghua is indispensable; to communicate with clients from other parts of the world, English is the expected lingua franca. This is the background and rationale for the language policy known as 'biliteracy and trilingualism'. Accordingly, one important goal of education is to enable secondary school-leavers and university graduates to read and write Chinese and English on the one hand, and to speak Cantonese, English and Putonghua on the other.

Despite the fact that Putonghua is the national language and the lingua franca of Chinese speakers in Greater China, its use in Hong Kong SAR remains rather limited. Putonghua is used – after Cantonese, before English – in official ceremonies such as celebrations of the National Day and trilingual announcements of mass transit railway (MTR) trains and some city buses. Radio Hong Kong operates a Putonghua station, but it is unclear how successful it has been in attracting a faithful audience. Putonghua is also increasingly heard in transactional communication between Cantonese-accented shopkeepers and visitors and tourists from mainland China. Beyond these contexts, it is unclear how widely Putonghua is used in the local community. There has been little research on the use of Putonghua in the workplace. In the education domain, great efforts have been made to promote Putonghua in school. For over a decade, Putonghua has been taught from primary school as a subject; at the end of Form 5 (Grade 11), Putonghua is one of the examination subjects in the Hong Kong Certificate of Education Examinations (HKCEE). It is also learned by more and more working adults in evening classes, largely for work-related purposes. All this helps explain why, according to the by-census in 2006, 40.2% of Hongkongers claimed to speak Putonghua as their 'usual' language (0.9%) or 'another' language (39.2%) – a marked increase from 25.3% ten years earlier (*Hong Kong 2006 Population By-census Main Report Volume I*, 2007: .44). This figure is on par with 44.7% of Hongkongers who claimed to speak English as their 'usual' (2.8%) or 'another' language (41.9%), up from 43% in 2001.

Compared with Putonghua, English has attracted far greater amounts of community resources. Miller and Li (2008) discuss a number of costly government initiatives to enhance the quality of teaching and learning of English in school from primary to tertiary levels, including two special schemes, Workplace English Campaign (WEC) and Continuing Education Fund (CEF), to encourage working adults to improve their English (among other languages such as Japanese and Korean; see Table 5.1).

The CEF, for example, is managed by the Student Financial Assistance Agency under the Education Bureau (EDB). It subsidises up to 80% of tuition fees for courses offered by recognised providers of continuing education, on condition that the courses are successfully completed. Language courses, especially English and Putonghua, are among the most popular courses for which reimbursement claims were made. In early 2007, for instance, over 350,000 applications for reimbursement were processed, with the net disbursement value in excess of one billion Hong Kong dollars (ca. US$128.2 million) (Miller & Li, 2008: 89).

Table 5.1 Hong Kong (SAR) government initiatives to enhance English

Provisions to enhance English in schools
• Reform of the curriculum guidelines for primary and secondary schools
• Redevelopment of the public examinations
• Introduction of the 'dual medium-of-instruction streaming policy' from Secondary 1–3 (Grades 7–9)
• Employment of Native English-speaking Teachers (NETs)
• Language Proficiency Assessment for Teachers (LPAT)
• English Enhancement Scheme
Provisions to enhance English in tertiary institutions
• Additional funding to universities for language enhancement programmes
• Reimbursement of fees to undergraduate students who take the IELTS (International English Language Testing System) test
Provisions to enhance English in the workplace
• Launching of the Workplace English Campaign (WEC)
• Launching of Continuing Education Fund (CEF)

Source: Adapted from Miller and Li (2008: 80).

Teaching of English: From Kindergarten to University

English is taught from kindergarten onwards. As a consequence of the compulsory nine-year education policy since 1978, school attendance up to Secondary 3 (Grade 9) is mandatory. With a minimum of eight 35- to 40-minute lessons per week from primary school, by age 15 the average teenager in Hong Kong will have received no less than 2000 hours of classroom input in English. The outcomes of learning are far from satisfactory. Basic literacy skills in English are generally attained, but at the end of secondary education (Secondary 5), relatively few school-leavers are able to hold a conversation in English fluently with confidence. Even those who manage to secure a place in one of the eight publicly funded tertiary institutions (around 20% of all Secondary 1 entrants) find it difficult to cope with English for academic purposes at the tertiary level. Research shows that many undergraduate students have difficulties understanding lectures delivered in English (Flowerdew *et al.*,1998, 2000), while their written outputs tend to be fraught with lexico-grammatical inaccuracies (see, e.g. Chan & Li, 1999; Li, 2000; Li & Chan, 1999, 2001), partly as a result of the cross-linguistic influence from their first language (L1), Cantonese. This makes it necessary for universities to strengthen the teaching of English. There is, for example, a three- to six-credit University English requirement for most undergraduate programmes across all disciplines, including students of Chinese Language and Literature. Still, dissatisfaction with Hong Kong students' poor English performance, university graduates included, is one recurrent topic in mass media. Employers complain that newly recruited local graduates are unable to cope with the actual needs for English in the workplace. In response to this 'complaint tradition' (Bolton, 2003; cf. Milroy & Milroy, 1985), the government provides a monetary incentive for undergraduate students to take the IELTS test before graduation. The IELTS expenses are reimbursed provided the student accepts having his or her IELTS score listed on their transcript. It remains unclear to what extent this incentive helps improve university graduates' English proficiency.

In short, there is no question that English is widely perceived as an indispensable asset, both in terms of its instrumental value for accessing higher education (local and abroad) and facilitating upward and outward job mobility. As shown in Table 5.1, various government initiatives, curricular and extra-curricular, have been made in the last decade to help improve Hongkongers' standards of English, but their effectiveness leaves much to be desired. Why? The explanations are partly linguistic and partly social. In the rest of this chapter, we will discuss two main factors: the tremendous typological and linguistic differences between English and Chinese on the one hand, and the lack of a conducive environment for practising and using English on the other.

Marked Typological Differences between Chinese and English

Owing to marked typological or cross-linguistic differences between English and Chinese, there are few useful L1 resources that Chinese learners of English could fall back on in the process of learning English. English is an Indo-European language, while Chinese belongs to the Sino-Tibetan family of languages (Gordon, 2005; http://www.ethnologue.com/ethno_docs/distribution.asp?by=family).

Phonologically, English and Cantonese differ tremendously in both segmental and suprasegmental features (Chan & Li, 2000; Hung, 2000,

2002). This helps explain why few Hong Kong Chinese learners of English are able to approximate native-like pronunciation. For instance, the phonemic distinction between pre-vocalic /n/ and /l/ in English is often ignored by Chinese learners, largely because these two consonants behave like free variants in the initial position of the Cantonese syllable (e.g. the second-person pronoun 你 is variously pronounced as nei^{23} or lei^{23}, with no risk of confusion in context).[1] The two languages also differ significantly in lexico-grammar. A large number of deviations from Standard English or English for Academic Purposes (EAP) norms may be accounted for by contrastive lexico-grammatical differences. A subset of these common 'errors' is listed in Table 5.2.

All these deviations from Standard English have been shown to be due, at least in part, to cross-linguistic influence (see, e.g. Chan, 2004; Li & Chan, 1999, 2001). There are other non-standard features that are more likely to be attributable to faulty or inadequate observation of the collocational patterns in the target language. Thus, in each of the following trios involving a transitive verb (*discuss, emphasise* and *blame*), it may be argued that the non-standard structure in (c) is the result of the learner mapping the collocational pattern in the corresponding nominalised structure supported by a 'delexical verb' in (b) (e.g. *have a long discussion about, place more emphasis on, put so much blame on*) to that in (a):

(1) (a) They discussed the project for two hours.
    (b) They had a long discussion about the project.
    (c) ?? They discussed about the project for two hours.

(2) (a) We should emphasise this more.
    (b) We should place more emphasis on this.
    (c) ?? We should emphasise on this more.

(3) (a) Don't blame her so much!
    (b) Don't put so much blame on her.
    (c) ?? Don't blame on her so much.

As for the orthographic system, English is alphabetic while Chinese is logographic (Erbaugh, 2002). There is no such thing as the Chinese alphabet; rather, a logographic Chinese character tends to be morphemic, and is generally pronounceable as a syllable, hence the term 'morphosyllable' (Bauer & Benedict, 1997: 296). Being a non-alphabetic system, there is no direct relationship between the way a morphosyllable is pronounced and the way it is written. Part of the learning of a Chinese

Table 5.2 List of common 'errors' in Hong Kong Chinese 'learner English'

Type of deviation	Example
Missing relative pronouns	I met two parents *attended* the interview yesterday.
too + Adj + to + VP	He is *too* happy *to see you*. (meaning '...so happy to see you.')
Periphrastic topic-constructions	*According to Tung Chee Hwa, he said that...*
Resumptive pronouns	She is the teacher *that she changes my life.*
Non-parallel structures	Its main functions are *file maintenance* and *storing information*.
Independent clause as Subject	*Snoopy is leaving* makes us all very happy.
Dangling modifiers	*Entering the stadium, the size of the crowd* surprised John.
There has/have	*There* will not *have* any paper in the printer.
Pseudo-tough movement	*I am difficult* to learn English.
On the contrary	John is a very diligent student. *On the contrary*, Mary is very lazy.
Concern/Be concerned about	The only thing I must *concern* is the style of clothes.
Somewhere has something	*Hong Kong has* a lot of rubbish.
Very + V	I like playing basketball. So I *very enjoy* it.

Source: http://personal.cityu.edu.hk/~encrproj/error_types.htm

morphosyllable thus involves learning its written form (形, $jing^{21}$), pronunciation (音, jam^{55}) and meaning (義, ji^{22}).

The above discussion serves to illustrate the tremendous typological and linguistic differences between English and Chinese at the phonological, lexico-grammatical and orthographic levels. This is why very little of what Hong Kong Chinese learners of English know about their L1, Chinese (i.e. spoken Cantonese and standard written Chinese), has any reference value in the arduous process of learning English. In the absence of facilitating factors such as extensive home support and a strong motivation to learn English, therefore, successful acquisition of English by Cantonese-L1 learners in Hong Kong up to a native-like proficiency level is relatively rare.

Further, since the majority of teachers of English are themselves Hong Kong Chinese, many of their proficiency problems are passed on to their students, leading to considerable problems in the quality of teaching and learning. This issue is currently being addressed by the SAR government, in that teachers of English at all levels are required to be subject-trained and to pass the 'Language Proficiency Assessment for Teachers' test (LPAT in English; more popularly known as the 'benchmark test', see Miller & Li, 2008). Nonetheless, given that English and Chinese have so little in common, typologically speaking, and that English is learned and used in Hong Kong more like a foreign than a second language (see below), the strong societal expectation of students exiting school with a high level of English proficiency, as enshrined in the well-intentioned language policy goal of biliteracy and trilingualism, is generally perceived as a great burden by Chinese students as they struggle their way up the education ladder. This is probably also true of mainland Chinese and Taiwanese students (see Gil & Adamson; Chen & Hsieh, this volume).

English in Hong Kong SAR: English as a Second Language or English as a Foreign Language?

Another major social factor that militates against the effective acquisition of English in Hong Kong is the lack of a conducive language-learning environment, an issue that is closely related to the question, 'Is English in Hong Kong more appropriately characterised as a second or a foreign language?'. The status of English in Hong Kong (SAR) has been variously characterised as **English as a Second Language** (ESL) or **English as a Foreign Language** (EFL) (compare, e.g. Bolton, 2003; Kachru, 2005; Li, 1999/2008; Luke & Richards, 1982; McArthur, 2001). A typical second language has the following characteristics (cf. Jenkins, 2003):

- being an official or co-official language;
- used as the medium of instruction (MOI) in school;
- widely used in such key domains as government, law, education and business;
- used by local people spontaneously for intra-ethnic communication.

These characteristics are largely true of English in former British colonies such as India, Nigeria and Singapore, where English continues to be highly visible in society after they declared independence. By contrast, a typical foreign language does not have these characteristics, viz.:

- not an official language;
- not used as the MOI, but taught as a subject in school;
- not widely used in such key domains as government, law, education and business;
- seldom used by local people among themselves.

One consequence is that being a foreign language, English is hardly visible in society. This is generally the case for English in EFL societies in Asia, such as China, Japan, Korea, Macao and Taiwan (compare Chen & Hsieh; Gil & Adamson; and Young, this volume). The situation in Hong Kong SAR is not as straightforward because it exhibits both ESL and EFL characteristics:

- English is a co-official language alongside Chinese[2];
- English is used as the MOI in about 30% of the secondary schools, but taught as a subject in primary schools and other secondary schools;
- English is widely used in such key domains as government, law, education and business, more commonly in print than in speech;
- English is seldom used by Chinese Hongkongers for intra-ethnic communication (except in Chinese-English mixed code).

Thus, English in Hong Kong does not fit conveniently into the traditional ESL-EFL dichotomy. This is one important reason why different views are held. The World Englishes scholar, Kachru (1997: 6, 2005: 90), for instance, regards English in Hong Kong (along with English in China) not as a second language, but a 'fast-expanding' foreign language (cf. Li, 1999/2008, 2000). His position differs manifestly from that of McArthur (2001) and Bolton (2003). For McArthur (1998: 53, 2001: 8–9), Hong Kong is one of 'the ESL territories' on a par with Bangladesh, Brunei, Ghana, India, Malaysia, Nigeria and Singapore. In his book-length account of Chinese Englishes, Bolton (2003) adopts an 'archeology of English' approach (see the preface of his book) to researching World Englishes by drawing principally on historical and textual evidence revealing forgotten traces of contact between English and the local language(s). After reviewing all the arguments for and against the emergence of 'Hong Kong English' as a 'new English' (Chapter 4), Bolton

(2003: 218) believes that significant forces towards the community's recognition of Hong Kong English are 'bubbling from below'. This conclusion is based on a detailed and systematic analysis of Butler's (1997: 106) five main criteria for diagnosing the emergence of a localised variety of English:

(1) A standard and recognisable pattern of pronunciation handed down from one generation to another.
(2) Particular words and phrases that spring up usually to express key features of the physical and social environment and which are regarded as peculiar to the variety.
(3) A history – a sense that this variety of English is the way it is because of the history of the language community.
(4) A literature written without apology in that variety of English.
(5) Reference works – dictionaries and style guides – which show that people in that language community look to themselves, not some outside authority, to decide what is right and wrong in terms of how they speak and write their English.

In Bolton's (2003) view, with the exception of (5), Hong Kong English already meets all the other criteria. Relative to the question, whether English in Hong Kong is more appropriately characterised as a second or a foreign language, Bolton's analysis is worth examining in more detail.

First, Bolton (2003) is certainly right that Chinese learners and users of English have a distinctive and phonologically well-defined 'Hong Kong accent' (cf. Hung, 2000, 2002), but it remains unclear whether this accent constitutes evidence of an autonomous variety. For one thing, few Chinese Hongkongers are willing to use English entirely for intra-ethnic (i.e. Chinese-Chinese) communication. More importantly, the linguistic features of the Hong Kong accent that do not conform to those of a non-standard-based model are generally perceived by teachers and learners alike as 'errors' in need of correction, rather than instantiations of a localised variety (Andrews, 2002; Bunton & Tsui, 2002; Li, 2000; Luk, 1998; Tsui & Bunton, 2000).

Butler's second criterion has to do with local, culture-specific words in English. As shown in Bolton's (2003, 288–297) careful documentation, many cultural aspects specific to Hong Kong (and elsewhere in Asia) have found expression in English, mainly through transliteration (lexical borrowing) or loan translation. But one crucial question is: Who are the users of the localised, acculturated English words? In Hong Kong, words like *moon cake*, *astronaut* (literally 'wife-empty-person', denoting 'an émigré who lives away from his spouse and family and who often flies between the host country and Hong Kong', cf. Bolton, 2003: 288), and *snake-head* ('leader of a human smuggling ring', Bolton, 2003: 296) are commonly used in local English media discourse, both print and electronic, but are seldom heard in Chinese-Chinese interaction in Hong Kong (with the possible exception of returnees; Chen, 2008). A list of Hong Kong-specific English words says nothing about who uses them. To the extent that the acculturated English words with a local flavour are not used among Hong Kong Chinese themselves, it seems more appropriate to see them as an extension of the 'World Standard English' lexicon, broadly as a result of globalisation and dictionary compilations by international publishers (McArthur, 2001: 15), in the same way that words like *curry, pizza* and *sushi* can no longer be seen as the exclusive property of peoples from whose cultures they originated.

Butler's (1997) third criterion concerns the presence of English in the local community over an extended historical period. In this regard, Bolton (2003) provides an impressive documentation and analysis of the history of contact between English and Chinese dating back to imperial China (since the late 17th century) and colonial Hong Kong (since 1842), especially the linguistic and sociolinguistic discussion of Chinese pidgin English (CPE). This is consonant with his appeal for examining archives and socio-historically significant documents with a view to establishing a conceptual link between earlier phases of the local(ised) variety of English and the present. All this is enlightening. Less convincing is the implied claim, through the continued use of a subset of vocabulary items specific to the region, that 'China English' and 'Hong Kong English' have had an existence that is co-extensive with that of the British colonisers' presence in China. Whether it is a pidginised variety (CPE) among the group of Chinese engaged in trading activities with English speakers in 'treaty-port China', or a learner variety acquired by Chinese pupils through proper schooling, there is no evidence of these Chinese users and learners of English communicating with one another in English (except for a minority of reform-minded Chinese literati such as Lin Yutang, who deliberately published magazine articles in English; see Chapter 5, Bolton, 2003).

Butler's fourth criterion concerns creative works in English written by local writers. Bolton (2003) lists a number of literary works written in English by Hong Kong writers, notably Xu Xi. However, neither the number of such Anglophile creative writers of Asian descent nor the amount of local literary work produced to date is comparable to that in other ESL societies like the Philippines. Rather, literature in English produced by local writers appears to be limited to a relatively small group compared with the size of the population (over seven million). As the veteran journalist C.K. Lau remarks[3]:

> An obvious indicator of English's failure to become entrenched in Hong Kong is that there is absolutely no English-language Hong Kong literature. The small number of available English titles focusing on Hong Kong life are almost all written by expatriates, and usually for an expatriate readership. Unlike Singapore, Hong Kong has not produced any popular local writers in the English language. For leisure reading, most Hong Kong Chinese prefer to pick up a Chinese-language publication because reading in English is a chore for them. (Lau, 1997: 111–112)

The placement of Hong Kong in the outer circle as opposed to the expanding circle has theoretical implications in Kachru's three-circle model, namely, 'norm-developing' (outer circle) vs. 'norm-dependent' (expanding circle). The above discussion shows that, while a number of typical ESL characteristics are true of the former British colony, there is nevertheless one feature that makes English here more like a foreign than a second language, namely, the fact that few local Chinese use English entirely and spontaneously for intra-ethnic communication – unlike Chinese Singaporeans in this regard (compare Tupas, this volume).

Chinese Hongkongers are generally reluctant to use or switch to English at the inter-sentential level in their informal interactions with each other (Li, 2008; Li & Tse, 2002). This may be explained by the intricate relationship between language choice and local identity. There is a widely shared perception that Cantonese is the unmarked language as it is the mother tongue of the overwhelming majority of Hong Kong Chinese. As Bolton (2003: xv) explains, one important purpose of his book is to plead for 'acceptance of a new space, or spaces, for the discourses associated with English in Hong Kong'. His advocacy for more intellectual space for discussing Hong Kong English is well taken, but given the functions assigned to English at present, it seems certain that English remains psycholinguistically detached (except in Cantonese-English mixed code; Li, 2008; Li & Tse, 2002) in the lifeworld of the majority of Chinese Hongkongers. Lau (1997) regards this as the 'social cause of Hong Kong people's poor English':

> the root cause of their poor English skills is social (...) For the majority of the Chinese population, a genuine English-speaking environment has never existed to encourage them to learn and use the language. (Lau, 1997: 109)

This, I believe, is one of the major hurdles resisting sociolinguists' efforts to characterise the status of English in Hong Kong as a bona fide second language or a new, localised variety.

The Medium of Instruction Debate: Stigmas and Dilemmas

Huge community resources have been allocated to promote Hongkongers' biliteracy and trilingualism. Lofty as it may seem, biliteracy and trilingualism remains a worthwhile language policy goal. Few would dispute that the sustained prosperity of Hong Kong SAR hinges on, among other things, a trilingual citizenry with a fairly high level of proficiency in English and/or Putonghua (in addition to the community language Cantonese), as well as a reasonably high level of literacy skills in Chinese and English, both being indispensable for assuring life-long learning in a service- and knowledge-based economy. What remains uncertain in the language-in-education debate is the most promising road map, which has the greatest potential to help us get to where we want to be, most efficiently and effectively.

One of the major controversies surrounding the Hong Kong SAR government's language-in-education policy concerns the choice of Cantonese or English as the MOI at the onset of secondary education (Grade 7). In principle, using English as the MOI gives students more exposure to this *de facto* global language, and so they are more likely to master English up to a higher level. Hong Kong parents are aware of such a putative advantage for their children which, however, is contingent on whether they are motivated to learn through the medium of English and the availability of home support in different forms of learning aid, such as dictionaries, books in English, private tutoring and language games (cf. 'English fever' and 'national obsession' with English in Taiwan, see Chen & Hsieh, this volume). The mother tongue education policy was implemented in September 1998, out of recognition that other things being equal, learning through one's L1 (Cantonese in the context of Hong Kong for the majority) facilitates understanding and learning, which is especially important for those who demonstrably do not have the aptitude and motivation to learn through an unfamiliar language. After lengthy debates amplified through the mass media, the Hong Kong SAR government, under Mr Tung Chee Hwa, decided to allow some 30% of all secondary schools (114 out of 411) to retain English medium of instruction (EMI) status. Instead of being praised for getting the best of both possible worlds, however, this 'streaming policy' has been criticised for undermining the credibility of the pedagogically well-intentioned mother tongue education policy, which, according to Tsui *et al.* (1999: 205–206), is vindication of the politico-educational agenda over the social and economic agendas after the handover. Worse still, since EMI is seen as more desirable and EMI students are widely perceived as more capable academically, that 'streaming policy' in effect engendered social divisiveness in that Chinese medium of instruction (CMI) students get socially stigmatised as 'second best'.

More recently, there is some evidence that more is at stake than social stigma. According to a longitudinal study conducted by Tsang Wing-kwong, students graduating from CMI schools are worse off compared with their EMI peers in terms of (a) their success rate of being admitted into Form Six and university, and (b) their Hong Kong A-level (university entrance) examination results (cited in Clem, 2008). Tsang tracked the academic performance of 37,277 students from Form One in 1998 and 1999 to the completion of their A-level (university entrance) examinations in 2005 and 2006. Their A-level scores were compared, factoring into the analysis a number of variables such as gender, prior academic performance, socioeconomic background, as well as the average academic performance and socioeconomic background of other students in the same school. The results showed that CMI students appeared to have an early advantage over their EMI peers from Form One (Grade 7) to Form Three (Grade 9), but the performance gap was gradually narrowed towards Form Five (Grade 11). In terms of meeting the minimal requirements for admission into local universities as measured by the student's A-level examination scores, CMI students were worse by a wide margin. Interestingly, those CMI students who switched to English-medium instruction earlier (e.g. Form Four) tended to fare better than those who did so later (e.g. Form Six), with the group who received CMI instruction throughout (i.e. from Form One to Form Seven) having the lowest success rate. Tsang is cited as saying that 'changing [to EMI] at Form Six is basically a disaster...The indicators are all negative' (Clem, 2008). Whatever trade-off effect there was as a result of mother tongue education, therefore, it did not quite offset the lack of proficiency gain in the English language. The findings led Tsang to conclude that, relative to gaining access to university education as one of the primary goals of secondary education, mother tongue education did not seem to be serving CMI students' best interests. Like other scholars (e.g. Poon, 1999), Tsang is in favour of allowing individual schools the freedom to decide on the MOI of particular school subjects (Clem, 2008).

Tsang's findings prompted the Education Bureau (EDB) to consult educational stakeholders, notably secondary school principals and teachers, for alternative policy options with a view to 'fine-tuning' the mother tongue education policy, which is due to be implemented from September 2010. To counteract the socially divisive and stigmatising effect it engenders, some 'fine-tuning' measures have been proposed by the EDB with a view to blurring the distinction between English- and Chinese-medium schools.

Biliteracy and Trilingualism Policy: Problems and Prospects

Two main factors – one linguistic and the other sociolinguistic – help explain why a high level of English proficiency as part of the Hong Kong language policy of biliteracy and trilingualism is likely to remain a remote if not unattainable goal. We have seen that enhancing Hongkongers' English through education is hugely expensive; relative to the multi-million dollars invested (directly) in schools, tertiary institutions and (indirectly) in providers of continuing education annually, the returns seem to be grossly disproportionate and far from satisfactory. Typologically, owing to tremendous differences between Chinese and English at practically all linguistic levels, from phonology and lexicogrammar to orthography, Cantonese-L1 learners' linguistic knowledge of their mother tongue (i.e. their vernacular Cantonese and standard written Chinese) is of little use in the arduous English-learning process. At the same time, it also helps explain why cross-linguistic influence tends to be characterised by negative rather than positive transfer.

In terms of the ways English is used in Hong Kong society, one of the perennial sociolinguistic realities is that, with the exception of a minority of returnees from English-speaking countries (Chen, 2008), bilingual Chinese Hongkongers – regardless of their proficiency level in English – tend to be reluctant to use English entirely for informal interaction with one another. For this reason, the status of English in Hong Kong is more like a foreign than a second language. This is bad news for local teachers and ELT practitioners because, relative to the goal of acquiring English, opportunities for the natural use of and exposure to English outside school premises are hard to come by. This is thus another major stumbling block for the government's costly initiatives to promote the use of English in society through education.

Leaders of local universities are aware of this problem. To cope with it, two strategies are currently used by all local tertiary institutions to different extents depending on the availability of resources. One strategy is to internationalise the student population on campus by enlarging the percentage of non-local, English-speaking and Putonghua-speaking students. In the presence of non-Cantonese speakers, a switch to English or Putonghua is natural in order that they would not be excluded from the conversation. Another useful strategy is language immersion, that is, to encourage students to spend one or more semesters in an English-speaking country.

As for the controversial MOI debate, recent developments suggest that the SAR government has finally recognised the detrimental effects of stigmatisation brought about by the socially divisive policy of assigning labels to schools as either English medium or Chinese medium. By creating and perpetuating a second-class syndrome among those who 'failed' to make it to EMI schools, such a 'streaming policy' has triggered a lot of ill feelings among different groups of stakeholders: CMI students, their parents, teachers and principals of CMI schools (Li, 2009). Today, there seems to be a growing consensus in the community that a more liberal policy that allows individual schools to decide which subjects are more appropriately taught in English or Chinese, or some combination of these, is pedagogically more sound and productive. The role of the education authorities may accordingly be redefined as one of monitoring individual schools' abilities to teach in English and evaluating the students' learning outcomes (Cheung, 2008).

Notes

1. Cantonese expressions are transliterated using $Jyut^{22}$ $Ping^{33}$ (粵拼), the LSHK (Linguistic Society of Hong Kong) romanisation scheme. The two digits in superscripts give some indication of the tone level and contour of the Cantonese syllable.
2. Article 9 of the Basic Law states that 'In addition to the Chinese language, English may also be used as an official language by the executive authorities, legislature and judiciary of the Hong Kong Special Administrative Region' (*The Basic Law of the Hong Kong Special Administrative Region of the People's Republic of China*, on WWW at http://www.lawinfochina.com/law/display.asp?id=1210).
3. In the intervening decade after Lau (1997) made these remarks, the literary scene in English produced by local writers has witnessed considerable growth, as shown in such new titles as *Woman to Woman and Other Poems* (Lam, 1997, third printing 2005), *Water Wood Pure Splendour* (Lam, 2001) and *City Voices: Hong Kong Writing in English 1945 to the Present* (Xu & Ingham, 2003; on WWW at http://www.xuxiwriter.com/ for many more titles). It remains unclear, however, how many bilingual Hong Kong Chinese readers of English have developed an active interest in the emerging home-grown literature in English.

References

Andrews, S. (2002) Teacher language awareness and language standards. *Journal of Asian Pacific Communication* 12 (1), 39–62.
Bauer, R.S. and Benedict, P.K. (1997) *Modern Cantonese Phonology*. Berlin and New York: Mouton de Gruyter.
Bolton, K. (2003) *Chinese Englishes. A Sociolinguistic History*. Cambridge: Cambridge University Press.
Bunton, D. and Tsui, A. (2002) Setting language benchmarks: Whose benchmarks? *Journal of Asian Pacific Communication* 12 (1), 63–76.
Butler, S. (1997) Corpus of English in Southeast Asia: Implications for a regional dictionary. In M.L.S. Bautista (ed.) *English is an Asian Language: The Philippine Context* (pp. 103–124). Manila: Macquarie Library.
Chan, A.Y.W. (2004) The boy who Mary loves him is called John: A study of the resumptive pronoun problem and its correction strategies. *Hong Kong Journal of Applied Linguistics* 9 (1), 53–69.
Chan, A.Y.W. and Li, D.C.S. (2000) English and Cantonese phonology in contrast: Explaining Cantonese ESL learners' English pronunciation problems. *Language, Culture and Curriculum* 13 (1), 67–85.
Chen, K.H.Y. (2008) Positioning and repositioning: Linguistic practices and identity negotiation of overseas returning bilinguals in Hong Kong. *Multilingua* 27, 57–75.
Cheung, A. (2008, 27 March) Mind our language. It's too early to write off mother-tongue teaching, but the choice should be left to schools. *South China Morning Post*.
Clem, W. (2008, 15 March) Research casts doubts on mother-tongue education. *South China Morning Post*.
Consciousness-raising approach to error correction in the ESL classroom. On WWW at http://personal.cityu.edu.hk/ ~ encrproj/error_types.htm. Accessed 12.9.08.
Erbaugh, M.S. (ed.) (2002) *Difficult Characters. Interdisciplinary Studies of Chinese and Japanese Writing*. Colombus, OH: National East Asian Languages Resource Center, The Ohio State University.
Flowerdew, J., Li, D. and Miller, L. (1998) Attitudes towards English as the medium of instruction among Hong Kong Chinese university lecturers. *TESOL Quarterly* 32 (2), 201–231.
Flowerdew, J., Miller, L. and Li, D.C.S. (2000) Chinese lecturers' perceptions, problems and strategies in lecturing in English to Chinese-speaking students. *RELC Journal* 31 (1), 116–138.
Gordon, R.G. Jr. (ed.) (2005) *Ethnologue: Languages of the World* (15th edn). Dallas, TX: SIL International. On WWW at http://www.ethnologue.com/ethno_docs/distribution.asp?by=family.
Hong Kong 2006 Population By-census Main Report Volume I (2007) Census and Statistics Department, Hong Kong Government. On WWW at http://www.censtatd.gov.hk/freedownload.jsp?file=publication/stat_report/population/B11200472006XXXXB0400.pdf&title=Hong+Kong+2006+Population+By-census+Main+Report+%3a+Volume+I&issue=-&lang=1&c=1. Accessed 28.9.08.
Hung, T.T.N. (2000) Towards a phonology of Hong Kong English. *World Englishes* 19 (3), 337–356.

Hung, T.T.N. (2002) English as a global language: implications for teaching. *The ACELT Journal* 6 (2), 3–10.
Jenkins, J. (2003) *World Englishes. A Resource Book for Students*. London and New York: Routledge.
Kachru, B. (1997) English as an Asian language. In M.L.S. Bautista (ed.) *English is an Asian Language: The Philippine Context* (pp. 1–23). Manila: The Macquarie Library.
Kachru, B.B. (2005) *Asian Englishes. Beyond the Canon*. Hong Kong: Hong Kong University Press.
Lam, A. (1997) *Woman to Woman and Other Poems* (3rd printing 2005). Hong Kong: Asia 2000.
Lam, A. (2001) *Water Wood Pure Splendour*. Hong Kong: Asia 2000.
Lau, C.K. (1997) *Hong Kong's Colonial Legacy. A Hong Kong Chinese's View of the British Heritage*. Hong Kong: The Chinese University Press.
Li, D.C.S. (1999) The functions and status of English in Hong Kong: A post-1997 update. *English World-Wide* 20 (1), 67–110. Reprinted in K. Bolton and Y. Han (eds) (2008) *Language and Society in Hong Kong* (pp. 194–240). Hong Kong: Open University of Hong Kong Press.
Li, D.C.S. (2000) Hong Kong English: New variety of English or interlanguage? *EA Journal* 18 (1), 50–59.
Li, D.C.S. (2006) Chinese as a lingua franca in Greater China. *Annual Review of Applied Linguistics* 26, 149–176.
Li, D.C.S. (2009) Towards 'biliteracy and trilingualism' in Hong Kong (SAR): Problems, dilemmas and stakeholders' views. *AILA Review* 22, 72–84.
Li, D.C.S. and Chan, A.Y.W. (1999) Helping teachers correct structural and lexical English errors. *Hong Kong Journal of Applied Linguistics* 4 (1), 79–101.
Li, D.C.S. and Chan, A.Y.W. (2001) Form-focused negative feedback: Correcting three common errors. *TESL Reporter* 34 (1), 22–34.
Lo, M. (2008, 5 November) Don't blame the government, says StanChart. *The Standard*, p. 10.
Luk, J. (1998) Hong Kong students' awareness of and reactions to accent differences. *Multilingua* 17 (1), 93–106.
McArthur, T. (2001) World English and world Englishes: Trends, tensions, varieties, and standards. *Language Teaching* 34, 1–20.
Miller, L. and Li, D.C.S. (2008) Innovations in ELT curricula and strategies of implementation in Hong Kong SAR. In Y.H. Choi and B. Spolsky (eds) *ELT Curriculum Innovation and Implementation in Asia* (pp. 71–100). Seoul: Asia-TEFL.
Milroy, J. and Milroy, L. (1985) *Authority in Language. Investigating Language Prescription & Standardization* (2nd edn). London and New York: Routledge.
Poon, A.Y.K. (1999) Chinese medium instruction policy and its impact on English learning in post-1997. *International Journal of Bilingual Education and Bilingualism* 2 (2), 131–146.
The Basic Law of the Hong Kong Special Administrative Region of the People's Republic of China (n.d.) On WWW at http://big5.chinalawinfo.com/eng.chinalawinfo.com/law/display.asp?id=1210. Accessed 1.10.08.
Tsang, S. (1997) *Hong Kong: Appointment with China*. London and New York: I.B. Tauris.

Tsui, A.B.M. and Bunton, D. (2000) Discourse and attitudes of English teachers in Hong Kong. *World Englishes* 19 (3), 287–304.

Tsui, A.B.M., Shum, M.S.K., Wong, C.K., Tse, S.K. and Ki, W.W. (1999) Which agenda? Medium of instruction policy in post-1997 Hong Kong. *Language, Culture and Curriculum* 12 (3), 196–214.

Xu, X. and Ingham, M. (2003) *City Voices: Hong Kong Writing in English 1945 to the Present*. Hong Kong: Hong Kong University Press.

Chapter 6

English Use and Education in Macao[1]

MING YEE CARISSA YOUNG

Introduction

Macao, formerly a colony of Portugal and now a special administrative region (SAR) of the People's Republic of China, is located at the Pearl River Delta on the south-eastern coast of mainland China, approximately 60 km southwest of Hong Kong. In 2009, Macao had a total area of 29.5 km^2 and an estimated population of 542,200 residents (Statistics and Census Service, 2010). Macao was the first European settlement in the Far East and the last colony in Asia (Evans, 2006). The year 1557 witnessed the first contact between Chinese people and Europeans and the beginning of the Portuguese rule over Macao. Saint Paul's College, the first university in South China and a tertiary institute that used English as one of the instructional languages, was founded in Macao by the Jesuits in the 16th century. Despite the fact that English was first used in Macao, English has never been an official language (Bolton, 2002).

While mainland China, Hong Kong and Macao are today part of the same country under China's 'One Country, Two Systems' policy, the history and roles of English in these three places have been quite distinct. The use of English in colonial Macao has been discussed elsewhere (Bolton, 2002; Evans, 2006; Harrison, 1984; Ieong, 1993; Liu, 1994; Sheng, 2004). This chapter mainly focuses on the language policy, English use and English language education in Macao after her return to Chinese sovereignty in 1999.

Adopting a Language Model for Macao English

Using the most common model of World Englishes, that is, the distinction between English as a native language (ENL), English as a second language (ESL) and English as a foreign language (EFL), English operates as an EFL in Macao. English is not the primary language of the majority of the population, nor is it an ex-colonial language. Moreover, English is seldom used or spoken in the normal course of daily life. While English is learned at school, students have little opportunity to use English outside the classroom. Despite the popularity of this model, as commented in the literature (Kirkpatrick, 2007), this model cannot describe the spread of English in the so-called 'EFL' regions, such as mainland China and Macao. While English is not actually spoken in Macao in daily life, the increasing role that English plays in Macao has been witnessed since her return to Chinese sovereignty.

Using Kachru's (1992) 'three circles' model, that is, the distinction of countries or regions in the 'inner circle', the 'outer circle' and the 'expanding circle', Macao is listed as being in the expanding circle, the same as China. As the model suggests, the roles of English would develop in expanding circle countries or regions. However, the model cannot clearly describe the extent to which English has been developing in postcolonial Macao. While both China and Macao are located in the same 'circle', it is noted that English actually develops in different directions in Macao and China. This is partly due to the historical roles played by English in this former Portuguese colony, and partly due to the lack of long-term language education policy and English promotional campaigns in Macao (Young, 2006).

The Influence of Political Changes on Language Policy in Macao

When the Portuguese started their influence in Macao in the 16th century, the Chinese language was the only official language of Macao. Portugal maintained a friendly political relationship with China until 1849, when the Portuguese Colonial Governor, Joao Ferreira do Amaral, was accused of declaring Macao a free port and was later killed in a local riot. The relationship between China and Portugal became tense, resulting in an increase of Portuguese influence in Macao. For the next one and a half centuries, the Portuguese language played the role of the only official language in the territory. According to Wong (2007), Colonial Governor Correiada Silva made laws in 1919 to implement Portuguese language education in all government and missionary primary schools. The Portuguese language was the sole language used in court and government. In addition, all contracts and legal documents were to be drafted in or translated into Portuguese.

The year 1987 saw the signing of the Sino-Portuguese Joint Declaration and some changes in Macao's language policy. In the 1980s, the public began to fight for the official status of the Chinese language and the formulation of a bilingual policy (Liu, 1994). In 1991, the Chinese language resumed its official status in Macao. Passed by the People's Congress of China on 31 March 1993, *The Basic Law of the Macao Special Administrative Region of the People's Republic of China* (1997), which serves as the constitutional law of postcolonial Macao, states that both Chinese and Portuguese are the official languages of Macao. In addition to Chinese, Portuguese may also be used in administration, government and law. In postcolonial Macao, the two official languages enjoy legal rights. All government documents are drafted in Chinese and Portuguese. However, unlike her close neighbour, Hong Kong, where the Official Languages Division monitors the implementation of the Hong Kong SAR Government's language policy in the Civil Service, there is no government department monitoring the language policy of the Macao SAR Government.

It is noticed that there is no mention of English language policy in the Basic Law. In fact, English has never enjoyed any official status in Macao. The increasing use of English in postcolonial Macao, for the most part, is driven by the strategic economic development of postcolonial Macao. Just before the handover, the Macao Government invited the Macao Development Strategy Research Centre and the Macao Association of Economic Sciences to examine the strategic development of the Macao SAR Government over the next two decades. The consultants set out the overall objective to establish Macao as 'a medium-sized international city under the principle of "One Country, Two Systems" that is fully open in China as well as the Asia Pacific Region through the hard effort of 20 years' (Ieong, 2000: 60). To achieve this main objective, eight long-term strategies are proposed. Among them the fifth strategy is to promote the learning of English:

> During the ruling of Portugal, Macao has failed to establish an English environment. However, ignoring the importance of English today means losing tremendous business opportunities. Also, without an English environment, Macao is unlikely to go internationalised. Hence, we should put forward this issue for public discussion and encourage every household to place emphasis on learning English. (Ieong, 2000: 97–98)

English Use in Macao

Interpersonal function of English

In Kachru's (1992) model, the interpersonal function of English refers to the use of English as a common language between speakers of various languages and dialects. There is no significant community of native English speakers in Macao (McArthur, 2002). According to the 2006 by-census (Statistics and Census Service, 2007), 1.5% of Macao people claim to use English as their usual language – a sharp increase from 0.8% a decade ago (Table 6.1). However, this rate is much lower than that in Hong Kong, as 44.7% of the Hong Kong people use English regularly (see Li, this volume). Nevertheless, English was, and still is, a neutral language for intercultural interactions among the Chinese, Portuguese and Macanese (i.e. mixed Portuguese and Asian ancestry) residents in Macao.

The role of English as the unmarked language for inter-ethnic communication has become more prominent as a consequence of the mushrooming gambling industry (known locally as 'gaming') in post-colonial Macao. Under Article 118 of the Basic Law, the Macao SAR Government has the full autonomy to formulate policies on tourism and recreation. In order to establish Macao as a prosperous internationalised city, the government decided to break up the monopoly of the local casino operator, the Sociedade de Jogos de Macao (SJM), and grant casino concessions to two more operators: the Wynn Resorts and Galaxy Resorts. The opened gaming market resulted in both competition and a significant increase of government tax revenue. In 2006, Macao overtook

Table 6.1 Percentage of usual languages used in Macao

Language	1991	1996	2001	2006
Chinese-Cantonese (%)	85.8	87.1	87.9	85.7
Chinese-Putonghua (Mandarin) (%)	1.2	1.2	1.6	3.2
Chinese-Other dialects (%)	9.6	7.8	7.6	6.7
Portuguese (%)	1.8	1.8	0.7	0.6
English (%)	0.5	0.8	0.6	1.5
Other languages (%)	1.1	1.3	1.6	2.3

Source: Statistics and Census Service (2007).

Las Vegas to become the world's most profitable casino destination. Nicknamed the 'Asian Las Vegas', the 33 casinos in Macao generated a gross revenue of US$15,047 million in 2009, compared to that of US$5,891 million in 2005 (Statistics and Census Service, 2010). The western-operated casinos and resorts, such as Venetian Macao and Wynn Macao Resort, recruit a large number of middle to senior management employees worldwide, resulting in a growing community of expatriates. To communicate with their superiors and English-speaking players, front-line employees, who are typically school leavers among the local permanent residents, must polish their English communication skills. As a result, the Macao Tourism and Casino Career Centre, managed jointly by two government-run institutes – Macao Polytechnic Institute and the Institute for Tourism Studies – offers specialised courses including casino English. In this particular sector, there is no doubt that English has become a more important medium of communication than before.

The growth of the gaming industry fuels the development of related tertiary industries, resulting in the increasing use of English. An obvious example is the use of English in tourism. In addition to Chinese-speaking tourists from mainland China, Hong Kong and Taiwan, Macao attracts non-Chinese and non-Portuguese speakers from Asia, the Americas, Europe and Oceania. The tourist information counters of the Macao Government Tourism Office provide brochures, city maps and leaflets in the two official languages as well as English. Staff members who can speak English are available. In hotels, airports, ferry terminals and scenic spots, tourists can find signs and notices in the two official languages and English. They can also communicate with staff members in these languages. Even taxi drivers, who are usually perceived to be less educated Cantonese speakers, are required to learn some basic English phrases to communicate with their passengers (Wong, 2007).

Nevertheless, English does not seem to be popular as a medium of interpersonal communication. While empirical research on people's daily use of English in colonial Macao is not available, a recent study on students' use of English outside the English language classroom in postcolonial Macao has revealed that 56.1% of the 502 local students surveyed do not speak English more than twice per week, and over half (50.5%) do not have any English-speaking friends (Young, 2007). This implies that the larger market demand on the use of English appears to be a result of the rapid development of the gaming and relevant service industries.

Regulative function of English

The regulative function is performed by English as a medium of the legal system and public administration (Kachru, 1992). In Macao, English is not a language of law because English is not spread through colonial manifestations. The legal system is Portuguese-based and is a product of the Portuguese strand of the civil law, continental or Roman-German family of legal systems. Legislation is the main source of law in Macao. The five classic codifications, namely, the Civil Code, the Commercial Code, the Civil Procedure Code, the Penal Code and the Criminal Procedure Code, which form the authoritative framework of Macao's legal system, were drafted in Portuguese. In the 1990s, there were voices from the public and local legal professionals that all laws should be translated into Chinese, but no action was taken (Ieong, 1993). Currently, the only codification that has an unofficial English translation version is the Commercial Code, which is often referred to by international businesses operating in Macao (Sheng, 2004).

In the public sector of Macao, it can be argued that English currently serves as an international language, in addition to the two official languages. A case in point is the Macao SAR Government website, in which Chinese, Portuguese and English versions are available. Another example is the inscription of the historic centre of Macao as a UNESCO World Heritage Site on 15 July 2005. The expansion in international trade and tourism involves communication between the Macao Government and her non-Chinese and non-Portuguese audience and partners. Chinese, Portuguese and English are used as working languages to promote the image of Macao as a historic centre. For this reason, English-knowing government officials are required to give press releases and statements in English – in addition to Portuguese and Chinese. Certain official documents and contracts also include an English version. These are some of the reasons that have contributed to the rise of English as the predominant foreign language in the regulative field in postcolonial Macao.

Imaginative/innovation function of English

According to Kachru (1992), the imaginative/innovation function entails the use of English in the fields of literature and media. In Macao, although English is more extensively used than Portuguese, it is not the dominant language in the media (Harrison, 1984). The use of English for creative purposes started to grow quietly, partly due to the political change and partly due to 'market demand'.

Regarding newspapers, *A Abelha da China*, a Portuguese-medium weekly newspaper first published in Macao in 1822, was the first 'foreign language' newspaper available in China. Despite the fact that native speakers of Portuguese accounted for 0.7% of the total population in Macao, and very few Chinese people in Macao were Portuguese literate, Portuguese newspapers survived because of government support. However, the readership of Portuguese-medium local newspapers shrank as a result of the political change. Meanwhile, a real demand for English newspapers emerged with the influx of tourists, expatriates and gamblers after the liberalisation of the gaming industry. In order to survive, some of these newspapers targeted the English readership. Some examples are the launch of an English supplement by *Ponto Final* in 1999 and the issue of a weekly English post by *Macau Hoje* in 2002. However, such attempts to expand the local market failed because of the lack of advertisers' support. A more successful example is *The Macao Post Daily*. Launched on 27 August 2004, this independent local English daily targets both English-speaking Macao residents and visitors. *The Macao Post Daily* had a satisfactory daily circulation record of 3500 copies during the first week of issue (Lam, 2004). Following the success of this paper, *The Macau Daily Times*, a local English daily with both print and online versions, was launched on 1 June 2007. Currently, other English daily newspapers with some coverage of Macao news are *The South China Morning Post* and *The Hong Kong Standard* – two independent Hong Kong papers that are on sale in Macao on the date of publication. *The China Daily (Hong Kong Edition)*, an English-language newspaper with its head office in mainland China, is also available in Macao.

The local television (Teledifusão Macau, TDM) and radio (Rádio Macau) services operate Chinese and Portuguese networks run by the local government. With the exception of a small number of imported English-medium television dramas and the broadcast of late evening English local news, most of the programmes are broadcast in Chinese and Portuguese. Other free-of-charge English-medium television channels received in Macao are Television Broadcasting Corporation (TVB) and Asia Television (ATV) from Hong Kong, China Central Television (CCTV) from mainland China and British Broadcasting Corporation (BBC) world service from Britain. A wide range of English-language cable TV channels are also available in Macao.

As the number of movie-goers decreases, the number of cinemas has dropped from thirteen in the 1960s to three: Cineteatro Macau, Weng Lok Cinema and the Macao Tower Convention, which screen movies in various languages including English. Like those in Hong Kong, most films screened in Macao carry subtitles. Those with English or Putonghua sound tracks carry Chinese subtitles, while those with Cantonese sound tracks carry English subtitles. Since the local Macao people are mainly non-Portuguese speakers, Portuguese-medium films are seldom screened. Special art and classic movies in various languages are screened at the annual international film festivals. For instance, the latest and well-equipped cinema in the Macao Tower Convention and Entertainment Centre hosted 'CineAsia', the international convention dedicated to the Asian cinema exhibition and distribution industry in December 2007.

As a result of the development of information and communications technology, many people, especially the younger residents in Macao, are now communicating with their family and friends through email, ICQ or blog. Most local households have access to the internet via broadband service. According to government statistics, there were 143,353 subscribers to the internet in 2009 (Statistics and Census Service, 2010). However, thus far, the spread of English through the Internet has not become very extensive. The use of English is far less popular than that of Chinese. Most local websites are available in Chinese. Chinese (Cantonese) is often used in local online discussion forums and blogs.

English Education in Macao

The instrumental function refers to the use of English as an instructional language in the education system of the community concerned (Kachru, 1992). Since the colonial era, the Macao Government has adopted a laissez-faire education policy. Over 80% of the schools are run by the Church, non-profit organisations and individuals (Rosa, 1989). These private schools have the freedom to choose their mode and medium of education. For this historical reason, Macao education features the co-existence of Portuguese, British and Chinese education systems. In postcolonial Macao, one of the major tasks of the government is to unify the education system. The Education and Youth Affairs Bureau (Direcção dos Serviços de Educação e Juventude, DSEJ) under the leadership of the Secretary for Social Affairs and Culture of the Macao SAR Government is responsible for the design, coordination, leadership, management and assessment of educational affairs at non-tertiary level. Over the past nine years, efforts have been made to improve the school curriculum and to meet the needs of society in the 21st century. A successful example is the implementation of Law No. 9/2006 'Fundamental Law of Non-tertiary Education System' (Macao Special

Administrative Region Government, 2007). Under this law, regular education consists of three years infant education, six years primary education, three years junior secondary and three years senior secondary education. Commencing on 1 September 2007, all students from all government schools and students from the 60 private schools that are integrated into the public school network are provided with 15 years of free and compulsory education. According to the Education and Youth Affairs Bureau (2009), in the academic year 2009/2010, there were 84,760 students studying in 80 schools that offer pre-primary, primary and secondary education. Among them, 10 are government schools while 70 are private schools. Some schools operate a Chinese-medium school unit and an English-medium school unit on the same campus to meet the needs of the students and their parents. Among them, 103 school units are Chinese-medium, 14 are English-medium and 6 are Portuguese-medium. In short, Chinese is the main medium of instruction whereas English is an important foreign language in the Macao education system. The colonial language, Portuguese, is taught as a compulsory language subject in government-run schools only. As a result, the majority of the local people are not Portuguese literate.

It can be argued that the use of English in the Macao education system is motivated by market and parental demands. Many parents believe that a good command of English is important for the future of their children (Tang, 2003; the 'parents' factor is also echoed in this volume, see Chapters 2–5). To fulfil the requirements of the parents and maintain their competitiveness, some prestigious private schools not only teach English as a compulsory language subject, but also use English as the medium of instruction. Since 'English-medium school' is somewhat a symbol of status, some schools concurrently operate Chinese-medium and English-medium units on the same campus in order to raise their reputation. The students' English proficiency level is therefore considered one of the indicators of the school's performance and credential (Mann & Wong, 1999). Overall, English is not used as the dominant medium of daily communication, but is taught as a language subject and used as a medium of instruction for certain school subjects in Macao. It somehow fulfils Kachru's definition of instrumental usage – 'English as a medium of learning in educational systems' (Bhatt, 2001).

A description of the English programmes in Macao schools is a difficult task. This is because Macao has never had a unified school curriculum. As stated in Law No. 11/91/M, both government and private schools shall have autonomy of teaching (Sou, 2008). The school principals and head teachers concerned enjoy freedom of curriculum development. They may set the English syllabus, select suitable textbooks, teaching and assessment methods to meet the needs of their students. As a result, the English proficiency levels and communication abilities of Macao students vary tremendously from school to school. In postcolonial Macao, the SAR Government still has no intention of unifying the educational system. However, to meet the needs of the recent rapid economic development of Macao, the Curriculum Development and Reform Committee of the Macao Education and Youth Affairs Bureau was formed in 2006 to act as an advisory body for curriculum reform.

But before any new laws on school curriculum are made, the syllabuses published in 1999 are still in effect. Currently, two sets of English syllabuses are available for government and private schools' reference. As shown in Table 6.2, the excerpts of the two syllabuses reveal differences in objectives, teaching approaches and course contents between government and private schools (Education and Youth Affairs Bureau, 1999a, 1999b). Overall, the English syllabus for government schools emphasises communication skills development while the one for private schools focuses more on the development of basic listening, speaking, reading and writing skills.

Unlike other regions in Greater China, Macao does not have any unified school-leaving examination that could provide a benchmark of the quality of students and schools (Bray & Koo, 2004). In order to explore the English proficiency of Macao students across schools, the Macao Education and Youth Affairs Bureau invited a group of 1013 students from 25 secondary schools to take a standardised English examination (Education and Youth Affairs Bureau, 2001). Results show that the final scores of the student-participants range from 0 to 96 marks (standard deviation: 18.24, mean: 54.1 marks). As shown in Table 6.3, the students are especially weak in their English listening comprehension skills.

Obviously, there is a gap between the English proficiency levels of the local students and the English language requirements of the local tertiary institutions (Bray et al., 2002). At the tertiary level, English becomes 'English as a virtual second language' as defined by McArthur (1998). English is a means to study other educational content areas and most academic disciplines in the 10 tertiary institutes that are recognised by the Macao SAR Government.[2] Higher education policies are initiated and formulated by the Tertiary Services Office (Gabinete de Apoio ao Ensino Superior, GAES). While this government department processes applications for new academic programmes, it gives freedom to tertiary

Table 6.2 Excerpts of English syllabuses of junior high schools in Macao

	Objectives	Contents	Teaching suggestions	Assessment methods
Government schools with Chinese as medium of instruction	To be able to introduce oneself.	Personal particulars.	Students complete pen pal application forms, listing personal particulars.	Worksheets about composition and pronunciation of vocabulary.
	To be able to use simple present tense, basic sentences and related vocabulary to describe one's family and school life.	Self-introduction (name, gender, age, nationality, address, telephone number, date of birth, affiliation, class, weight, height, appearance, etc).	Using short passages about students' family status and school life as reading comprehension exercises.	Dictation and understanding of the meaning of vocabulary.
	To increase understanding of classmates.	Grammar: personal pronouns, verb to be, verb to have, etc.	Based on the above passages, students make recordings of self-introductions at language laboratories. The teacher evaluates students' speaking and communication skills (pronunciation, tone, grammar, tenses, etc.).	In-class oral and listening comprehension exercises.
	To build confidence in speaking English.			Reading comprehension exercises.

Table 6.2 (Continued)

	Objectives	Contents	Teaching suggestions	Assessment methods
	To consolidate the use of personal pronouns.			Sentence making or composition based on examples of sentences or passages.
	To be able to replace personal nouns with suitable personal pronouns.			Written tests (formative evaluation).
	To use verb to be and verb to have to describe oneself.			
Private schools	To be able to perform simple self-introduction.	Vocabulary of greetings and self-introduction.	The teacher demonstrates self-introduction using simple English, and then asks students about their personal particulars (name, age, hobbies, etc.)	Oral exercises.
	To be able to express one's ideas using previously learned basic grammar.	'Yes-no' questions and common questions.	The teacher plays recordings about greetings and simple conversations on self-introduction	Compositions.

Table 6.2 (*Continued*)

	Objectives	Contents	Teaching suggestions	Assessment methods
	To make basic greetings.	Revision of questions like 'Do you like to read books?' and 'What's your name?'	Revision of simple sentences on self-introduction like 'Good morning', 'My name's Tim Wong'.	Reading comprehension.
	To be able to use complete 'yes-no' questions and common questions.	Simple replies like 'Yes, I am' and 'No, he doesn't'.	Students imitate the content of the recording to introduce each other.	Formative tests.
		Revision of greetings in the morning.		Listening comprehension exercises.

Source: Education and Youth Affairs Bureau (1999a, 1999b).

Table 6.3 English test results of Macao secondary school students ($n = 1013$)

Tested areas	Contents	Format	Time allotted (min)	Average scores (%)
Reading	Comprehension of two short texts	18 multiple-choice questions	45	58
Writing	Description of five pictures	80 words	30	56
Listening	Comprehension of statements and dialogues in American English	30 multiple-choice questions	15	48

Source: Education and Youth Affairs Bureau (2001).

institutes in terms of curriculum development. To facilitate the effective use of English as a medium of learning, the government-run University of Macau established the English Language Centre in 2002 to provide counselling services to help students enhance their report and essay writing skills. In 2003, the MPI-Bell Centre of English was established by the government-run Macao Polytechnic Institute and the Bell Educational Trust. The centre recruits a global team of qualified teachers among native speakers of English to tailor a wide variety of learner-centred English language courses and international English examination preparation courses for the local students and the public. In the private sector, the Macau University of Science and Technology requires all first-year undergraduates to take at least 240 hours of English courses to improve their ability to understand English-medium lectures and communicate with native and non-native English speakers. The university strategically recruits native English-speaking teachers to teach oral English courses – a scheme that is similar to the native-speaking English teacher schemes in Hong Kong and Japan (Lai, 1999).

Conclusions

It can be argued that the large demand for English-knowing employees in the job market promotes the learning in and the learning of English in Macao. As English has surpassed Portuguese to be the most important foreign language, the Macao SAR Government has made some efforts in promoting the use and education of English. However, since the colonial government adopted a less intrusive policy over educational issues, the English proficiency levels of educated Macao people vary enormously.

Future challenges include the formulation of a long-term English language policy to raise the academic standard of English in Macao in order to reach the goal of establishing Macao as a medium-sized internationalised city by 2020. With reference to the experience of Greater China, some possible strategies include the launch of large-scale English promotional campaigns that are similar to 'Beijing Speaks Foreign Language to the World' in Beijing and 'Speak Good English Movement' in Singapore (Young, 2006). Another possible move is to learn from the experience of the 'Native-Speaking English Teacher' scheme in Hong Kong schools and import native English speakers as English teachers. In fact, certain Macao tertiary institutions have hired native speakers to teach English subjects. However, without government supervision, the qualifications of teachers and the quality of teaching may vary. The third possibility is the introduction of public examinations in the English language, but such a move may involve unification of English syllabuses across schools and 'intrusion' into the administrative freedom currently enjoyed by school managements.

As stated in other chapters in this book, the sociolinguistic situations of countries and regions in Greater China are different. However, the demand of English-knowing citizens for economic development is similar. As such, joint research projects that investigate the development of the English curriculum in Greater China may contribute not only to the research body, but also to the cultivation of English-knowing people in Macao and her close neighbours.

Notes

1. In spelling this city, both "Macao" and "Macau" are used interchangeably. The author uses "Macao" throughout this chapter and follows the official titles of the organisations concerned.
2. Currently, 10 Macao higher education institutions are recognised by the Macao SAR Government. Among these institutions, the University of Macau, Macao Polytechnic Institute, the Institute for Tourism Studies and Macau Security Force Superior School are run by the government. Private tertiary institutions include Asia International Open University (Macau), the University of Saint Joseph (formerly Macau Inter-University Institute), Kiang Wu Nursing College of Macau, Macau University of Science and Technology, Macau Institute of Management and Macau Millennium College. In the academic year 2008/2009, a total of 31,249 students were registered at these institutions (Tertiary Education Services Office, 2009).

References

The Basic Law of the Macao Special Administrative Region of the People's Republic of China (1997) (In Chinese.) Macao: Macao Foundation.

Bhatt, R.M. (2001) World Englishes. *Annual Review of Anthropology* 30, 527–550.

Bolton, K. (2002) Chinese Englishes: From Canton jargon to global English. *World Englishes* 21 (2), 181–199.

Bray, M., Butler, R., Hui, P., Kwo, O. and Mang, E. (2002) *Higher Education in Macao: Growth and Strategic Development*. Hong Kong: Comparative Education Research Centre, The University of Hong Kong.

Bray, M. and Koo, R. (2004) Postcolonial patterns and paradoxes: Language and education in Hong Kong and Macao. *Comparative Education* 40 (2), 216–238.

Education and Youth Affairs Bureau (DSEJ) (1999a) English syllabus for junior high schools (government schools with Chinese as the medium of instruction). On WWW at http://www.dsej.gov.mo/crdc/course/Junior/word/Jeng99.pdf.

Education and Youth Affairs Bureau (DSEJ) (1999b) English syllabus for junior high schools (private schools). On WWW at http://www.dsej.gov.mo/crdc/course/Junior/word/Jeng99_N.pdf.

Education and Youth Affairs Bureau (DSEJ) (2001) Research on academic ability of foundation education in Macao. On WWW at http://www2.dsej.gov.mo/~webdsej/www/dsejnews/2001/12/report/index.htm.

Education and Youth Affairs Bureau (DSEJ) (2009) The general situation of non-tertiary education in Macao in school year 2009/2010. On WWW at http://www.dsej.gov.mo/~webdsej/www/func_viewnews_layout1_page.php?board_name=enews&search_style=0&pageis=0&start_msg_date=2005-08-30&end_msg_date=2010-06-30&howcount=1&pt=http://&mode=c&nolimit=&board_name=enews&&msg_id=26.

Evans, S. (2006) The beginning of English language teaching in China. *Asian Englishes* 9 (1), 42–63.

Harrison, G.J. (1984) The place of English in Macao and a theoretical speculation. *Journal of Multilingual and Multicultural Development* 5 (6), 475–489.

Ieong, S.S.L. (1993) Reflections on the language issues in Macao: Policies, realities, and prospects. ERIC Document No. ED368168.

Ieong, W.C. (2000) *Macao 2020: The Long Term Objectives and Development Strategies in 20 Years*. Macao: Macao Development Strategy Research Centre and Macao Association of Economic Sciences.

Kachru, B.B. (ed.) (1992) *The Other Tongue: English across Cultures* (2nd edn). Urbana, IL: University of Illinois Press.

Kirkpatrick, A. (2007) *World Englishes: Implications for International Communication and English Language Teaching*. Cambridge: Cambridge University Press.

Lai, M.L. (1999) Jet and net: A comparison of native-speaking English teachers schemes in Japan and Hong Kong. *Language, Culture and Curriculum* 12 (3), 215–228.

Lam, I.F. (2004) The survival strategies of Portuguese newspapers in Macao after the handover (in Chinese). *Media Digest*, October 2004. On WWW at http://www.rthk.org.hk/mediadigest/20041014_76_120137.html.

Liu, X.B. (1994) *Shuang Yu Jing Ying Yu Wen Hua Jiao Liu*. (In Chinese.) Macao: Macao Foundation.

Macao Special Administrative Region Government (2007) *Lei n.° 9/2006 - Lei de Bases do Sistema Educativo Não Superior.* (In Portuguese and Chinese.) Macao: Government Printing Bureau.

Mann, C. and Wong, G. (1999) Issues in language planning and language education: A survey from Macao on its return to Chinese sovereignty. *Language Problems and Language Planning* 23 (1), 17–36.

McArthur, T. (1998) *The English Languages.* Cambridge: Cambridge University Press.

McArthur, T. (2002) *The Oxford Guide to World Englishes.* Oxford: Oxford University Press.

Rosa, A. (1989) Macau: Education in the period of transition: An overview and prospects. ERIC Document No. ED-90/CONF-401/COL-54.

Sheng, Y. (2004) *Languages in Macao: Past, Present and Future.* Macao: Macao Polytechnic Institute.

Sou, C.F. (2008) Curriculum reform in Macao: Background, progress and prospects. Paper presented at the Conference Series on Education Development in Chinese Society – Curriculum and Instruction, Macao, 22–24 November 2008.

Statistics and Census Service (DSEC) (2007) *Global Results of By-census 2006.* Macao: Statistics and Census Service.

Statistics and Census Service (DSEC) (2010) *Macao in Figures 2010.* Macao: Statistics and Census Service.

Tang, F.H. (2003) Improving English language teaching and learning in Macau's schools. In Y.L. Zhang, R.I. Chaplin, J.V.H. Ao and N.W. Law (eds) *Proceedings of International Seminar on English Language Teaching and Translation for the 21st Century* (pp. 209–224). Macao: Macao Polytechnic Institute.

Tertiary Education Services Office (GAES) (2009) *Data of Higher Education in Macao: Number of Staff and Students for the Academic Year 2008/2009.* Macao: Tertiary Education Services Office.

Wong, Y. (2007) *Ao Men Yu Yan Yan Jiu.* (In Chinese.) Beijing: The Commercial Press.

Young, M.Y.C. (2006) Promoting the teaching of English in Macao through the experiences of Singapore, Beijing and Hong Kong. *Journal of Youth Studies* 9 (2), 151–162.

Young, M.Y.C. (2007) Macau perspectives on native English teachers. Paper presented at the 33rd Annual International Conference of the Japan Association for Language Teaching, Tokyo, Japan, 22–25 November 2007.

Part 2

Convergence and Divergence of English Language Use and Education in Different Regions in Mainland China

Chapter 7
The 'English Curriculum Standards' in China: Rationales and Issues

XIAOTANG CHENG

Introduction

This chapter outlines some of the recent changes and issues in the teaching and learning of English as a foreign language (EFL) in primary and secondary schools in mainland China. In the last few decades, English language education in China has undergone constant changes, particularly with regard to teaching methodology. However, it is generally agreed that the most dramatic and pervasive changes from theoretical underpinnings to real classroom practice have taken place in the last decade and these changes have mainly been brought about by the design and implementation of the new English Curriculum Standards (ECS) (MOE, 2001, 2003). As is always the case, these changes are accompanied by controversial issues that arise out of the nationwide implementation of ECS.

The design and implementation of the new ECS is part of the overall reform of basic education in China, which was initiated by the Chinese Ministry of Education (MOE) in 1999. A central task of this reform was to design new *standards* for all school subjects, a concept that was expected to replace the traditional *syllabus*. For many people, this was just another round of syllabus revision and the change of terminology from 'syllabus' to 'standards' was of little significance. Professionals familiar with the literature on curriculum design, however, would understand that this change of terminology was clearly an indication of the endorsement of the 'standards' movement, which has dominated educational discussions since the 1990s. Standards are descriptions of specific targets that students should be able to reach in different domains of curriculum content, which are usually stated in the form of competencies (Richards, 2001: 132–133).

In 1999, the MOE commissioned several groups of education specialists (known as 'Standards Groups') to draft the standards for all the subjects in compulsory education (primary and junior high schools, age 6–15). In 2001, the trial version of these new standards was released and put into pilot implementation. At the same time, the drafting of standards for senior high schools (age 16–18) started. In 2004, the standards for senior high schools started to be used in four provinces. Following the MOE's guidelines, the number of schools using the new standards increased year by year. By September 2009, all primary and junior high schools and about 80% of senior high schools will be using the new standards.

The implementation of the new ECS entails changes in many things, such as textbooks, teaching approaches and methods, and assessment criteria and methods. Although the implementation of the new ECS is believed to have positively impacted on ELT in China, it is not without problems and controversies. For example, the targets specified in the ECS are said to be unattainable uniformly given the size of the country; the approaches and methods advocated in the ECS are not fully accepted and practiced by teachers. This chapter discusses the changes and issues that have been brought about since the new ECS was promulgated and implemented.

Learning and Using English in China

English is the most widely learned and used foreign language in China. More people are now learning English in China than in any other country. Within the formal (state) education sector, an estimated 176.7 million Chinese students studied English in 2005 (Graddol, 2006). The underlying ideology behind this pervasive scale of learning English is that as a global language, English is a necessary tool that facilitates access to modern scientific and technological knowledge and information in countries and regions where English is used as a native or second language. Learning English is seen as a way to enable China to join the global village and to strengthen its economy. It is widely believed that learning English will enable Chinese citizens to access international research and development, to use advanced methods in industry and business and to learn from foreign countries for the economic prosperity and growth of the country (Dai, 1999; Hu, 2001).

Due to its widely perceived importance, in the past three decades, English has been a compulsory subject for almost all junior high schools, senior high schools and colleges and universities. In 2001, with the introduction of the ECS, English became a compulsory subject in primary schools from Grade Three (age 8) onwards, though in some cities (e.g. Beijing, Shanghai and Guangzhou) it is offered from Grade One (age 6). The class time for teaching English varies from 80 to 200 minutes per week depending on the actual arrangements made by local educational authorities and specific schools (Chen, 2008; Wang, 2007).

It is commonly agreed that the ECS not only extended English provision to primary schools, but also substantially transformed the methodology used in English language education. Xiahou and Rao (2007) provide a good summary of the traditional pattern of English education in China. For a long time, English education has been dominated by a teacher-centered, book-centered method, and an emphasis on repetition, reviewing and rote memory. The teacher is regarded as the 'fount of knowledge'. The cultural norm in English education is that the teacher transmits knowledge and students accept and learn that knowledge. In the classroom, teachers devote almost all their effort to explaining texts in detail, analysing grammar, paraphrasing sentences, asking detailed questions about the texts and making students practice patterns, read aloud and retell the text until they very nearly, if not literally, learn every word of the texts by heart. Such teacher-dominated and text-focused classroom teaching places a great emphasis on linguistic details and accuracy. For most Chinese students, there is a keen interest in the exact understanding of every word, a low tolerance for ambiguity and a focus on discrete points and specific syntactic constructions.

Under the traditional pattern of teaching and learning English, instead of learning English as a tool for doing things in everyday life, students at all levels study English as a required academic subject that is a part of the state education programme shaped by rigid and mandatory top-down educational policies and by teaching practices sanctioned by tradition (Liu, 1998; cited in Xiahou & Rao, 2007). Based on this centralised curriculum, almost all English textbooks are designed to teach grammar, reading and writing, with little emphasis on listening and speaking. Another feature in traditional EFL teaching is that much of EFL teaching takes places in the classroom, with little exposure to the language outside class. The limited class time may be just enough to help students understand how the language works, but it does not allow them to practice using it (Xiahou & Rao, 2007).

The traditional pattern of teaching and learning English was widely criticised as a methodology that produces only test-takers rather than competent English users. Neither high school leavers nor university graduates holding certificates in English were able to function properly in English for life or work purposes. The situation started to change in the 1990s, when the communicative approach was introduced to the

English classroom in China and more emphasis was put on developing students' practical language skills, particularly oral skills. However, ELT in China was still seen as unable to meet the ever-growing need for more English language talent (Dai, 1999). The demand for competent users of English was largely due to China's entry into the WTO, rapid economic development, increased international cultural and intellectual exchanges and tourism. In the early 1990s, the Chinese government made a decision to make English a key part of its strategy for economic development. The decision also meant changes to the traditional methodology in teaching and learning English.

English Curriculum Standards Rationale and Effectiveness

Rather than totally rejecting the traditional approaches and methods used in ELT in China, the main aim of the new English curriculum is to shift from overemphasising the transmission modes of teaching and learning with a focus on grammar and vocabulary to a methodology that facilitates the development of students' overall ability in language use (MOE, 2001, 2003). In order to do so, the ECS attaches great importance to activating students' interests in learning, relating the course content to the students' life experiences and cognitive stages of development, promoting learning through their active involvement in the process of experiencing, practising, participating in activities, cooperating with each other and communicating with the language. The overall goal is to develop students' comprehensive language competence by making learning a process during which they form positive attitudes, develop thinking skills, improve cross-cultural awareness and develop effective learning strategies so as to gradually become independent learners (Wang, 2005). Over the past few years, it is commonly observed that the ECS has been welcomed by teachers, researchers, educational administrators and parents, and positive changes and results have been widely reported (e.g. Chen, 2008; Liu, 2008).

Revisiting the rationale for teaching and learning English

For a long time before the 1990s, learning English meant mastering knowledge about English, particularly with regard to pronunciation, vocabulary and grammar. Practical skills, such as listening, speaking, reading and writing, were virtually ignored. Starting in the early 1990s, when the communicative language teaching (CLT) approach was introduced to China, ELT gradually transited from knowledge-based teaching to communicative competence-orientated teaching.

Communicative competence became the buzz word in the 1990s (ironically, during that period, the CLT fever cooled down internationally). After about 10 years' debate on the attainability of communicative competence, ELT educators and researchers in China apparently came to the agreement that the real question is not whether communicative competence is attainable for the majority of students, but whether communicative competence is *the* goal we should be aiming for. Given the fact that only a small proportion of those who learn English in China actually use English later in life and for work purposes, it is easy to refute the claim that the aim of learning English is to master it as a tool for communication (see further discussion on this issue below). According to the new ECS, developing communicative competence is only one of the five learning outcomes of the English curriculum, with the others being developing learning strategies, cross-cultural awareness and positive values and attitudes. As Liu (2007) argues, 'such a theoretical framework of communicative competence needs to be expanded to address both global needs and local contexts, if English Language Training in China is to be successful'.

Following this thread of thinking, the ECS states that language is not only a tool for communication, it is also a tool for thinking, a tool for learning and a tool for social participation. The aims of learning a foreign language should not be limited to the mastery of knowledge and skills in the foreign language so that students can communicate in the target language. Like other school subjects, such as mathematics, music, art and PE, foreign language learning is part of the overall development of the students. Through learning a foreign language, the students can develop positive attitudes and values, enrich their life experiences, broaden their world vision and enhance their thinking skills (MOE, 2001, 2003).

The rethinking of the rationale for teaching and learning English necessarily leads to changes in curriculum targets, teaching methods and approaches, teaching materials and assessment and evaluation systems. Encouragingly, according to a recent survey (Huang, 2009), an increasing number of English teachers implementing the new ECS gradually understand and accept the rationales advocated by the ESC and there is a high degree of conformity between their theoretical understanding and their actual teaching practice in the classroom.

Resetting in the curriculum targets

In accordance with the rethinking of the rationale for teaching and learning English, the targets specified in the new English curriculum have been expanded from mastering knowledge and skills to developing students' comprehensive competence in using the English language. It is crucial here to understand 'using the English language' in a broader sense than 'using English for communicative purposes'. For example, students may learn other school subject knowledge through English. They may need to obtain information in English when solving a problem. They may become aware of cultural differences when learning and using English. They may develop more learning strategies through learning English. Besides, the learning and teaching of English should contribute to the students' development in thinking skills.

According to the new ECS, comprehensive competence in English is built on development in the following five areas: language skills, language knowledge, affect and attitudes, learning strategies and cross-cultural awareness. Good language skills include listening, speaking, reading and writing (the four skills). Primary school students are expected to start with 'skills' such as playing English games, performing short dramas, singing and chanting, and viewing (video). Then they move on to more 'serious' practices such as identifying the main idea or important information while reading or listening and conveying information through speaking. In senior high school, besides the four basic skills, students are expected to develop critical thinking skills in English.

Sound language knowledge includes pronunciation, vocabulary, grammar, functions and topics. The ECS states that sound language knowledge is not merely the foundation for developing language skills. Rather, knowledge in its own right *is* part of the curriculum standards. The ECS warns against the over-teaching of knowledge and the practice of teaching knowledge without meaningful context.

Affect refers to interests, motivation and self-confidence in learning English; attitude refers to students' attitudes towards the English language, people who speak English, cultures in English-speaking countries and the teaching and learning of English. Positive attitudes are believed to facilitate English learning by enhancing students' motivation and interest, self-confidence and perseverance, cooperative spirit and teamwork skills, and national and international awareness. Language learning is most effective when students' affective factors (such as interest, motivation and attitudes) are taken into full consideration and they hold positive attitudes and values relevant to the target language.

Effective learning strategies include thinking strategies, strategies for monitoring learning, communication strategies, and strategies for locating and using learning resources. The ECS repeatedly states that learning to learn is perhaps more important than the learning of certain areas of knowledge and skills. When learning strategies are incorporated into the language curriculum, it will help students to become independent and autonomous language learners, which is fundamental for life-long learning.

Cross-cultural awareness includes cultural knowledge, cultural understanding and cross-cultural communication skills. Given the fact that language cannot be separated from culture, students are expected to understand English-related cultures and use English with cultural sensitivity.

It is important to note that while these five domains of targets are stated in separate categories, they are inter-related and inter-supportive for each other. Compared with the targets set in the previous English syllabuses, the targets specified in the new ECS are wider in scope and higher in terms of education outcomes.

Advocating new learning and teaching methods

The issue of teaching methodology has always been a controversial one in English teaching in China. Teaching approaches and methodology, however effective they are claimed to be, are subject to criticism as learners, resources, etc., differ from one context to another. Within the ELT circles, opinions diverge greatly as to what teaching methods should be advocated or recommended to teachers. In the early 1990s, when the *English Syllabuses for Middle Schools* (MOE, 1992, 1993) were drafted, because of lack of agreement on which teaching method(s) should be recommended, the syllabuses did not have a section on teaching principles or teaching methods. Rather, they ended up with a list of issues that teachers should pay attention to when implementing the syllabuses.

When the new ECS was drafted (from 1999 to 2001), the issue of teaching methods was brought up again. The discussion focused on two suggestions. The first was that since the ECS mainly sets the learning and teaching targets, it should give teachers the freedom to use whatever methods to achieve the goals and targets, though some teaching suggestions could be made. Given the fact that there are too many language teaching approaches and methods and none has proven to be effective in all contexts, the advocates for this proposal strongly opposed singling out any particular teaching method(s) to be recommended to teachers all over the country. The rationale behind this view was that officially recommending teaching methods would deprive teachers of the freedom to teach creatively. This is understandable because in China officially 'recommended' things are often interpreted as 'mandatory'.

The second suggestion was that as a national guidance document (expected to be a key one for the new century), the ECS should not only set new learning targets, but also suggest ways to achieve these targets. Recommending teaching methods may not be necessarily understood as requiring all teachers to teach in the same way or using only the recommended methods in the current context. The fact that none of the existing teaching methods and approaches has proven to be 'universally' effective should not prevent a national curriculum from spelling out the merits of these methods and approaches. In fact, language teaching research and second language acquisition research in the past 30 years have had many positive effects on language teaching practice. For example, the communicative approach and task-based language teaching (TBLT) have produced very positive results in many parts of the world (e.g. Van den Branden, 2006; Willis & Willis, 2007). There is no reason why these methods and approaches should not be recommended to English teachers in China.

After rounds of debate, the ECS group finally agreed on the second option and decided that the ECS advocate process-orientated language learning and teaching approaches, such as experiential learning and cooperative learning. In this approach, students are encouraged to experience the language, learn the language by self-discovery and participate in discussion and negotiation activities. It also advocates the task-based approach to language learning and teaching in which students learn the language by completing assigned tasks with that language.

Changes in textbook design and adoption

The textbook is often seen as of primary importance in language education in China by policy makers, administrators, teachers, parents and students. There is the common analogy of textbooks to the 'Bible' and the belief that everything in the textbook is correct and everything in the textbook is supposed to be taught and learned. In China, textbooks are not only taken as a teaching tool, they also represent aims, values, methods and philosophy in foreign language teaching and learning. Indeed, very few language education scholars and theorists disagree that textbooks are the most powerful tool in spreading new methodological ideas and in shaping language teaching and learning practice (Richards, 2001; Tomlinson, 1998, 2008). Therefore, developing new and good textbooks is considered the most important part of the curriculum reform and choosing the 'right' textbook has always been a big issue for individual schools and students.

During the 1970s and 1980s, most English textbooks in China were grammar orientated. First, grammatical items were selected and sequenced. Then dialogues and texts that contained the targeted grammatical and lexical items were chosen. If it was difficult to find appropriate dialogues or texts that would serve the purpose, the textbook writers would rewrite existing dialogues and texts by inserting certain grammatical items into them, or contrive materials for this purpose.

In the past 30 years, grammar-translation syllabuses, audio-lingual syllabuses, situational syllabuses and the functional-notional syllabus have been designed and applied one after another. Corresponding textbooks have been written according to these syllabuses. However, the effectiveness of a type of syllabus depends very much on its suitability for the context in which it is used, and 'decisions about a suitable syllabus framework for a [language] course reflect different priorities in teaching rather than absolute choices. In most textbooks there will generally be a number of different syllabus strands, such as *grammar* linked to *skills* and *texts, tasks* linked to *topics* and *functions*, or *skills* linked to *topics* and *texts*' (Richards, 2001: 164, italics original). Therefore, the notion of an integrated syllabus, also called the multi-syllabus, has come into being. Designing a multi-syllabus does not mean the simple combination of elements from different types of syllabuses. Rather, it is a matter of choice of priority.

Currently, the practice of adhering to one type of syllabus throughout a language programme is rare. Rather, syllabus designers tend to resort to a multi-syllabus. There are two ways for syllabus designers to do so. First, they can design a multi-syllabus, incorporating features of currently popular syllabuses. Second, they can choose to adopt a specific type of syllabus for specific stages of the programme. For example, a syllabus might be organised grammatically at the first level and then the grammar is presented functionally. Or the first level of organisation might be functional with grammar items selected according to the grammatical demands of different functions (Richards, 2001: 164).

The trends in syllabus design are often reflected in materials development. Since the early 1990s, following the 'cooling down' of the CLT fever, materials developers have changed their claims about their materials. While still emphasising the goals of developing learners' communicative competence, materials developers have made explicit claims about the value of incorporating grammar and vocabulary study in textbooks. Besides, most textbooks have also made a point of embedding learning strategy training (Tomlinson, 1998).

Current trends in textbook writing in China following the promulgation of the ECS can be summarised as follows. Along with the evolution of approaches to materials development, textbooks have evolved into much more complex objects. Many textbooks currently in use are no longer a single student's book accompanied by a teacher's book. Rather, they consist of a whole set of materials, including the student's book, workbook, the teacher's book, cassettes, CD-ROMs, an evaluation (test) book, the readers, etc. These materials are designed in such a way that they 'provide a richer experience of language learning and offer the learner choice of approach and route' (Parish, 1995; cited in Tomlinson, 2001: 70). Besides, these materials remove much of the teacher's burden involved in the process of creating or adapting teaching materials.

Remarkable technical advancement has brought sophistication and a great proliferation of textbooks. Most textbooks have a colourful and glossy appearance, though there has been a warning against textbooks that may be more eye-catching but have little content and methodological validity (Masuhara, 1998).

Chinese textbook publishers cooperate with foreign publishers. There are generally two modes of cooperation. The first one is that a Chinese publisher buys the copyright of a series that has already been published by a foreign publisher and republishes it in China with adaptations made by Chinese writers. The main purpose of the adaptations is to make the series fit the Chinese context of ELT, in particular the requirements of the ECS. The second mode of cooperation is that a Chinese publisher and a foreign publisher jointly commission a team of writers to create a new series according to the needs of the students and the requirements of the curriculum.

Currently, with more textbooks available on the market, students and schools have more choices as to what textbook to use. However, the procedure of developing and adopting textbooks for primary and secondary schools is a very complicated and rather top-down process in China. According to the regulations set by the MOE, if publishers intend to develop a textbook (usually a series of books), they should first commission a team of writers to write a proposal (including writing plans, sample lessons or units, features, underlying theoretical assumptions, etc.). Then, the MOE invites publishers to submit their proposals and sample lessons (the MOE has plans to do so twice a year, but they don't seem to be able to fulfil this commitment). On receiving the proposals and sample lessons, the MOE commissions a panel of experts to evaluate them. Only when a proposal is accepted (approved) by the MOE, can its publisher proceed to develop the series. When the series (or part of it) is finished, it must be submitted to the MOE for quality inspection before publication. The publisher may be requested to revise the book based on comments made by the inspection panel.

Every year, the MOE announces a list of textbooks that have been inspected and approved by the inspection panel. From the list, the education department of provincial or city governments chooses one or two textbooks for the schools. In order to encourage some degree of diversity in textbook adoption, the MOE suggests that for each subject at least two different series should be used in one province. Some provinces do not follow this recommendation though, the result of which is that all students in the province may use the same book. However, it can be argued that this is a much improved practice as compared to the past when students in the whole country were using one single textbook.

Issues Under Debate

The new ECS has been implemented for eight years in the country. As discussed above, during this period, some of the projected changes have taken place and evidence of positive outcomes has been widely reported. There is consensus that compared with the past, students have generally shown more interest in learning English; the classroom atmosphere is more active; teachers are more capable of using a variety of methods; and students' competence in using English is generally higher (Chen, 2008). Despite all these, policy makers and practitioners have often confronted questions and issues as listed below.

Should every student be required to learn English at all?

It is usually taken as a fact that a large number of students may not use the language for communication after graduation, thus many people, including students themselves, find it hard to see the point of learning a foreign language at all. These people would often ask the question: if English has little practical value other than a requirement for university entrance or graduation, why shouldn't students use that time to learn some other useful knowledge and skills?

Foreign language education scholars and policy makers in China have repeatedly pointed out that the purpose of learning English (or any other foreign language) is not only to master another tool for communication; it is part of the overall development of all students (MOE, 2001, 2003; Chen, 2008; Cheng, 2008; Cheng & Gong, 2005). Based on the bilingualism research findings presented below, they argue that learning additional languages aids students' cognitive development and broadens their vision. Furthermore, learning a foreign language at an early age opens up a whole new dimension for children and greatly benefits their reading and writing in their own language. Like music education, learning a foreign language contributes significantly to the development of individual intelligence and cognition. Hence, English education is not just about language, it is about making a person a better thinker.

It is a commonly accepted claim that language and mind are intrinsically inter-related. To a large extent, human beings' cognitive development depends on language development. What evidence do we have to support the claim that learning additional languages further stimulates the cognitive development? On what basis can we say monolinguals do not have the same cognitive advantage as bilinguals or multilinguals? Let us take a look at some research findings as reported in the literature.

(1) Learning a second language changes the brain. Studies have shown that acquiring a second language actually changes the brain and increases mental acuity. Mechelli *et al.* (2004) at University College London conducted a study on the language region of the brain. The research results show that the grey matter in the language region of the brain in the left inferior parietal cortex was larger in people who speak two languages than in those who speak only one. Besides, the grey matter in young bilinguals' (before 5) brain has a higher level of density than that in older bilinguals (10–15 year olds).

Bialystok and colleagues (Bialystok *et al.*, 2005; Bialystok & Shapero, 2005) at York University, Canada, have also studied the effect of bilingualism on a variety of aspects of cognitive development for children between the ages of approximately 4 and 8. The results show that bilingual children have a more advanced ability to solve problems that contain potentially 'misleading' perceptual information than monolingual children who are at about the same developmental stage. This processing advantage has been shown across a wide range of problem types, including both verbal and non-verbal domains. The results point to the pervasive influence of an experiential factor on the course of cognitive development.

Bialstok *et al.* (2006) have also studied the effect of bilingualism on adults. The executive (mental) processes normally decline with healthy aging, as control over cognition becomes more effortful and response times become slower. Lifelong bilingualism protects individuals against this decline by reducing the rate of natural slowing that comes with age.

These studies have shown that the bilingual advantage found in adulthood increases in magnitude with age, as bilinguals maintain higher levels of cognitive control beyond 60 years old. Senior adults who were fluent in two languages were sharper mentally. Language acquisition, in particular, has a protective effect on the brain, not only on language-related skills such as vocabulary, but also on non-verbal and cognitive skills. The studies have shown that the better the proficiency in the second language, the more the language region of the brain grows.

(2) Learning a second language improves learning of other subjects. Studies have shown that learning a second language can help students to improve their learning of other knowledge and their analytic and interpretive capacities. Research in the USA has shown that mathematics and verbal SAT scores increase with each additional year of foreign language study, which means that the longer one studies a foreign/second language, the stronger their skills will become for succeeding in school.

In China, a study conducted in Beijing (Wang, 2007) has shown that students enrolled in the English Experiment Classes performed significantly better not only in their English examinations but also in examinations in other subjects such as mathematics and Chinese. This study was conducted in seven primary schools in Beijing where some students enrolled in the English Experiment Classes when they entered the school while others enrolled in normal classes. The teaching of children in the experiment classes differed from that of normal classes in that they had more exposure to English (five periods per week), learning materials were more diverse and the teachers were trained to use more flexible and more effective teaching methods. The students in the normal classes were attending fewer English classes (two to three periods per week). Wang (2007) reports that students in the experiment classes were not only more active in class, they also achieved better grades in all subjects, not just in English. Although one may argue that these students' better performance may be attributed to factors such as more exposure and better teaching, it clearly indicates that the enhanced experience of learning English contributes to better overall cognitive development. It should be noted, however, that research studies in this area are still rare in China and there is urgent need for such research.

What targets should be set for English learning?

According to the new ECS, English teaching in primary and secondary schools should enable students to eventually develop all-round language competence, which basically means that when students finish high school, they should be able to use English in their future work and life. This target has been criticised as unrealistic for three reasons:

(1) The aims of English learning in primary and junior high school are to learn basic English knowledge and skills, which will set a good foundation for English learning at later stages, e.g. senior high school and university. Some claim that the notion of 'setting a good foundation' leaves room for different interpretations. It can be argued that even the learning of English in senior high school should be aimed at 'setting the foundation' rather than developing skills to use the language.
(2) Thinking in English and developing integrated language skills are not realistic for high school students. Chinese students do not have an English learning environment. Even the majority of teachers of English have not mastered such skills. How can they help the students to develop these skills?
(3) Another argument against the English learning targets is that China is too big a country. It is unsuitable and/or unfair to require all students to reach the same targets. Different parts of China have different levels of development. Even students in one place have diverging needs. How can students achieve the same learning targets?

Supporters of the ECS argue that learning basic language knowledge is not enough if the purpose of English teaching is to enable students to function in English in the future. As an official aim statement, the ECS should set such a target that may be challenging but essential. In the 21st century, students should be expected to be equipped with the skills to obtain and convey information through English, to express their opinions and feelings and recount their experiences in English. They should be able to think in the global language.

Although China does not have an English learning environment (few EFL countries do, I suspect), students today have a variety of English learning resources (materials and facilities); they have various channels to learn English. Besides, the overall qualifications of English teachers are improving. The latest development in resources and teacher training makes the target, 'integrated language competence' and 'the skills of thinking in English' attainable.

As for the last counter argument, the ECS has indeed taken into account the uneven educational development throughout the country and the diverging needs of students. Although it is a 'National

Standards', it makes it explicit that it does not require all students in all regions to fulfill the same targets. It is explicitly stated in the ECS that local educational authorities can choose a suitable level as required targets for their students in different localities. The reality is that no local authority would overtly claim they are happy to choose a lower level of target requirements for their students.

What teaching approaches are suitable for the Chinese English language teaching context?

As has been mentioned above, the ECS does not prescribe one single teaching methodology for the whole country, but proposes several approaches that prove effective in practice in the world. These approaches include experiential learning, discovery learning and TBLT. However, it has proved that promoting such approaches is a daunting task. Take TBLT for example. Since the late 1980s, TBLT has become such a hot topic that some people are now saying we are experiencing an 'age of tasks'. TBLT is developed and practiced in many parts of the world and it helps provide students with opportunities to learn a language by engaging in authentic, practical and functional use of the target language for meaningful purposes. The underpinning assumption is that the most effective way to learn a language is by engaging in real language use in the classroom (Willis & Willis, 2007). In TBLT, students learn a language by using the language to do things. To be more specific, in TBLT, learners are encouraged to activate and use whatever language skills and knowledge they already have in the process of completing a task. The use of tasks will also give a clear and purposeful context for the teaching and learning of grammar and other language features.

Although discussions about TBLT started in the late 1980s, it was not until 2001 that TBLT actually attracted the attention of teachers across the country. In that year, the MOE promulgated the ECS, suggesting TBLT as one of the major English teaching approaches in schools. However, despite efforts to promote TBLT through lectures, seminars, demonstration lessons and journal articles, many teachers feel perplexed by this new approach. It is generally believed that there are two reasons for the difficulty in TBLT promotion. First, there exists some doubt about TBLT for the classrooms in China. Second, although there is abundant research on tasks and task-based learning, the literature on the practical application of TBLT in the classroom has not been made accessible to Chinese teachers.

The doubt is shown first of all by a common argument that many advocated learning and teaching approaches and methods, such as experiential learning, discovery learning and now task-based learning, may not be suitable for ELT in the Chinese context. These approaches are mostly developed in western countries for the ESL contexts, not for the EFL contexts. Some teachers predict that these approaches may be popular now, but they will lose popularity sooner or later. The National Standards should not single out a certain approach or method.

Much of the distrust of TBLT also arises from different interpretations of the approach or a lack of understanding of what constitutes a task. For example, many English teachers in China do not see differences between traditional exercises, activities and tasks. They believe that tasks are whatever the students are doing in the classroom, including traditional language drills. When doing these exercises does not make any difference in terms of raising teaching efficiency, some would jump to the conclusion that TBLT does not work. Other teachers think that TBLT emphasises learning by doing and pays no attention to the learning of grammar. This is obviously not the case. As Willis and Willis (2007) point out, practitioners who appropriately adopt the approach certainly recognise the importance of grammar. TBLT activities are almost always followed by one or more form-focused activity to deal with grammatical points in their practice.

There are some other practical reasons for the resistance to TBLT. For example, many teachers perceive a loss of classroom control when doing TBLT, which is often considered a deficiency in teaching. Other teachers are concerned about the amount of time required to prepare task-based lessons or the skills and material resources required to do so. Therefore, some teachers simply give up after a few unsuccessful attempts. Besides, the existing examination system does not allow teachers enough freedom to follow the TBLT approach. It is often believed that TBLT aims at helping students to develop language competence, but the examinations are still mainly testing students' mastery of knowledge.

To summarise, there are still areas in need of attention in implementing TBLT in China. There exists a huge gap between the curriculum as experienced by students and teachers, and the curriculum designed by curriculum specialists in response to policy documents. This gap begs further research and discussion that will hopefully provide some insights for policy making and curriculum designing to narrow the disparities between practice and perceptions.

Conclusion

This chapter has summarised the rationale of the new ECS and issues in the teaching and learning of English in Chinese schools brought about by the process of implementing the new curriculum for basic education in China. As any reform will necessarily encounter disputes and resistance, it is not surprising that China's top-down reform of basic education faces many challenges and problems. In the case of English teaching and learning in Chinese schools, however, substantial changes are evident at both theoretical and practical levels. It will take more time and effort for English education policy makers and researchers to convince the public that the theoretically sound curriculum would lead to changes for the better, not for worse, and it will still be some time before the benefits of the changes become obvious.

References

Bialystok, E., Craik, F., Grady, C., Chau, W., Ishii, R., Gunji, A. and Pantev, C. (2005) Effect of bilingualism on cognitive control in the Simon task: Evidence from MEG. *NeuroImage* 24, 40–49.

Bialystok, E., Craik, F. and Ryan, J. (2006) Executive control in a modified antisaccade task: Effects of aging and bilingualism. *Journal of Experimental Psychology* 32 (6), 1341–1354.

Bialystok, E. and Shapero, D. (2005) Ambiguous benefits: The effect of bilingualism on reversing ambiguous figures. *Developmental Science* 8 (6), 595–604.

Chen, L. (2008) Towards a multi-language, high-quality, coherent foreign language education program. *Foreign Language Teaching in Schools* 31 (11), 1–5. (In Chinese)

Cheng, X. (2008) On the suitability of the new English curriculum for basic education. *Curriculum, Teaching Materials and Method*, Issue 1, 44–49. (In Chinese)

Cheng, X. and Gong, Y. (2005) On the theoretical basis for English Curriculum Standards. *Curriculum, Teaching Materials and Method*, Issue 3, 66–71. (In Chinese)

Dai, W. (1999) Issues on the strategy of cultivating high-quality foreign language talents for the 21st century. *Foreign Language World*, Issue 4, 1–3. (In Chinese)

Graddol, D. (2006) *English Next*. London: British Council.

Hu, W. (2001) Lessons from foreign language education planning in China. *Foreign Language Teaching and Research* 33 (4), 245–251. (In Chinese)

Huang, Z. (2009) The conformity between English teachers' teaching principles and their actual teaching behaviour under the new English curriculum. *English Teaching in Schools*, 32 (1), 31–36. (In Chinese)

Liu, D. (2008) Development of English textbooks during the 30 years of reform and opening-up. *English Teachers*, Issue 10, 3–8. (In Chinese)

Liu, J. (ed.) (2007) *English Language Teaching in China*. London and New York: Continuum International Publishing Group.

Masuhara, H. (1998) What do teachers really want from coursebooks? In B. Tomlinson (ed.) *Materials Development in Language Teaching* (pp. 66–71). Cambridge: Cambridge University Press.

Mechelli, A.,Crinion, J., Noppeney, U., O'Doherty, J., Ashburner, J., Frackowiak, R., and Price, C. (2004) Neurolinguistics: Structural plasticity in the bilingual brain. *Nature* 431, 757.

Ministry of Education (MOE) (1992) *English Syllabus for Full-time Junior Middle Schools of Nine-year Compulsory Education.* Beijing: People's Education Press. (In Chinese)

Ministry of Education (MOE) (1993) *English Syllabus for Full-time Senior Middle Schools.* Beijing: People's Education Press. (In Chinese)

Ministry of Education (MOE) (2001) *English Curriculum Standards* (for 9-year compulsory education and senior high schools). Beijing: Beijing Normal University Press. (In Chinese)

Ministry of Education (MOE) (2003) *English Curriculum Standards* (for senior high schools). Beijing: People's Education Press. (In Chinese)

Richards, J. (2001) *Curriculum Development in Language Teaching.* Cambridge: Cambridge University Press.

Tomlinson, B. (ed.) (1998) *Materials Development in Language Teaching.* Cambridge: Cambridge University Press.

Tomlinson, B. (2001) Materials development. In R. Carter and D. Nunan (eds) *The Cambridge Guide to Teaching English to Speakers of Other Languages* (pp. 239–260). Cambridge: Cambridge University Press.

Tomlinson, B. (ed.) (2008) *English Language Learning Materials: A Critical Review.* Continuum International Publishing Group.

Van den Branden, K. (ed.) (2006) *Task-based Language Education.* Cambridge: Cambridge University Press.

Wang, Q. (2005) Primary English teachers' perceptions of learner-centre approach in English language teaching in China: A preliminary survey study. In Q. Wang (ed.) *English Teacher Education in 21st Century: Research and Development* (pp. 31–64). Beijing: Beijing Normal University Press.

Wang, Q. (2007) Report on the Primary English Curriculum Innovation Project. Unpublished project report. Beijing Normal University. (In Chinese)

Willis, D. and Willis, J. (2007) *Doing Task-based Teaching.* Oxford: Oxford University Press.

Xiahou, F. and Rao, Z. (2007) Making native-English-speaking teachers aware of challenges and adapt themselves to EFL teaching in China. *STETS Language & Communication Review* 6 (1), 29–33.

Chapter 8
Primary School English Language Teaching in South China: Past, Present and Future

YUEFENG ZHANG and JINJUN WANG

Introduction

Geographically speaking, South China refers to the drainage area of the Pearl River covering both Guangdong province and Guangxi Zhuang Autonomous Region. The Pearl River Delta has favourable conditions for developing foreign trade because of its convenient transportation network, and its proximity to Hong Kong, Macao and the South China Sea. Therefore, it was one of the first regions to implement China's 'open door' policy in the late 1970s and has become one of the most advanced economic hubs and a major manufacturing centre of China.

Guangzhou (the capital city of Guangdong province), Shenzhen, Dongguan, Huizhou and Foshan are the major cities located along the Pearl River. Except for metropolitan Guangzhou, they are all middle-sized cities and in many ways typify cities in the region. Since ancient times, Guangzhou has been China's most significant port for external exchanges and cooperation with other countries. As early as the Ch'in and Han dynasties (221 BC–220 AD), Guangzhou was the starting point of the Silk Road sea route. In the Dong Han dynasty (25 AD–220 AD), Buddhism was introduced to the hinterland from here. During the Southern dynasties (420 AD–589 AD), Da Mo landed here from India and founded the Chinese Zen. During the Ming and Qing dynasties (1368–1911), Guangzhou became a major port. In more recent times, Guangzhou was commonly known as the first window for Chinese through which to watch the world.

This chapter reviews the history and the current situation and foresees the future development of primary school English language teaching (ELT) in Guangdong province, with a special focus on the second wave and third wave of English as proposed in Chapter 1. It can help us understand the major developments of primary ELT in South China.

English Language Teaching in Guangdong in the Second Wave (1759–1949)

The development of ELT in China is greatly influenced by the changing status and role of English language in society, which is contextualised in China's economic, political and societal situations and her relations with the rest of the world (Adamson, 2004; Zhang, 2005). Although the second wave was characterised by the influx of the language through colonialism of Africa and Asia, including Hong Kong, by western powers, the spread of English in China was driven more by a reaction against colonialism. Faced with the threat posed to national integrity by the technological strength and imperial impulses of industrialised nations as they sought to expand their maritime trading bases and political spheres of influence, Chinese authorities adopted the policy of self-strengthening by accessing the technology of these nations – a process that would be facilitated by learning one of the principal western languages. This policy proved controversial, and the role and status of English fluctuated significantly at different times as political and economic circumstances changed. Altogether, there were three main stages of ELT development in Guangdong, including the late Qing dynasty era (1759–1911), the Republican era (1911–1949) and the early People's Republic of China (PRC) era (1949–1976).

English during the late Qing dynasty (1759–1911)

The Industrial Revolution in the 18th century resulted in a number of western countries seeking access to China. The Chinese government, concerned about preserving cultural integrity while engaging in trade with these foreign merchants, nominated Canton (modern-day Guangzhou), being close to the South China Sea and to military fortifications, as the sole port for foreign trade in 1759 (Hsü, 1990). Foreigners who wished to reside in Canton were restricted to a small area of Shamian Island, where they were subjected to serious limitations. These foreigners were not allowed to communicate with the Chinese unless supervised by *compradores* (local business agents who were registered with the authorities and acted as Chinese-English translators) or to learning Chinese. The *compradores* were probably the first Chinese to learn English on their native soil. However, they were often despised in their villages and communities and English was perceived as a barbaric tongue only for doing business with English-speaking countries.

The Opium Wars of 1839–1842 resulted in Britain forcing the Chinese government into signing the Treaty of Nanjing and the Treaty of Tianjin, and astonished the Chinese government with the advanced state of science and technology in western countries. In the late Qing dynasty, English was serving two controversial roles in society. On the one hand, it was considered a vehicle for gaining access to western science and technology in order to protect the sovereignty of the country. In 1861, the imperial government established the *Tongwen Guan* (literally 'School of Combined Learning'), an institute of translation in Beijing. This was the very first official organisation to offer ELT in mainland China. In 1864, the Guangzhou branch of the *Tongwen Guan* was established, with English Language as one of the three core courses. This institution laid a very solid foundation for further development of ELT in Guangdong. By the late 1870s, graduates from the *Tongwen Guan* began to gain appointments within the imperial civil service or even diplomatic postings overseas (Spence, 1980) and the status of the school, and therefore of studying English, rose accordingly. Missionary organisations were another force in the promotion of English. In 1844, missionary schools were established in Tianjin, Shanghai, Ningpo and other treaty ports.

On the other hand, English was also seen as a threat to the nation's cultural integrity. Anti-foreign hostility towards the English language arose among sections of Chinese society – the gentry, most notably, whose status and power were derived from traditional social and political structures. These people organised mass campaigns or violent anti-foreign movements (such as the Boxer Uprising of 1900–1901) and, at times, had sought to eradicate its traces from China. Much of the violence was directed against missionaries, whose Christian teaching and the Bible (which were often, necessarily, linked to the teaching of English or other foreign languages) were perceived as a threat to the mixture of Taoism, Buddhism, Shintoism and Confucianism, the state philosophy that embraced religious, governmental, social and familial affairs in China (Adamson, 1998, 2002).

These anti-foreign sentiments formed a strong counterpoint to the trend towards strengthening China militarily, economically and diplomatically through technical transfer from the west. The conflict between the parties of these two controversial views was sometimes upgraded to violence, which endangered the stability of the society. To achieve a compromise, some scholars, most notably Zhang Zhidong, sought to encapsulate in the Hundred Days' Reform the principle of *zhongxue wei ti xixue wei yong*

(Chinese essence, western practice), which advocated the retention of Confucian ethics, but with the values-free adoption and adaptation of western economic, military and technological techniques (Ayers, 1971). Thus, anti-foreignist sentiments could be assuaged somewhat, as the fundamental state philosophy would be preserved (Adamson, 1998, 2002). During the Late Qing dynasty, English courses were only offered in higher senior primary schools with favourable conditions (Xin Hui Xian, 2005).

English during the Republican era (1911–1949)

The Republican era was marked by efforts to establish a new state in a less hostile international environment with regard to English-speaking countries. However, the Republic, founded on 1 January 1912, was marked by political uncertainty. The brief provisional presidency of Dr Sun Yat-sen was followed by the appointment of Yuan Shikai as President of the Republic of China, but Yuan's inclinations appeared monarchical rather than republican. After his death, China experienced a further breakdown in law and order: warlords established control of regions of the country and it was only in 1928, with the setting up of a Nationalist Party government in Nanjing, that a semblance of unity was restored. Even then, the relative stability was short lived, with the outbreak of the Sino-Japanese War in 1937, followed by the Civil War that culminated in 1949 with the founding of the People's Republic of China (Adamson, 1998, 2002).

The study of English was still controversial because it acted as a conduit for the introduction of new philosophies, religions and social theories to modernists, but was strongly resisted by traditionalists as a threat to Confucius cultural heritage. A major advocate of learning from the industrialised world was Dr Sun Yat-sen. At times, he lived abroad in order to study foreign languages (particularly English), literature, politics, mathematics and medicine. His goals, encapsulated in the Three People's Principles, were the development of Chinese nationalism, freedom from domination by the Manchu Qing dynasty as well as from foreign powers, democracy and socialism. He sought to create a modernised China that existed on an equal footing to the industrialised nations, but which synthesised Chinese tradition with new imported ideas. In the early days of the Republic, studying abroad, most notably in the USA, grew in popularity (Keenan, 1977). Furthermore, Chinese people in the major cities experienced wider exposure to English than previously, through the increased availability of foreign newspapers, journals and films, with the result that the popularity of English learning was heightened.

The US policy backing the Nationalist Party in the Chinese civil war resulted in the ambivalent attitude of the Chinese Communist Party towards the USA and her allies that was to set the tone for the early decades of the PRC, who abhorred the anti-Communist stance of the US government and retaliated in 1949 by announcing that it would seek solidarity with the forces of socialism to combat imperialism.

Influenced by the political instability in the whole country during the Republican era, the development of ELT in Guangdong was also very limited. English was only offered as a selective course in some special primary schools such, as the Tangxia primary school in the Tianhe district of Guangzhou (Cai, 2004).

English in the early People's Republic of China (1949–1976)

The first three decades of the PRC was considered to be part of the second wave as the post-colonial period for China. Right after the establishment of the PRC, many western countries did not recognise the PRC. By contrast, there was a strong link with the USSR in terms of both economy and politics. Because of Soviet influences, Russian was the primary foreign language while English was the second foreign language in the 1950s. English was considered useful only to transfer western technology and attain cultural information, and retained low official status (Adamson, 1998). The development of ELT was limited to some secondary schools and a few private primary schools. Then, as Sino-Soviet relations deteriorated in the late 1950s, China began to build up ties with some western countries. English was considered a useful tool to communicate with the western world. It began to replace Russian as the main foreign language in China in the early 1960s (Lam, 2002) and served the purpose of improving national economic construction and achieving modernisation with a higher official status (Adamson, 1998). In 1963, the Ministry of Education (MOE) suggested that some full-time primary schools with favourable conditions could offer foreign language courses in senior grades. However, metropolitan areas such as Guangzhou began to offer English courses in most primary schools in the next few years.

However, this did not last long, as the Cultural Revolution (1966–1976) swept China and English was rejected as an imperial language. English learners were condemned as 'spies of imperialism' and English teaching 'collapsed' (Hughes, 2001: 174). It was only after China normalised relations with the USA in 1976 that English started to regain its importance, renewing ties with the west from then on (Lam, 2002). The Cultural Revolution did not seem to interrupt English language education in Guangzhou for as long as other places in China. In 1969, when most cities in inland China were still in chaos, Guangzhou started to provide English courses once again to school children (Lu, 2002).

English Language Teaching in Guangdong in the Third Wave (1977 onwards)

The third wave of English, which is characterised by globalisation and the mobility of people, began spreading in China from 1977 onwards, especially after Deng's tour of the southern provinces in 1984. The rapid development of the economy and trade with other countries in Guangdong has bestowed unprecedented importance on English and ELT has been rapidly expanded in primary school sectors.

With the shift from a politics-orientated society into an economy-orientated one, the economy of South China increased more rapidly than other regions in the country. Since 1989, Guangdong province has held first position in China's economic statistics, and has played a phenomenal role in the nation's transformation into an economic superpower. By 2006, 181 of the world's top 500 multinationals had invested in 649 local companies in the province of Guangdong and foreign companies had established 261 research and development centres there. The cumulative total of the actual absorption of foreign capital up to 2006 in Guangdong province reached US$289.5 billion, accounting for a quarter of the total foreign investment in China (*Guangdong Sheng Dui Wai Mao Yi*, 2008). In 2007, the value of exports from Guangdong province rose to US$369.25 billion, and the amount of exports and imports amounted to US$634.05 billion, which represents 29.2% of the import and export value of the whole country (*Guangdong Sheng Ren Min Zheng Fu*, 2008a). In 2008, the GDP in Guangdong province was RMB 3569.646 billion yuan, that is, US$5369 per capita (Liang, 2009).

In the meantime, enterprises in Guangdong province also began to invest overseas. By 2007, 1804 corporations had been established abroad, covering more than 90 countries and regions (*Guangdong Sheng Ren Ming Zheng Fu*, 2008b). Every year, hundreds of thousands of people attend the biannual China Export Commodities Fair held in Guangzhou. The 100th Fair held in 2006, for example, attracted 192,691 purchasers from 212 countries and regions. Among them, 40,596 were from Europe and 26,021 from America. The turnover at this Fair alone reached US$34.06 billion (Du *et al.*, 2006). Tourism is also well developed in South China. Guangdong's tourism income accounts for a quarter of that of China. In 2008, the total tourism income in Guangdong province was RMB

264.13 billion yuan (US$38.2 billion), of which the international tourism receipts were worth RMB 9.175 billion yuan (US$1.3 billion), and the number of international tourists amounted to 6,160,000 (*Guangdong Sheng Tong Ji Ju*, 2009). It is also worth noting that more people in South China than anywhere in the country could afford to travel abroad. In 2008, there were 2,497,053 outbound tourist journeys organised through travel agencies in Guangdong province (*Guangdong Sheng Lv You Ju*, 2006).

Hand in hand with these economic developments, English has been gaining momentum as the main foreign language of the nation's political, academic, industrial and commercial communities (Lam, 2002). In 1982, it was also stipulated as the main foreign language in secondary education and one of the key subjects in the entrance examination to university. The grasp of English is a crucial determinant for access to higher education inside and outside China and well-paid employment, especially in the commercial sector (Adamson, 1998; Dzau, 1990; Liu, 1995). Citizens' mastery of English contributes importantly to realising the four modernisations and promoting the country's international status in the world (Adamson, 2002; Lam, 2002). As the major foreign language used to communicate with foreign investors and business people, English plays a vital role in the development of South China and there has been an ever-increasing demand for English in the whole region. In some cities, such as Guangzhou and Shenzhen, the requirement for English proficiency is explicitly set out in official documents for people who aspire to become civil servants. In principle, they must possess a CET (College English Test – a nationwide examination that is administered for university students all over the country) Band 4 certificate (Wu, 2003). In-service civil servants are also required to learn English and pass the English test. In 2002, Guangzhou's Personnel Bureau stipulated that all civil servants under 45 years old must receive English training and take English tests. The test results of an individual would be taken as a significant reference for his/her promotion (*Guangdong Sheng Ren Shi Ting*, 2002).

The expansion of English language teaching to primary schools

The need for English in society has hugely stimulated English provision in the region. English teaching is a multimillion-dollar business and provision of English is one of the most crucial selling points for school recruitment. Owing to its geographical location and unique position in international exchanges, South China education authorities have attached great importance to primary school English teaching.

In the early 1990s, the Guangzhou Education Bureau made the policy that the time for English teaching in primary school for grade one should be at least two periods per week, three for grade two to grade five, and four for grade six (*Guangzhou Shi Jiao Yu Ju*, 2007). Shenzhen City even outplayed Guangzhou by offering at least four periods of English lessons from grade one in primary schools. Following this, many cities in South China also began offering English courses from grade one onwards in the 1990s (*Guangdong Sheng Jiao Yu Ju*, 2004), a whole decade before ELT in primary schools nationally became commonplace.

In some foreign language primary schools in Shenzhen, students even have up to nine English language lessons every week, which outnumber the time for other subjects, including Chinese language. Some schools also employ native English speakers to teach oral English and create an authentic environment for students to use English. However, not all native English speakers have received training in teaching English and the quality of their teaching is questionable. In 2005, one of the authors met a native English speaker who taught English in a primary school in Shenzhen. He had been a waiter in South Africa and had not received any teacher training before he came to China. Although teachers in the school knew that he taught poorly, parents liked him very much because he was a native speaker.

As mentioned above, to further encourage language use by the students, many extra-curricular English lessons or activities are often offered as electives after school or over the weekend. Some schools regularly hold English festivals or open days to create opportunities for pupils to use the language for communication. Leading these learning and teaching initiatives are foreign language schools, international schools and some provincial (or municipal) key schools in the secondary sector. Many primary schools follow suit to create an environment where English can be used for interactions between pupils. For example, the Chaotian Primary School of Guangzhou pays much attention on cultivating pupils' awareness in using English. From 25 to 31 December 2006, an English festival was held in this school. During the festival, the school was immersed in English posters, broadcasts and notice boards, and pupils were encouraged to use English in conversations. Every day, following the morning exercises, an English teacher led all pupils in speaking English loudly on the playground. Every afternoon a few pupils with excellent and fluent oral English hosted a campus broadcast with an English teacher. There were also competitions and contests in English song singing, drama, storytelling and similar activities (*Chaotian Xiao Xue*, 2006).

Training English language teachers

Such an expansion has produced a great need for more English language teachers. In addition to some traditional tertiary institutions, such as the South China Normal University, which trains teachers including English teachers, the Guangdong Normal College of Foreign Languages was established in 1978 to train English teachers mainly for primary schools in Guangdong. To date, this college has produced over 5000 graduates who have become primary English teachers. Furthermore, the higher salaries and more favourable working conditions offered by the schools in South China have attracted many secondary school English language teachers from inland China.

In order to enhance in-service teachers' professional development, a Primary School English Teaching and Research Office is set up in each education bureau at the district or county level. This office is responsible for the organisation and management of teaching and research activities, examination affairs and teacher training. With the help of primary school English teaching and research groups in sub-districts or in schools, the teaching and research office can conduct its work, including provision of teaching guidelines, experience exchange, teaching observation and evaluation (*Guangzhou Shi Jiao Yu Ju*, 2008). Its work includes inviting experienced English teachers or experts to advise English teachers in a particular school according to what they have observed, and help teachers better understand the curriculum standards and the textbooks and improve their teaching (*Tan Gang Xiao Xue*, 2005).

Since the 1980s, many training programmes have been organised for teachers. From time to time, theory-based seminars are conducted by national education experts, teaching and researching personnel from local education bureaus or locally famous English teachers. The contents of training include knowledge of advanced educational theories, new curriculum policies or innovative textbooks. Sometimes, training is also available for specific teaching approaches such as the communicative approach and the task-based language teaching approach, and other practical teaching skills, such as teaching stories and songs, vocabulary teaching, microteaching and phonics.

Another popular training activity for in-service teachers is public lessons. In order to improve the teaching skills of primary school English teachers, education bureaus, education research organisations and primary schools themselves often organise teaching competitions or public lessons taught by primary English teachers. For example, public lessons are organised several times a year to demonstrate good teaching by different teachers from various schools in Shenzhen. After the lesson, the teacher trainers, university scholars, district researchers or some experienced teachers would do post-lesson evaluation to highlight the teachers' strengths.

Furthermore, primary school English teachers are also encouraged to conduct research and write papers. Every semester, excellent research papers are identified through public appraisal (*Zhan Jiang Shi*, 2007). Furthermore, some non-governmental organisations are also engaged to conduct primary school English teaching and research through such activities as teacher training or seminars. For example, the International Cooperative English Teaching and Research Center at the South China Normal University holds annual international symposia to discuss the future development of China's primary school English teaching from the perspective of internationalisation of education (Feng, 2007). All of these have helped primary school English teaching in Guangdong to hold its leading position in China (*Guang Dong Wai Yu*, 2008).

English language teaching pedagogy

Along with the changing roles of ELT in the mainland, different English language pedagogies have been adopted in the national curriculum documents since the establishment of the PRC (see Table 8.1). Chinese curriculum developers have tried to integrate some western pedagogy with traditional Chinese teaching methods that mainly emphasise the use of repetition drills and memorisation (Adamson, 2004). These imported foreign ideas included Kairov's Five Steps from the Union of Soviet Socialist Republics (USSR) in the 1950s and other international trends, such as the grammar-translation method (GTM) in the 1950s, the audiolingual method (ALM) in the 1960s, communicative language teaching (CLT) in the 1990s and, more recently, the task-based approach (TBA) in 2001.

Although there have been some progressive pedagogies, such as CLT and TBA, recommended by the national curriculum since the 1990s, it is found that the traditional teacher-centred, grammar-based method is still the dominant pedagogy used by English language teachers in China due to the constraints of many inhibiting factors (Hu, 2002; Liao, 2000; Tang & Absalom, 1998; Zhang, 2005). This was the case in respect of primary English teaching in South China, which was not deemed effective. Linguistic knowledge was overstressed while communicative competence was overlooked. As a consequence, 'dumb English' was commonplace. However, over the past two decades, it is widely claimed

Table 8.1 The intended pedagogies in curriculum documents in the PRC

Curriculum series	Intended pedagogy
1. 1957	Grammar-translation method (GTM); teacher-centred; focus on accuracy and written language; memorisation; Kairov's Five Steps
2. and 3. 1960	GTM; teacher-centred; focus on written language, pronunciation and grammatical structures; memorisation
4. 1961	Reading aloud, memorisation, GTM and audiolingualism (ALM)
5. 1963	Reading aloud, memorisation, oral practice, sentence writing, students' independent learning, GTM, ALM
6. Cultural Revolution	Mainly GTM and partly ALM
7. 1978	ALM and GTM
8. 1982	Predominantly ALM, GTM and partly functional/notional approach
9. 1993	Eclectic CLT, structural-functional/notional, with some ALM, the Five Steps
10. 2001	Task-based approach (TBA)

Source: Adapted from Adamson (1998, 2001, 2004).

that South China stands out in primary school English teaching in China because it has made major innovations in teaching methodology, teacher training, teaching and research activities, hardware and facilities, textbook compilation and so on. Quality teaching and learning can be illustrated to a certain extent by the outstanding performance of pupils in the influential national English contests, such as the 'Star of Outlook English Talent Competition' (Guan, 2008). Pedagogical innovation was also a major theme of the new national English Curriculum Standards (ECS) implemented in 2001.

Teaching resources

Textbooks suitable for local situations are important for primary school English teaching. Now in South China, the prevailing primary English textbooks include national textbooks issued by the MOE, local textbooks compiled by local education bureaus (usually also designated for use in local primary schools), experimental textbooks compiled by experts from reputable universities, textbooks written by commercial publishers such as Longman Limited (Hong Kong) and authentic English textbooks imported from abroad. These textbooks are all claimed to integrate the rationale of the new curriculum standards and new theories of modern foreign language teaching. For instance, the textbook designated for use in all primary schools in Guangzhou, *Success with English*, pays much attention to pupils' psychological characteristics and developmental needs, and stresses the cultivation of pupils' interest in English learning and positive attitude towards English learning. The textbook also takes the historical approaches of English teaching in Guangzhou into consideration, and sets a reasonably high goal of English learning for pupils. While it incorporates new theories of ELT, such as the activity approach and task-based learning, the importance of linguistic competence is not forgotten. Of the three units in each of the seven modules of each graded booklet, the first two units focus on the drilling of linguistic knowledge and skills, while the third unit emphasises, in particular, the development of pupils' comprehensive competence (Lu, 2008).

Besides textbooks, there are many other teaching materials, including multi-media disks, tapes, CDs, work books, wall maps and flash cards available to teachers. In addition, primary school English teaching resources also include supplementary books and web resources. Supplementary books are often compiled by relatively small publishing houses to match the prevailing primary school English textbooks. Web resources may be offered by the local governmental websites, such as Xinhua Resource Pool for English Teaching, which mainly serve primary schools in South China (*Ju Jiao Hua Nan*, 2004). Some organisations and companies also provide web resources for English teaching, such as MP3 English Learning website (http://www.abc9388.com), which offers audio materials based on primary school English textbooks. There are also some private websites and blogs, such as Peng Xuehong's blog (Peng, 2006), which offer a variety of personal resources for primary school English teaching.

The English Curriculum Standards (2001)

Since the late 1990s, the force of globalisation has further enhanced the importance of the English language. English, which is the most widely used language in the world, is increasingly and extensively affecting

Chinese people's daily life and work, and is playing a more important role than ever in the mainland (Adamson, 2002). Increasing numbers of Chinese people are now learning English in order to acquire a higher education and improve their career prospects (Zhang, 2005). China's entry into the WTO in 2001, the Beijing Olympics in 2008 and the Shanghai Expo in 2010 all boosted the trend of learning English throughout the country.

In 2001, China's MOE published the ECS. The ECS is designed to meet the challenges of the 21st century. For the first time, ELT was stipulated as a compulsory subject from at least grade three in primary schools all over the country. The new curriculum emphasises six principles: addressing the needs of all pupils and stressing their full development; setting up integrated but flexible targets; giving priority to pupils in the teaching process and catering for their individual differences; teaching through activities and stressing pupils' experience and involvement; stressing process evaluation to accelerate pupils' development; and enabling learners to exploit resources to learn English (Chen *et al.*, 2002). These six principles are built on contemporary education philosophies and challenge traditional teaching approaches.

Since the promulgation of the ECS, there have been some further developments in ELT in South China. Some primary school English teachers carried out action research projects that involved pupils more in the teaching process. Local education bureaus also organise research forums, or seminars for English teachers to exchange their experiences in implementing the new curriculum (Zhao, 2008). As the new curriculum stresses the creation of supportive environments for English learning, and activity-based learning, more teachers are often found to incorporate some innovative activities in class such as Simon Says, listening and guessing games, Chinese whispers and so on (Feng & Wang, 2007). Some primary schools in South China teach pupils how to conduct simple research in class. An (2005), as a classroom teacher, developed activities to cultivate pupils' capability to conduct a simple survey in English through distributing questionnaires to their classmates in order to investigate their appearance, height, weight and age. Teachers often encourage pupils to participate in singing contests, speech contests, oral English contests and band tests organised nationwide, in a province, in a city, in a county, in a town, or in a school, to arouse pupils' enthusiasm to learn English, and to increase the attractiveness and social influence of schools.

Since the implementation of the new curriculum, assessment of English learning in primary schools has begun to change from summative assessment of language knowledge only to an increasing emphasis on formative evaluation for learning in South China. The Primary School English Education Section of Guangzhou Education Bureau and some primary schools, for example, are conducting research into how English teaching can be enhanced through an effective evaluation mechanism, which consists of both summative and formative assessment. Their work on evaluation in English teaching and research helps many primary schools realise that assessment should not be taken as the goal, but as a means to enhance English learning. The ultimate goal is to guarantee the teaching quality, to monitor and enhance pupils' English learning, to increase pupils' interest in English learning, to enhance the improvement of the quality of English learning and to enhance the change from an emphasis on scores to competence (*Ying Yu Ke Zu*, 2005).

English Language Teaching in Guangdong in the Future: Opportunities and Challenges

As described above, globalisation has further accelerated the spread of English and boosted the provision of ELT in South China, which has further consolidated the region's leading role in the development of ELT in the country. As the new curriculum reform has created more opportunities for ELT to expand more vigorously, English education also faces many challenges in its future development. Some of the major challenges, as the following section shows, have hampered the development of primary school ELT in Guangdong province.

Negative wash-back of examination-orientated education

Although the implementation of the new curriculum has brought about many changes that appear positive, traditional examination-orientated language education has not disappeared. Many primary schools give priority to high scores in examinations as they argue that these are closely linked with their reputation in society (*Tian He Qu*, 2006). While pupils are encouraged to participate in various English contests, they are under enormous pressure to gain high scores in examinations. In many situations, contests exacerbate the pressure on pupils instead of stimulating their interest. Indeed, examination results remains the most important criterion for education bureaus and society to evaluate the English teaching level of a primary school and for schools to appraise English teachers (*Zhong Xing Xiao Xue*, 2007).

Because of the enormous pressure placed on teachers and pupils to achieve high scores in examinations, formative assessment is usually ignored, though it is encouraged in the new curriculum. Examination-orientated English language education, which is seen as unavoidable for schools, has fundamentally affected the implementation of the new curriculum at the primary level. As a result, many teachers tend to stick to a teacher-dominated, form-focused and grammar-based way of teaching and ask students to do many form-focused pattern drills and exercises in order to prepare for examinations.

Lack of teacher training

Whether the ECS succeeds or not relies mainly on whether all the stakeholders can understand the rationales and put them into practice, especially the stakeholders in schools. It is a huge project to provide training for the new curriculum to all the principals and teachers from all the schools, as there is still a big gap between the intended curriculum and the existing teacher practice (Zhang & Hu, 2010; Zhang & Adamson, 2007). Although the ECS was written by knowledgeable educators and scholars at Beijing Normal University, there has been a limited, sporadic and unsystematic introduction and dissemination of the new curriculum to schools and teachers due to the lack of teacher trainers who really understand the new curriculum well. In some primary schools, there was an attempt to experiment with the new curriculum in some research projects. However, little consistent technological or theoretical support was given to these schools or to the teachers in charge of the projects, which normally failed to produce effective outcomes (Zhang, 2005, 2007).

Without sufficient support from trained-up teacher trainers to help disseminate, monitor and support the innovative curriculum reform, it is hard to guarantee that the new curriculum can be successfully disseminated and implemented in the way it is intended in all schools.

Inequality in English provision

The area of South China is about 450,000 km^2, of which the Pearl River Delta covers just 41,698 km^2. The English teaching level in primary schools in the Pearl River Delta area represents the highest level in South China, but there are many underdeveloped areas with poor English provision. In Guangdong, primary schools can be classified as consisting of three levels in terms of English provision. The first level schools are those located in big cities and some in small and medium-sized cities as described above. These schools possess the most advanced material resources and qualified English teachers. Even for this level of schools, teachers still need more training and time to put the new curriculum into practice. The second level schools are those in small cities and towns outside the Pearl River Delta. These schools are less well resourced with regard to advanced hardware and qualified English teachers. The third level schools are located in remote rural areas. These schools are badly in need of hardware and English teachers. Many rural primary schools have to employ teachers of other subjects as part-time English teachers. Inequality in English provision caused by unbalanced development is no doubt a major challenge.

To sum up, historically, South China has always been a gateway of the country for exchanges with other countries since ancient times. With the rapid spread of English in the world and the special strategic position of South China, English has gained even more prominence in society and in primary schools. From the days of the *Tongwen Guan* to present times, despite all the ups and downs caused by political and societal changes, South China has maintained its leading role in conducting ELT in all sectors, with primary schools being a pioneering area. The promulgation of the ECS has boosted the further development of ELT in South China, particularly in the Pearl River Delta region. However, given the above-mentioned challenges, primary English education in South China is in need of further fundamental reform of the assessment system, more training for different stakeholders and more support to the rural areas in order to achieve a more balanced and comprehensive development.

References

Adamson, B. (1998). English in China: The junior secondary school curriculum 1949–94. Unpublished PhD thesis. University of Hong Kong.
Adamson, B. (2001) English with Chinese characteristics: China's new curriculum. *Asia Pacific Journal of Education* 21 (2), 19–33.
Adamson, B. (2002) Barbarian as a foreign language: English in China's schools. *World Englishes* 21 (2), 231–243.
Adamson, B. (2004). *China's English*. Hong Kong: Hong Kong University Press.
An, F.Q. (2005) Our Class Survey I. (In Chinese) On WWW at http://www.szjy.edu.cn/Show.asp?ArticleID=1575&ClassID=79. Accessed 21.9.08.
Cai, W.L. (2004) Tangxia primary school started to offer English course in the Republic of China. *Yang Cheng Jin Gu* 2004 (1), 60. (In Chinese)
Chen, L., Wang, Q. and Cheng, X.T. (2002) *Illustration of Standards for Full Time Compulsory English Curriculum*. Beijing: Publishing House of Beijing Normal University. (In Chinese)
Du, J., Tang, X.Y. and Zhong, X. (2006) The turnover in this session reached to 34.06 billion US dollars, Guangzhou exceeded one billion US dollars for the first time. (In Chinese) On WWW at http://gz.dayoo.com/gb/content/2006-10/31/content_2672263.htm. Accessed 21.9.08.
Feng, A.W. (ed.) (2007) *Bilingual Education in China—Practices, Policies and Concepts*. Clevedon: Multilingual Matters.

Feng, Z.J. and Wang, J.J. (2007) Integrate English – A bilingual teaching model in Southern China. In A.W. Feng (ed.) (2007) *Bilingual Education in China— Practices, Policies and Concepts* (pp. 147–165). Clevedon: Multilingual Matters.

Guan, X.D. (2008) 'Star of Outlook English Talent Competition' of Shenzhen drew up the Curtain. (In Chinese) On WWW at http://blog.sina.com.cn/s/blog_58fbdde90100943g.html. Accessed 21.9.08.

Guangdong Sheng Lv You Ju [Guangdong Provincial Tourism Bureau] (2006) Outbound tourists organized through travel agency. (In Chinese) On WWW at http://www2.visitgd.com/GovernmentAffair/images/News/2006/0623/20066231500414613.xls. Accessed 21.9.08.

Guangdong Sheng Ren Shi Ting [Guangdong Provincial Department of Personnel] (2002) Guangzhou requires civil servants take English tests, master at least 1,000 words. (In Chinese) On WWW at http://www.gdrst.gov.cn/info/Information.asp?InfoID=187167165254777418. Accessed 21.9.08.

Guangdong Sheng Tong Ji Ju [Statistics Bureau of Guangdong Province] (2009) The Report on Economic and Social Development of Guangdong Province in 2008. (In Chinese) On WWW at http://210.76.64.38/tjgb/t20090225_64168.htm. Accessed 21.9.08.

Hu, G. (2002) Potential cultural resistance to pedagogical imports: The case of communicative language teaching in China. *Language Culture and Curriculum* 15 (2), 93–105.

Hughes, H.J. (2001) Review essay: China's new revolution. *English Studies* 2, 172–176.

Ju Jiao Hua Nan [Focusing on South China] (2004) The first online warebase of primary school English teaching resources is about to be born. (In Chinese) On WWW at http://shenzhen.ccw.com.cn/ywzl/200204/0401_12.asp. Accessed 21.9.08.

Lam, A. (2002) English in education in China: Policy changes and learners' experiences. *World Englishes* 21 (2), 245–256.

Liang, G.H. (2009) GDP per capital in Guangdong province rose to 5,369 US dollars. (In Chinese) On WWW at http://www.tfol.com/10026/12702/12703/2009/1/22/10703809.shtml. Accessed 21.9.08.

Liao, X. (2000) How communicative language teaching became acceptable in secondary schools in China. (In Chinese) On WWW at http://iteslj.org/Articles/Liao-CLTinChina.html. Accessed 12.8.04.

Lu, Z.G. (2002) The final report of compiling Guangzhou junior high school experimental English textbook. (In Chinese) On WWW at http://www.cbc21.com/subject/english/html/050202/2002_12/20021203_2051.html. Accessed 21.9.08.

Lu, Z.G. (2008) Analysis of primary school English textbook SUCCESS WITH ENGLISH Book 3. (In Chinese) On WWW at http://ps-english.guangztr.edu.cn/Article/ShowArticle.asp?ArticleID=61. Accessed 21.9.08.

Peng, X.H. (2006) A notice of online teaching and research — application of phonic in primary school English teaching. On WWW at http://www.thjy.edu.cn/pengxuehong/article/376/633146763170000000.aspx. Accessed 21.9.08.

Tang, D. and Absalom, D. (1998) Teaching across cultures: Considerations for western EFL teachers in China. *Hong Kong Journal of Applied Linguistics* 3 (2), 117–132.

Wu, Y.R. (2003) English level to register for the civil servants must be over CET B and 4. (In Chinese) On WWW at http://news.sina.com.cn/s/2003-10-24/0904978656s.shtml. Accessed 21.9.08.

Xin Hui Xian Li Shi Bian Ji Wei Yuan Hui (2005) Section 2: Basic Education. (In Chinese.) On WWW at http://wylib.jiangmen.gd.cn/jmhq/list.asp?id=4382. Accessed 21.9.08.

Ying Yu Ke Zu [Teaching Section of English Course] (2005) A summary of a research project about developmental evaluation – implications of foreign teachers' evaluation art on ours. (In Chinese) On WWW at http://www.gze.net.cn/view.jsp?NewsID=5014. Accessed 21.9.08.

Zhang, Y. and Hu, G.W. (2010) Between intended and enacted curriculums: Three teachers and a mandated curricular reform in mainland China. In K. Menken and O. García (eds) *Conceptualization for Language Policy in Education* (pp.123–142). New York: Routledge, Taylor & Francis.

Zhang, Y. (2007) TBLT-innovation in primary school English language teaching in mainland China. In K. Van den Branden, K. Van Gorp and M. Verhelst (eds) *Tasks in Action: Task-based Language Education from a Classroom-based Perspective* (pp. 68–91). Cambridge: Cambridge Scholars Publishing.

Zhang, Y. and Adamson, B. (2007) Implementing language policy: Lessons from primary school English. In A. Feng (ed.) *Bilingual Education in China* (pp.166–181). Clevedon, Buffalo, Toronto: Multilingual Matters.

Zhang, Y. (2005) The implementation of task-based approach in primary school ELT in mainland China. Unpublished PhD thesis, The University of Hong Kong.

Zhao, S.H. (2008) A notice of study for teaching and research persons of counties and districts in the first half semester of 2008. (In Chinese) On WWW at http://ps-english.guangztr.edu.cn/Article/ShowArticle.asp?ArticleID=92. Accessed 21.9.08.

Zhong Xing Xiao Xue [Zhongxing Primary School] (2007) English group of Zhongxing primary school won the title of Excellent English Group in Guangzhou. (In Chinese) On WWW at http://www.gze.net.cn/view.jsp?NewsID=12154. Accessed 21.9.08.

Chapter 9
English Immersion in Mainland China

HAIYAN QIANG, XIAODAN HUANG, LINDA SIEGEL and BARBARA TRUBE

The Context of English Immersion in China

The China, Canada, United States, English Immersion (CCUEI) project did not come about as the result of a 'top-down' official directive for reforming English education in China's basic education (elementary and secondary) school system, nor was it the result of any education professionals' impulsive research interest. Three important contextual factors contributed to the birth of English immersion in China as described below.

Heightened recognition of the value of English

China's economic reform since the late 1970s has set as its central goal to achieve its aim for modernisation. During the 1980s, the country was repositioning itself in the new global economy with a series of 'Out' and 'In' new economic policies. Chinese businesses were urged to brave 'out' to the world, and foreign investments and manufacturers were encouraged to come 'in' to China. In this environment, the English language suddenly gained unprecedented recognition. English was undeniably accepted as the most common language to communicate scientific, technological, academic, diplomatic, tourist and international trade information (Kelly, 2003). The language was valued as an indispensible communication tool to bridge China and its people to the outside modern world. The ability to understand and speak English, therefore, was widely recognised as giving individual citizens an advantage in employment opportunities and career advancement. The English competency of the nation's citizenry as a whole was also recognised as a prime condition for the country to secure a foothold in competing in the global marketplace, a prerequisite for China's grand plan towards modernisation.

Strengthening English education thus became not only an integral part of the education reform, but also part of the national strategic plan for economic development. As explicitly pointed out by Deng Xiaoping in the early 1980s, then the leader of the central government, education must take the lead in repositioning the country to 'face the modernization, face the world, and face the future' (Project Team, 2008: III). At the turn of the century, the central Ministry of Education (MOE) initiated a series of education policies to reform the nation's basic (elementary and secondary) education. Among them was a document entitled 'English Curriculum Standards for the Public School System', published in 2001. According to this policy, all elementary schools must schedule English as a 'core' subject, a required course for all students beginning in the third grade (Han & Liu, 2008). Reform proposals were also solicited for improving English instruction and learning in the school settings. In fact, in the 1990s, many local schools had already begun to offer English language as a subject to early grades, as early as kindergarten and first grade, with the use of a variety of English textbooks, commercial reading materials and media. Parents eagerly embraced the school reform direction, wanting their young children to have a jump start in learning English in an 'authentic' environment. The English immersion pedagogy, which emerged as an innovative teaching strategy, was welcomed from the outset by the school administration and parents as a 'right idea in the right time', and as a response to the nation's economic and political agenda of China's modernisation.

Dissatisfaction with traditional English language teaching in China

Although China has a history of formal English education for over 100 years (Fu, 1986), many regard the outcome as 'getting half the result with twice the effort'. Research and test results showed that students in general performed better in reading comprehension and writing English than using English to communicate. Poor communication skills, argued by many, may be a fair reflection of the fundamental flaws of traditional teaching methods that had been dominating English education in schools for so long (Li, 1996). In the new economic order, improving students' English communication skills was seen as a critical challenge facing the education professionals. This urgency was made clear by Li Lanqing, the then Vice Premier in charge of education; '[The failure of] foreign language education is directly impacting on the nation's open economic policies ... Researchers must be urged to test out the most scientific and efficient ways to popularize English, to create and improve ELT methods that are most suitable for the Chinese education system' (Li, 1996). In the mid 1990s, the national MOE issued a series of documents to encourage and support reform ideas in English language teaching (ELT). With the headlines of 'Let a hundred flowers blossom and a hundred schools of thought contend' and 'Apply theory to practice', the MOE emphasised an outcome-based reform approach, welcomed 'out of the box' thinking and encouraged free exploration of good practices in English education for the school system (Qiang & Zhao, 2001: 7).

Exposure to the Canadian French immersion model

It was in this social context that the Canadian French immersion programme was first introduced to China and attracted the serious attention of Chinese researchers. In 1996, under the authorisation of the Chinese Financial Department of Foreign Trade, the Canadian International Developmental Agency (CIDA), the Chinese National Education Commission and the Canadian University Society, and with financial support from CIDA, many Special University Linkage Consolidation Projects (SULCP) were initiated in China. One of the joint projects was 'Women and Minorities as Educational Change Agents', led by Professor Ruth Hayhoe, a comparative educator specialising in Chinese education. Eight universities from China and Canada participated in the project. In the sub-project on minority bilingual education studies, the Canadian team, led by Professor Linda Siegel, systematically introduced the theory and practice of French immersion education in Canada to Chinese partners at a workshop held in Xi'an. The workshop marked the first time ever when the concept of immersion education was exposed to Chinese educators.

The first Canadian French immersion programme was launched in Canada in 1965 at kindergarten level and extended up through the end of secondary education. With its successful results, the immersion model expanded dramatically during the following two decades. By the 1990s, it was implemented in over 2000 primary and secondary immersion classes for about 300,000 students. The model established its status as a well-developed teaching pedagogy that had made an enormous impact on research and practice in the field of foreign language and bilingual education.

The Canadian model has since been adapted in other countries in more than 10 languages, including Australia, Singapore, Holland, South Africa, and the USA. Reports on these programmes show positive results and a wide acceptance of the model (Qiang & Zhao, 2001: 5–6). For example, according to a survey by the Center for Applied Linguistics in 2006, a total of 263 schools in 33 states of the USA implemented various types of immersion programmes, including the full, partial or two-way immersion types (Lenker & Rhodes, 2007). Findings from the programmes in the USA and other countries indicate similar positive results and issues as reported on the Canadian model.

With the successful Canadian French immersion programme as a reference model, questions were raised in China: Could this model meet Chinese students' needs of English? What might be the major challenges in implementing it? Are the challenges surmountable in the school reality? What modifications must be made prior to using the model? A Xi'an-based research team led by Professor Haiyan Qiang, a member of the SULCP, was heavily engaged in deliberating these questions. Answers were not straightforward, but the determination became evident, due largely to the Chinese belief that 'the stone from another mountain can be used to polish one's own jade'. With a great deal of excitement and awareness of the challenges ahead, the research team decided to propose introducing the Canadian French immersion model in Xi'an schools in 1997, and thus began the journey of experimenting with the North American immersion model in the Chinese school context.

The Development of English Immersion in China

The Chinese English immersion programme was initiated as a sub-project of the China-Canada SULCP project under the heading 'An Experiment of English Immersion Teaching'. To formally recognise the contributions from the Canadian partner, the programme shortly announced a name change to the 'China-Canada English Immersion collaborative (CCEI)' at its first conference in Xi'an in June 1997. Led by Professor Haiyan Qiang, director of the CCEI, the first conference was devoted to planning for the immersion experiment in the Xi'an area schools. Canadian scholars from the University of British Columbia and the University of Toronto were present at the conference to offer consultations on theoretical understanding of the immersion model and practical matters such as school selection, scheduling, teacher qualifications and English immersion instructional strategies. A group of principals and teacher leaders from selected kindergarten and elementary schools in Xi'an were invited to learn about the immersion teaching concept, observe model teaching and engage in the initial planning sessions. At the end of the conference, eight kindergartens pledged to be part of the first immersion experiment group beginning in the fall of 1997.

In each of the eight kindergartens, a special experiment class was organised with 30 five-year-old children selected from the existing class groups[1] by consensus of the parents. The partial immersion model was used in all eight sites, meaning that the children were immersed in an English environment 50% of the time for each school day. The teachers were selected based on their bilingual competency. Prior to the school year, they received intensive training to learn how to use the integrated approach, which incorporates language acquisition with subject learning in the experimental class.

The very early phase of the programme, despite its inexperienced researcher and teachers and the 'Do as we learn, and Change as we do' approach throughout the first year, nevertheless enjoyed its initial success. Although no formal evaluation was conducted for the first year, many positive anecdotal comments from the parents and teachers were received, indicating that children's receptive and expressive language skills emerged in the English environments. *Ad hoc* observations made by teachers and researchers suggest that the children obviously enjoyed the activity-centred and integrated teaching strategies. Most children appeared to have little problem following teachers' directions in English, and in comparison with children in other regular classes, they appeared more comfortable speaking in English with a noticeably larger vocabulary in their communication with teachers and peers.

Inspired by the success of the first year, the programme was extended to five elementary schools in Xi'an in 1998. The selection of schools in the second year was more strategic to ensure a fair representation of all elementary schools in the area. Of the five schools chosen for the programme, two schools enrolled students mostly from factory worker families; whereas two other schools enrolled students whose parents typically worked in universities or for the provincial or local governments; and for the remaining school, students represented a mix of all socio-economic classes. With parents' permission, first graders were selected at random to form one or two experiment classes in each school to implement the immersion programme. Some students came from the immersion kindergarten, but most had no prior English learning experience at all. As with the kindergarten practice, the partial immersion model was used, so students gained the all-English learning environment for about half of their school day. Integrated teaching materials were used during the immersion hours to cover the content in the subjects of science, moral education and social studies, physical education, music and visual arts.

Students in the immersion experiment stayed together as a cohort throughout their six-year elementary education. They were offered an option of departing the programme any time per request by parents, but very few did. In 2004, the immersion project saw its first graduating group from the elementary schooling. During these years, the immersion programme was evolving to become an increasingly structured and comprehensive school reform project. With the unexpected addition of American teacher educators joining the immersion team in 2000, the programme gained needed resources and renewed energy. The American partnership has since provided both theoretical and technical support, including developing and sharing related research updates, supervising classroom instruction, offering teacher workshops, developing evaluation tools for teaching observation, and writing and editing immersion textbooks. In acknowledging and encouraging the continued support from American colleagues, in 2002, the Chinese immersion project was officially renamed the China-Canada-US English Immersion Collaborative programme (CCUEI).

Graduation of the first immersion group from elementary schools was heralded as a success story in the Xi'an area. Test scores in English and other subjects reflected positively on the CCUEI programme, and alleviated the concern of some parents that the English-only environment may hinder student learning in other subjects. Responding to the parents' appeals to continue their children's immersion education to the higher level, the Education Bureau of Shaanxi Province officially approved continuation of the English immersion programme in three 'key' secondary schools in Xi'an. By 2007, the first group of immersion students graduated from the middle school level. One of the three schools continued to implement the immersion experiment to the high school grades.

Over time, the Xi'an experience with the immersion programme gradually spread to other parts of China. Currently the CCUEI model is implemented in and undergoing research in 50 experimental schools, ranging from kindergarten, elementary to secondary levels in some major metropolitan school districts. The experiment has been recognised as a key collaborative research project by the participating universities and schools. It has also been approved as priority research projects and supported by a number of national level offices in education, including the Department of International Affairs and the Department of Social Sciences of China's MOE. It is also listed in 'The Tenth Five Year Plan for

Educational Studies' as a Priority Project by the National Center for Foreign Language Teaching and Research.

The Teaching Principles of English Immersion in China

As mentioned previously, the early phase of the CCUEI project was focused on available research on secondary language immersion, with the intent to construct its own theoretical framework. The popular Canadian French immersion model and other foreign language immersion models were carefully studied and shared. The CCUEI collaborative members examined the essential characteristics of foreign language immersion, as summarised by Johnson and Swain (1997) based on their case studies of immersion education in a wide variety of countries around the world:

(1) The second language (English language) is a medium of instruction.
(2) The immersion curriculum parallels the local first language (Chinese) curriculum.
(3) Overt support exists for the first language.
(4) The programme aims for additive bilingualism.
(5) Exposure to the second language is largely confined to the classroom.
(6) Students enter with similar (and limited) levels of second language proficiency.
(7) The teachers are bilingual.
(8) The classroom culture is that of the local first language community.

The project participants believed that these characteristics properly captured school realities in China and agreed to hold the CCUEI practice true to these characteristics in designing and developing the programme. In an effort to strengthen its theoretical foundations, the developmental and cognitive learning theories of Piaget and Bruner and the social-linguistic theories of Vygotsky (c.f. Siegel, 2000) were brought in to formulate assumptions underlying the immersion practice:

- Young children learn languages easily and enjoy the experience. They do not experience the inhibitions and embarrassment of older children or adults.
- Language should be learned in an interactive way. Communication is important.
- The teaching of subject areas should be integrative.
- Language learning should be about everyday life.
- Children should enjoy the experience. (Siegel, 2000)

It is important to note that the above theoretical assumptions would be new to many of the project's participating members, especially some school practitioners, including principals and teachers. This was because English teaching in China was historically predominated by a teacher-centred approach, using the drill and skill delivery method. To accept the immersion approaches, which emphasised students' active involvement in learning based on constructivist learning theories, would signify a fundamental departure from the traditional way of instruction to which most of the immersion teachers were accustomed. To meet this challenging paradigm shift, the project team took three measures. First, regular training sessions were offered to model immersion teaching practices by expert English immersion teachers followed by structured group critiques based on immersion theories. Such kinds of training and classroom teaching observation/discussion occurred once a week or once every other week or at least once a month depending on the needs of each immersion school. Second, responsibility was delegated to immersion schools where the principal or a vice principal should be in charge of the project, and the most experienced immersion teacher should be the leader of the immersion teaching/research group in his or her school. The leader was the school-based project coordinator who would function as a liaison person to bridge communication among the immersion schools and teachers and the CCUEI teams in immersion teaching delivery. And third, a set of five teaching principles, as listed below, were developed and implemented by the CCUEI to guide classroom instruction, curricular design, lesson planning and teacher evaluation:

- Integration of teaching objectives in language acquisition and subject content, i.e. the integrated approach.
- Monolingual immersion teaching practices.
- Literacy blocks with listening skill development first.
- Activity-orientated teaching and learning.
- Whole-student approach.

Integration of objectives in English language and subject content

Foreign language immersion aims at learning outcomes in both areas of foreign language acquisition and subject content learning. In the literature, it is this dual learning principle that distinguishes immersion from other foreign language learning approaches. Learning the target language is achieved by using the target language as the sole instructional medium for learning the subject content. Thus, students learn

English in an indirect way through its integration while gaining knowledge of subject content. The immersion teachers were trained to be keenly aware of the dual purpose of immersion lessons, and were required to adopt suitable strategies to reflect this integrated purpose.

Monolingual immersion teaching practices

Immersion teachers were required to use only English to communicate with their students in the classroom. This is also a distinctive feature of immersion as opposed to other traditional ways of teaching English. The CCUEI presented three reasons for emphasizing this principle: (1) to provide an enriched language environment by maximising the English language input for students; (2) to decrease teachers' inclination of 'direct teaching' of the English language by making the language as the communicative tool in a quasi-natural environment in which the children can acquire English 'naturally'; and (3) to require teachers to improve their own communication skills with the English language, because none of the CCUEI immersion teachers were native speakers of English. By immersing students in the monolingual English atmosphere, immersion teachers help the students avoid the mother tongue interference, offer them more opportunities in language acquisition, develop their English language dispositions and form their habits of thinking and speaking in English. Thus, an authentic environment is firmly set up for the learners, enabling them to communicate with each other in English freely and frequently, thereby improving their English skills through sufficient practice.

Literacy blocks with listening skills first

Informed by research in first and second language acquisition, this principle defines the sequence of language learning and teaching skills. With a recognition that listening skills are valid both for comprehension and for introducing new materials, the focus of immersion teaching begins with listening skill development, moves on to speaking and then incorporates reading, and later writing. Immersion teaching in kindergarten and/or the early grades focuses primarily on improving children's listening comprehension and some speaking, chanting and singing of the target language. Adhering to the principle of 'listening first', the CCUEI model curriculum for the primary grades uses a wide variety of multimedia-supported resources that provide visual and auditory cues and activities for enhancing children's English listening sensitivities. Instructional activities described in the curriculum begin with those that are most often based on listening, and move on to speaking with high interaction and engagement in the use of the English language during activity-based strategies. The curriculum for the primary grades gradually introduces reading activities designed to enhance children's listening and speaking skills development and their competencies of deep understanding and critical thinking in the target language. The writing-related activities become more common when students reach the intermediate grade levels of grades three or four.

Activity-orientated teaching and learning

The activity-orientated instruction principle is developed based on modern social cognitive theories (Vygotsky, 1986) and the applications in the second language learning environment, as described, for example, in 'task-based' pedagogy theories (Ellis, 2003). Accordingly, significant learning occurs through frequent and systematic interactions between learners and focused learning tasks (mostly listening and speaking tasks). The immersion teacher can contribute to this learning most significantly by providing needed scaffolding appropriate to the student's language ability and keeping the task focused on the knowledge elements in question. In the CCUEI curriculum, the focused tasks are described in various activity forms, including whole group, individual, pair or small group; and in various activity types, including dictation, simulation, demonstration and role play. Students are expected to constantly engage in those instructional activities toward the goals of acquiring English and the subject content. Additionally, through the skill-building pedagogies of various cooperative learning strategies, students in CCUEI classrooms acquire the socio-cultural dispositions to embrace English language acquisition, a third goal of the programme.

The whole-student approach

The whole-student approach principle signifies the current CCUEI project's fundamental teaching philosophy. Students' overall development, in English language cognition, subject area knowledge, as well as socio-cultural competencies (see Figure 9.1), is the ultimate concern of the project, thus the end of the immersion pedagogy. The CCUEI philosophy seeks to engage students through strategies that address physical, cognitive, aesthetic and socio-cultural skills that are appropriate to the age and developmental stage of the student. Students participate in a range of communication modes that provide multiple means of expression, including kinaesthetic and aesthetic. Engagement is designed to incorporate moral education principles, which enhance students'

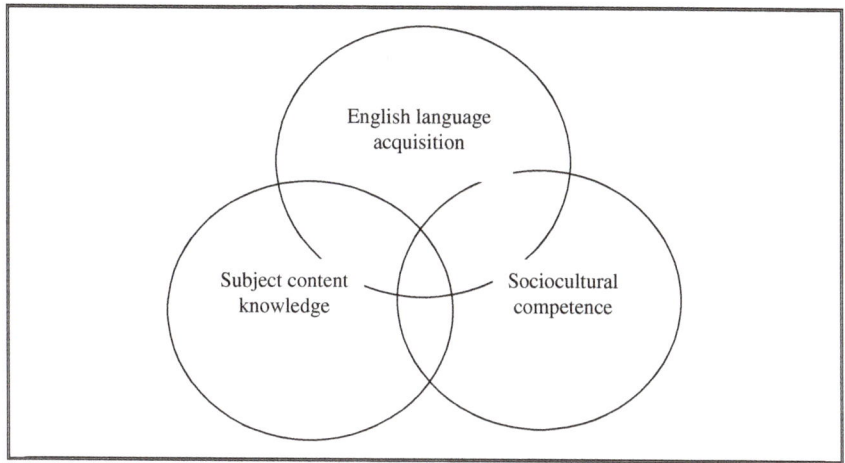

Figure 9.1 The whole-student principle

capacities for empathy, respect and tolerance for multiple perspectives. These perspectives involve retaining respect for the Chinese culture and language as well as understanding and respect for the diverse cultures of the English language communities. Engagement serves to motivate students' levels of curiosity, creativity, perseverance and responsibility in order that they become confident, self-directed, self-disciplined and goal-orientated learners (Huang & Trube, 2006). Teachers expect and support students in order to cultivate their confidence to actively engage in the learning activities that traditional teaching seldom offers: interact with learning content and express what they know and are able to do, speak out in front of the class, collaborate with partners on projects, communicate with peers on listening and speaking tasks and negotiate in a small group for the roles in a group performance. The immersion teacher development training and workshops stress this whole-student philosophy and exemplify the imparting of it. Issues related to students' needs, motivation, interests, attitudes, behaviors and individual differences are examined at both theoretical and pedagogical levels.

English Immersion Curriculum Models

One of the early challenges facing the CCUEI project was to find appropriate curricular materials for the immersion classrooms. A number of options were researched and tested, including (1) adopting textbooks used by immersion or regular schools in Canada or the USA,

(2) adopting children's commercial reading books used by some ESL programmes in selected Asian countries, and (3) translating the Chinese textbooks into English as the main text with additional commercial reading materials as supplements. Much discussion took place in deliberating over these choices. It was agreed that none was the right answer to serving the goals of the programme in subject areas and English, and meeting the needs of the Chinese learners. Subsequently, a bold decision was made that the project would develop its own curriculum for all participating schools to use. With grant support from the central MOE and membership universities and schools, a special task force was quickly assembled to develop the CCUEI curriculum guidelines. Learning objectives in the guidelines closely reflected the national curricular standards in the subject areas related to the immersion programme for grades kindergarten (age three) through six (age eleven) (CCUEI, 2001).

Integrated curriculum for kindergarten grades

The immersion experiment at the kindergarten level begins at different ages/grade levels depending on each kindergarten's conditions. Some begin with the three-year old group (lower class), others with the five-year old group (upper class). The partial immersion model was used in most immersion kindergartens. About half of each school day, teachers engage children in the immersion environment. To increase children's opportunities for contact with the second language, the integrative, theme/project-based curriculum was designed by a team of educators knowledgeable about research on how children learn. The curriculum integrates content from the traditionally divided subject areas of health, society, language, science and arts. An effort was made to place emphasis on selected knowledge elements that are related to children's daily lives, as indicated in the immersion curriculum guidelines for the kindergarten age groups, such as 'arts and language', 'science and society', 'health and life', 'art expression', 'games and entertainment' and 'environment protection'.

Theme-based units characterise the kindergarten curriculum structure. A total of 16 thematic units were included and organised to reflect the school calendar, natural and social events, as suggested by the example unit titles, such as Getting to Know Each Other, My Body, Clothing, Seasons and The New Year. Activities for each unit follow a consistent format under each theme, featuring listening and speaking activities supported by visuals and other multimedia inputs. Both the teacher version and the student version of the curriculum were written. The teacher version details learning objectives, resources and strategies for reaching the objectives, including suggested activities using concrete materials for manipulation and play. The student version highlights key subject knowledge concepts and English expressions related to the content knowledge, related visuals and/or graphic organisers, and a letter for parent involvement (Qiang & Zhao, 2001).

Two-phase curriculum development for primary grades

Development of the CCUEI curriculum model for the primary grades (grades one and two in elementary schools) took place in two phases. The first phase was marked as the *early half subject* model, beginning in September 1998 through July 2001. Students participated in the immersion environment for around 15 hours a week (about three hours per school day). Subjects included in the immersion experiment were music, arts, science, physical education, moral education and English language. Except for the English class, in which the same textbook was used as in non-immersion classes, translated English versions of the corresponding Chinese textbook were used for the other five subjects in the immersion classes. The immersion teachers made efforts to supplement teaching of these subject contents with needed instructional activities in the English language learning, similar, as often observed, to the 'sheltered English' method in North America. A downside was that teachers reported being overwhelmed by the heavy load of translating texts and its impact on their effective preparation for immersion teaching (Huang & Trube, 2006).

The second phase of curriculum development for the primary grades began in September 2001, as a *partial integrative curriculum* model. The shift to this model was driven primarily by two considerations. First, it was a response to the then top-down curriculum reform movement in basic education in China, calling for 'thematic teaching' in elementary schools. Local schools were encouraged to integrate subjects across the curriculum for instruction, except the core courses of Chinese and mathematics. The CCUEI group seized this opportunity with the proposal for the partial integrative curriculum model in immersion schools. The model embraced two implementation schemes: integrated thematic curriculum for primary grades (first and second), which integrates the subjects of science, social studies (moral education), music, physical education and arts; and subject-specific immersion teaching for social studies (including moral education) and science, respectively, for upper grades (third and above). The second consideration for the curriculum model shift was driven by research conducted in North America, which supports the use of the integrated curriculum model in foreign language immersion programmes. Both the Canadian French immersion and foreign language immersion programmes in the USA reported unequivocal success in adopting integrated curriculum materials (Cummings, 2008). Such an approach, as recognised by CCUEI collaborative members, would help create an enriched language environment in which developmentally appropriate and culturally relevant strategies could be implemented to reach the trio objectives of English acquisition, subject knowledge and students' socio-cultural development.

The progress of the CCUEI programme in schools parallels the evolving process of curriculum development, from English transition of Chinese materials to the creation of an integrated curriculum across various subjects. Drawing on the experience of curriculum development from the Canadian and USA partnerships, the CCUEI curriculum writing task force followed the Chinese national standards in the related subject areas to ensure coverage of the required knowledge elements for each grade level. Numerous meetings were devoted to discussion, reflection and decision making related to the structure and development of each content area text. Researchers and practitioners with expertise in teaching the subject content areas and English, including native English speakers, were consulted and assigned to small writing teams for drafting specific units and lessons. The review and revision phases were typically engaged in by the entire writing task force. Each revision was then field tested in the immersion classrooms before another round of authentic assessments, discussions and subsequent revisions took place for development of the final version of the curriculum. At the time of this writing, the CCUEI programme has completed and published its *Curriculum Integration in the English Immersion* for primary grades (first and second) and *Moral Education and Social Studies in the English Immersion* for third grade, and is currently field testing the curriculum in the fourth and fifth grades.

School-based immersion curriculum in middle schools

Restricted by the long established 'test-driven' educational philosophy and practice in China, the decision on immersion curriculum at the middle school level has been restricted to local schools, rather than being centrally developed and shared throughout middle school levels of the CCUEI project. The participating middle schools voiced their need to have direct control over the curriculum and negotiated the use of specific textbooks or teaching materials in their immersion classrooms. As such, a variety of English immersion courses, such as 'Science and Life' and

'Social Studies' were offered by secondary schools based on the needs and resources of different individual schools. The choice of teaching materials varies from the adapted Chinese version of foreign textbooks to locally developed materials by the immersion teachers group with support from CCUEI members.

Programme Evaluation

To measure the effectiveness of the CCUEI programme, a number of studies were conducted and have emerged in the literature (Fang, 2001; Chi & Zhao, 2004; Huang & Trube, 2006; Yan & Zhao, 2007; Zhao et al., 2007; Knell et al., 2007; Cheng et al., 2010). Although varied in their focal aspects or grade level in the programme for investigation, the studies have generally looked at the following outcomes of student learning:

- Language awareness – measure of awareness and recognition of phonological elements of English words.
- Cognitive competence – measure of the connection between short-term memory and cognitive activities through fast picture naming and sentence span tasks.
- English pragmatics – measure of student use of English language in the given social context, orally and in writing.
- Academic performance – measure of the impact of English immersion as a predictor of students' development in the first language (Chinese) and performance in other subject areas as well as social development.

The first formal evaluative study was conducted three years after the programme was introduced in a kindergarten. Designed by CCUEI researchers, the measurements included pictures, word lists and interview questions to test students' English phonological awareness, word recognition and pragmatics (use of English words in a scenario as presented in pictures). Data were collected from an experimental group and a control group for comparison. The results revealed positive growth in the experimental group in all measures when compared to the control group. The immersion children responded more quickly to the English language cues, answered with a higher level of correct responses and demonstrated a better understanding of English vocabulary in the provided visuals (Fang, 2001).

Consequently, encouraged by the initial success of the immersion practices, when the programme reached its sixth-year mark, a similar study was conducted at the elementary school level. Chi and Zhao (2004) reported the data collected from a partial immersion elementary group and a control group. It was found that the immersion class, as a whole, performed significantly better in English phonological awareness, listening, speaking and vocabulary development. In a separate study (Huang & Trube, 2006), immersion teachers reported that, in general, immersion students show more active learning behaviours in the classroom. In comparison with the non-immersion students, the immersion students were more willing to engage in group work, more capable of participating in discussions, appeared to enjoy learning better and showed more creativity in instructional activities. Furthermore, students in the immersion class ranked higher in the end-of-year test results in the other subjects of Chinese and mathematics than students in the non-immersion class.

Knell *et al.* (2007) also reported a study in an elementary school in the Xi'an area where the partial immersion method was first implemented. One hundred and eighty three students of early grades (1–3) participated, with about half from the immersion classes. The students were tested for their proficiency levels in English and Chinese measures. The English measures included oral interview, vocabulary, work identification, work list, letter recognition and onset-rhyme detection. The Chinese measures included phoneme deletion, character identification and vocabulary. The study found an overall 'additive' effect of the programme: the immersion students performed better in the English language acquisition without showing regression in the learning of their native Chinese language. Specifically, the study found that the immersion students performed better in English vocabulary, phonological awareness, word identification and oral proficiency. The study also found a comparable performance between the immersion and non-immersion students in their Chinese language development, in Chinese character recognition and phonological identification.

Cheng *et al*'s. (2010) recent study attempted to find out (1) the advantages of the immersion students over non-immersion students in second language (English) acquisition, and (2) the possible negative impact of the programme on its students' learning in Chinese and mathematics. Nearly 1000 students participated in the study, among which 68% were immersion students in grades two, four and six of several immersion schools, with the remaining 32% non-immersion students in these same grades. The Cambridge English for Young Learners test was used for measuring English achievement. Curriculum-based tests were used to measure Chinese and mathematics achievement. Data analysis of the test scores showed that English immersion students scored higher in English achievement than non-immersion students at each grade, and more noticeably so as they move after grade 4. Likewise, the immersion students outperformed non-immersion students in the Chinese and mathematics tests in all three grade groups. Cheng *et al.* (2010) thus concluded that the immersion methodology could be seen as effectively facilitating student language proficiency, literacy and numeracy without detrimental effects on their first language learning and mathematics. It can be argued that English language proficiency developed through the immersion programme is a good predictor of student learning in a subject area such as mathematics.

In addition to the aforementioned studies, which compared learning outcome in immersion students with non-immersion students, other studies focused on the immersion teaching method per se, by comparing it with other teaching methods. Zhang and Yan (2007) reported a study in a kindergarten where three teaching methods were used to teach children's English development: the immersion method, the phonics method and the whole-word method. It was found that children showed the best word-recognition ability with the immersion method. Zhao *et al.* (2007) reported another kindergarten level study in which three models of English teaching were compared: the immersion model, the traditional English teaching as a subject model in which the Chinese language was the instructional language and the English teaching as a subject model in which only English was used for instruction. The same verbal test was given to three different groups of children receiving the three models, and it was found that the immersion students showed the best oral communication skills in answering the test questions.

Challenges Facing the Immersion English Programme

The annual CCUEI conferences have become a structured venue for the exchange of research findings and teaching practices among members of the collaboration, as well as contributions from other scholars interested in the fields of English for speakers of other languages (ESOL), English as a second language (ESL) and topics of English immersion teaching and learning. The conferences typically include sessions on immersion teaching demonstrations, post-observation group critique and large group discussions of immersion strategies. Conference proceedings provide additional opportunities for participants to reflect and document their experiences and contribute to the collective professional development of the participants.

Four themes have emerged from these voices, concerning the challenges now facing the project. First, teachers need more structured professional development focusing on improving their English communication skills and using the activity-based instructional methods. All the immersion teachers in the project are native Chinese speaking English as a foreign language. Although they all have the college level credential of English education, fluency and flexibility in using English to manage the activity-based immersion instruction is reported as particularly challenging (Huang & Trube, 2006). Second, development of immersion curriculum resources needs to proceed more quickly in order to meet programme implementation needs in immersion schools. Resources available for the curriculum development have not kept pace with growth in terms of both the number and the grade levels of the immersion schools. Late arrival of curriculum materials inevitably hinders teachers' preparation for instruction (Zhao & Chi, 2004). Third, issues concerning the relationship between subject content and English in immersion programmes must be further explored. This challenge becomes more pressing when the immersion pedagogy is used at higher grade levels (third grade and above). Many questions can be raised, including: how do teachers ensure meeting curriculum standards in the content areas (e.g. science or social studies) with English as the sole instructional language? How can the immersion teacher simplify the language expressions without watering down the content knowledge? A study comparing immersion programmes in Hong Kong with CCUEI immersion programmes, focused on the content-language dilemma and reported that CCUEI programmes tend to tilt more towards meeting language objectives than teaching content objectives (Hoare & Kong, 2006). The challenge of appropriately meeting content teaching objectives needs to be properly addressed as the project continues its efforts in developing and revising the curriculum. Finally, after more than a decade of practice in schools, the programme is ready for a systematic and comprehensive evaluation to examine the programme's effect in achieving its trio goals in English language acquisition, subject content knowledge and student socio-cultural development. Only with the aid of scientific analyses of assessment data, can specific achievements be verified and areas of improvement identified in order for the further development of the CCUEI project.

Note

1. Chinese children typically begin kindergarten at age three and spend three years in the kindergarten, through lower, median and upper grades. The five year olds who participated in the first group of the immersion programme in Xi'an were all in the upper grade.

References

CCUEI (2001) CCUEI curricular guidelines grades K-6. Unpublished manuscript.
Cheng, L.Y., Li, M., Kirby, J. R., Qiang, H.Y., and Wade-Woolley, L. (2010) English language immersion and Students' academic achievement in English, Chinese and mathematics. *Evaluation and Research in Education*, 23(3), 151–169.
Chi, Y.P. and Zhao, W. (2004) The report of English immersion in elementary schools in China. *Comparative Education Studies* 7, 13–18. (In Chinese)
Cummins, J. (2008) Immersion education for the millennium: What we have learned from 30 years of research on second language immersion. On WWW at http://www.iteachilearn.com/cummins/immersion2000.html. Accessed 15.12.08.
Ellis, R. (2003) *Task-based Language Learning and Teaching*. Oxford: Oxford University Press.
Fang, J.M. (2001) English immersion instruction for children and their cognitive development. In H.Y. Qiang and L. Zhao (eds) *Studies on Second Language Immersion for Children* (pp. 62–68). Xi'an: Xi'an Jiao Tong University Press. (In Chinese)
Fu, K. (1986) *Zhong guo wai yu jiao yu shi* [*The History of Foreign Languages Education in China*]. Shanghai: Shanghai Foreign Languages Education Press. (In Chinese)
Han, B.C. and Liu, R.Q. (2008) Wo guo ji chu jiao yu wai u jiao xue de hui guy u si kao: zheng ce yu mu di [Reflections on China's English education at the basic education level: Policies and goals]. *Journal for Foreign Language Teaching and Research Bimonthly* 40, 2. (In Chinese)
Hoare, P. and Kong, S. (2006) One country two systems: Immersion in Xi'an Guangzhou and Hong Kong. In Y.P. Chi (ed.) *Proceedings for English Immersion Pedagogy in Chinese Context* (pp. 14–24). Xi'an: Shaanxi People's Education Press.
Huang, X. and Trube, B. (2006) English immersion teacher evaluation and feedback form (EI-TEFF): Collaborative development process. In Y.P. Chi (ed.) *Proceedings for English Immersion Pedagogy in Chinese Context* (pp. 3–13). Xi'an: Shaanxi People's Education Press.
Kelly, T. (2003) From lingua franca to global English. On WWW at http://www.globalenvision.org/library/33/655/. Accessed 1.2.09.
Knell, E., Siegel, L.S and Qiang, H.Y. et al. (2007) Early English immersion and literacy in Xi'an, China. *The Modern Language Journal* 91 (3), 395–417.
Lenker, A. and Rhodes, N. (2007) Foreign language immersion programs: Features and trends over 35 years. On WWW at www.cal.org/resources/digest/flimmersion.html. Accessed 7.2.09.
Li, L.Q. (5 September 1996) Gaijin waiyu jiaoxue fangfa, tigao waiyu jiaoxue shuiping [Improving foreign language teaching methodology to raise the standard of foreign language education]. *China Education Daily*, p.1. (In Chinese)
Liang, X.H. (2009) On the features of the first English immersion program CCUEI in mainland China. In H.Y. Qiang, X.B. Liu. X.l. Yang and C.L. Yu (eds) *Exploration and Innovation: English Immersion Education in China* (pp. 62–71). Macao: Science Education and Culture Press.
Project Team of Thirty Years Education Reforms and Development in China (2008) *The Rising of a Country through Education*. Beijing: Educational Science Publishing House.

Qiang, H.Y., Huang, X.D. and Siegel, L. (eds) (2004) *Curriculum Integration in the English Immersion: Book for Students [1B]*. Xi'an: Xi'an Foreign Language Media Press and Xijing People's Press. (In Chinese)

Qiang, H.Y., Huang, X.D. and Siegel, L. (eds) (2004) *Curriculum Integration in the English Immersion: Teachers' Book [1B]*. Xi'an: Xi'an Foreign Language Media Press and Xijing People's Press. (In Chinese)

Qiang, H.Y., and Yu, C.L. (2007/2008) *Moral Education and Social Studies in the English Immersion (3A/3B)*. Xi'an: Shaanxi People's Education Press. (In Chinese)

Qiang, H.Y. and Zhao, L. (eds.) (2001) *Studies on Second Language Immersion for Children*. Xi'an: Xi'an Jiao Tong University Press. (In Chinese)

Siegel, L. (2000) Introduction. In H.Y. Qiang, L. Zhao, and L. Siegel (eds) *English Immersion for Children* (pp. 1–2), Xi'an: Xi'an Jiao Tong University Press.

Vygotsky, L.S. (1986) *Thought and Language* (rev edn). Boson: MIT Press.

Zhang, L. and Yan, R. (2007) Impact of different teaching approaches on English word-reading ability for children. *Early Childhood Education (Educational Sciences)* 6, 8–11. (In Chinese)

Zhao, W., Zhang, L., Li, W.G. and Gao, X.M. (2007) A research report on the results of English immersion in Shanghai kindergartens. *Early Childhood Education* 6, 12–14. (In Chinese)

Chapter 10
Family Background and English Learning at Compulsory Stage in Shanghai[1]

WEICHENG ZOU and SHAOLIN ZHANG

Background

China began to reopen itself to the world in the late 1970s and since then, enthusiasm for learning English has turned into a national movement. In today's Shanghai, which is known as a Chinese gateway city to the rest of the world, amidst the Chinese drive for modernisation, an individual's ability to use English means greater opportunities for education, employment and personal development and this is reported extensively in the literature and mass media (*Shanghai Times*, 2003; Li, 2003).

Given this social milieu, expectations of English language teaching outcomes are high, and there is great pressure on schools and English language teachers to meet these expectations. Studies show that the choice of foreign language teaching (FLT) in Asia has been 'a movement of diversification' (Lambert, 1999: 153), yet in Shanghai, English is *the* foreign language being taught in schools at all levels and in higher education institutions. As a primary foreign language being taught in the city, English learning consumes a vast amount of resources both inside and outside schools and has a profound influence on the life of the local residents.

In the last two decades, English language learning in Shanghai can be characterised by two tendencies: 'younger and higher'. That is, children are being pushed to start learning English at a younger age, and parents have higher expectations for outcomes in terms of language proficiency. In the past, schools had an option to start English teaching either from grade one or grade four. However, today, all schools in Shanghai are required to offer English from grade one (SHMEC, 2005).

The shift towards the emphasis on English language teaching is drastic, reflecting a dramatic rise of standards for teaching outcomes. About a decade ago, the goal was to teach about '1940 words and phrases and a basic reading ability for a high school graduate' (MOE, 1996).[2] According to the new Curriculum Standards of English Teaching for High Schools of Shanghai, issued by the Shanghai Municipal Education Commission, high school graduates are required to have 'a satisfactory command of English in four skills (listening, speaking, reading, and writing) with no less than 4200 words in vocabulary' (SHMEC, 2005). In the past two decades, a series of reforms have been launched by the educational administration at the municipal level to promote new initiatives to improve English education. The English teachers at local schools are required to update their English language skills and teaching pedagogies in classrooms through various training programmes provided by governmental and non-governmental bodies in FLT. While some schools have organised short courses for teachers to study abroad in Britain, Canada, Australia, New Zealand, Singapore and the USA, these opportunities are limited, and the majority of the teachers have to rely on their own resources and efforts to meet the demands.

As a response to the social pressures of English teaching, many schools in Shanghai have begun introducing native English-speaking teachers into their classrooms. These teachers used to be found only in tertiary institutions, but today, they are found at almost every level of education. According to a study by Zhang (2008), among 30 kindergartens, 30 primary schools and 30 middle schools, students have some exposure to the teaching of English by trained native English-speaking teachers, with an average teacher-student ratio of 1 to 200 in kindergartens, 1 to 700 in primary schools and 1 to 1000 in secondary schools. The difference in ratio is related to the way these teaching programmes are funded. As kindergartens are not subject to the governmental regulation regarding fees, they tend to hire more foreign teachers than primary and secondary schools as the latter ones are under strict governmental restrictions prohibiting the collection of fees from parents.

Due to governmental restrictions on fee charges, a new type of school came into being in the early 1990s to meet the high demand for English. This type of school, called *Min Ban Xue Xiao*, literally 'People Managed Schools' (henceforth MBS), operates on non-governmental resources, though it is required to comply with official curriculums and guidelines. While admission to the state schools is based on catchment areas with little financial burdens on children's families, admission to MBSs is on a competitive basis and attending such a school is financially challenging for most families.[3]

Under such circumstances, the pressure on parents in Shanghai is obvious. For many of them, English is more than just a school subject; it permeates into many aspects of social life. The perception originates from the general social environment, the availability of educational opportunities and the prospects of their children's future employment in an increasingly competitive society.

This perception may also be derived from their memories of the past. Historically, Shanghai was one of the port cities under the heavy influence of foreign cultures, and for a century until 1949, English enjoyed a prestigious status in business, politics, education and social life. Young people in those years competed to master English in order to be admitted into the missionary universities where English was the medium of instruction and to find high-paying jobs in railways, banks and telegraph companies. Socio-politically, even in those years, English was often associated with Chinese national humiliation as it was seen as a symbol of imperial conquest of the old China. Ironically, however, a sense of superiority was often evident in people with the ability to use the language for real communication in Shanghai. This social psychology can easily be found in movies, novels and folk stories about life in old Shanghai and in many autobiographies by renowned Chinese scholars in English, such as those published in the collection of memoirs by more than 40 scholars in China (Li & Liu, 1988).

Popularity of English in Shanghai

Such social prestige associated with English, held back for over 30 years for political reasons, began to resurface in the late 1970s. Memories of the past glory of the language did not fade altogether from the minds of the local residents. Probably more quickly than those elsewhere, parents of school children in Shanghai realised the importance of the language in modern society. Indeed, in today's Shanghai, English is omnipresent. First of all, in the mass media, there is a special television channel in English, three English newspapers targeting expatriates in the city, two English newspapers taking students as their target readers, and over 55.5% of advertisements and commercials are bilingual in Chinese and English (Zhang, 2008). Furthermore, millions of public signs, business names and even political slogans are translated into English. The traditional values and the social status associated with English have apparently recurred and become even more evident in society. In this social environment, the majority of parents naturally attach great importance to English learning for the future of their children.

Perceived values aside, parents are under direct pressure to push their children to learn English. This pressure comes from numerous English examinations, ranging from tests for children in kindergartens, schools and universities, to examinations for the general public in the city. The certificates from these examinations are generally perceived by parents as key to various opportunities to move ahead in education, leading to better employment in the future. One of the most crucial examinations for children is the examination taken at the end of compulsory education when students are streamlined by the examination results in Chinese, mathematics and English into two types of senior secondary schools: one orientated towards vocational training and the other towards academic higher education. The outcome of this streamlining correlates to the incomes of the students when they enter the job market (Yin, 2004).[4]

Socioculturally, Chinese parents tend to believe that children learn best under pressure, thus examinations are the means to a better end (Fang & Ruan, 2005). In this sense, one can argue that this helps explain why education in China is basically examination orientated. Many parents are found to push their children to take various examinations both inside and outside school regardless of the purpose of the examination. For example, it is not uncommon in Shanghai that children at a young age are found in Test of English as a Foreign Language (TOEFL) or International English Language Testing System (IELTS) training classes just because parents want their children exposed to English as much as possible.

The following list illustrates the extent of the popularity of English examinations in Shanghai.

(1) Examinations for children:
- Shanghai Tongyong Child English Certificate Tests (spoken and written tests), sponsored by the government of Shanghai.
- Cambridge Young Learners English Tests (YLE), sponsored by the British Council.

(2) Examinations for tertiary students
- College English Tests – Bands 4 and 6 (CET-4 and CET-6), administered by the Ministry of Education for university students.
- Tests for English Majors – Bands 4 and 8 (TEM-4 and TEM-8), administered by the Ministry of Education for students majoring in English.

(3) Examinations for vocational students or the general public
- The Public English Test System (PETS) sponsored by the Ministry of Education for students in vocational schools, or the general public.
- The Test of English for International Communication (TOEIC) sponsored by The Educational Testing Service (ETS) for employment purposes.
- Cambridge Business English tests (BEC Preliminary, BEC Vantage and BEC Higher) sponsored by The University of Cambridge Local Examinations Syndicate.

(4) Examinations for the general public
- Shanghai Tongyong English Tests, sponsored by the government of Shanghai.
- State Tests for Promotion, sponsored by the national government for promotion in job titles in workplaces.
- Shanghai Intermediate and Advanced Interpreting Certificate Tests, sponsored by the government of Shanghai.
- State Intermediate and Advanced Interpreting Tests, sponsored by the Chinese government.
- The Business Language Testing Service (BULATS), sponsored by the British Council in collaboration with the Chinese government for Chinese civil servants.

(5) Examinations for studying abroad
- The TOEFL, sponsored by ETS for higher education.
- The Graduate Record Examination (GRE), sponsored by ETS for higher education.
- The IELTS, sponsored by the British Council for both academic and non-academic purposes.

As the list of examinations indicates, English examinations can impinge on the life of every local resident in Shanghai. The message to parents is clear: children need the ability to use English in order to move ahead from kindergartens to universities or from ordinary jobs in the workshop to professional work in the city's skyscrapers.

To help their children meet future demands, parents try their best to find every possible opportunity at a high cost. For example, they may send their children to elite MBSs, especially those featuring English teaching, and/or outsource extracurricular classes and activities in English. As the demand for these schools and the types of activities increases, a huge market for English teaching and learning has gradually emerged in Shanghai. For extracurricular classes and activities in

English, for example, parents usually select one or several of the following for their children[5]: (1) private tutors, such as retired teachers, teachers who are moonlighting and university students; (2) remedial classes provided by the school in the state system at a very low cost as the price is under the control of the education authorities; (3) remedial English classes offered by commercial businesses; (4) English classes for general purposes taught by trained professionals or English native speakers; (5) English competition training classes for very young children and secondary school students; (6) Summer/Winter camps of English language learning provided by trained professionals or English native speakers; (7) studying abroad programmes; and (8) any other opportunities that may give children the chance to learn or practice English, such as volunteer work for international activities. The cost of these classes or programmes can vary greatly with the size of the classes and the quality of the teachers.

The context outlined above clearly suggests that in Shanghai the social impact of English can hardly be overestimated. As children are expected to attain higher levels of English proficiency, the education system has to evolve to meet this demand. The current state system cannot meet the drastic needs of the learners. Many parents would naturally look for supplementary English education opportunities for their children. One implication of the situation where supply does not meet the needs is that supply is often dependent on the socioeconomic (and often political as well) power of those who need. That is, social class may affect one's outcome in foreign language learning. In the literature on FLT in general, however, as Macaro (2003: 101) points out, there is a 'distinct lack of research which compares social class with foreign language learning'. This chapter aims to take an in-depth look at how parents' social, cultural and economic status affects the learning outcomes of their children.

Theoretical Model

This study adopts Stern's (1983: 338) model of language learning. On the basis of several studies, Stern developed a model consisting of five important variables. Among the five are (1) social context, (2) learner characteristics and (3) learning conditions. These three are represented as determiners of (4) the learning process and, through it, of (5) the learning outcome.

Each of these five variables is of considerable complexity in itself. Relevant to this study in particular are the variables of social context and the learning conditions of the students in Shanghai. According to Stern

(1983: 338), the social factor covers a broad range of sociocultural and socioeconomic factors in addition to a sociolinguistic factor. Sociocultural and socioeconomic factors could influence the learner's motivation, attitude and beliefs about the value of a foreign language and methods to learn it. Furthermore, they could also influence the availability of opportunities in which learners could be exposed to useful, meaningful instruction and access the practice suitable to their language level. In other words, the social, cultural and economic conditions of learners' families may have an influence on learning conditions, and as a result, the quality of learning outcome.

Historically, family background has been regarded as an important factor influencing the opportunities in education. Scholars in the West have long researched into how race, social class, financial conditions and cultural background influence the chances to access modern education (Burstall et al., 1974; Musgrove, 1979; Okano & Truschiya, 1999; Stern, 1983) and have shed light on the issues surrounding learners' family background. Many of these studies have calculated quantitatively 'the likelihood of educational failure such as school dropping-out rates, or course failure, or documented the underperformance of one demographic category compared to another on a host of academic measures, including Grade Point Average (GPA), high school completion, and most often, performance on standardized achievement tests' (O'Connor et al., 2009: 1).

Studies (e.g. Zhao, 2000) in China reveal that inequalities in the Chinese educational system were mainly shown in the opportunities to access higher education before 1976. Admission to universities was determined according to political background, rather than academic merits. This system was challenged in 1977 when the reform and opening-up policies reinstated the higher education system with a merit-based admission. According to the study by Li (2003), the educational opportunities in China have become more and more unevenly distributed since 1978 and the impact of family background and other institutional factors[6] on the acquisition of educational opportunities has increased. As her study shows, the educational levels that people have acquired in recent years have been the combined result of parents' occupation, educational background and the urbanisation of the place where people live in different periods since 1949 when the People's Republic of China was founded. These studies show that family background influences motivation and conditions that, in turn, influence the outcomes of learning in schools.

A recent sociological study in Shanghai reveals an emergent correlation between the levels of education and incomes of a family. The survey carried out in 2003 (Yin, 2004) reports that high income families have a significantly better educational background than those in the low income categories. While 81.9% of the high income families have at least a university degree, there are only 42.3% for the mid-income families, and less than 10% for the low income families. Among the low income families, only about 50% have a middle school diploma, meeting only a minimum requirement, i.e. the nine-year compulsory education of the country. Furthermore, according to the same study, the income level is also related to categories of professions or trades. Those who enjoy high incomes are mostly found in the group of professionals, or those who work in state businesses with better economic benefits, or those who are private entrepreneurs or civil servants in governmental departments. Low income groups are typically found in those who work in service sectors, on the factory floors, or those unemployed or on welfare. This finding seems to point in the direction of change in Shanghai that one's educational background, to a great extent, can account for one's economic conditions although the old system has not been completely phased out.

However, the relationship between a family's socioeconomic conditions and education is by no means straightforward. A study carried out by Wang (2004) investigated a group of high school students and their families in an inland province in China. According to this research, there is no correlation between the outcomes of language learning and the tuition fees the family paid to college student tutors. What affects the learning outcomes most is the general academic environment of the family, and how supportive the parents are in advising learning strategies to their children. Despite discrepancies in research results, we see one finding in common: the educational background of the family seems to serve as an important indicator of a learner's performance in language learning.

Stern warns (1983: 277) that the relationships between socioeconomic and sociocultural factors and language learning cannot be seen as self-evident. Studies have sometimes found very clear relationships between them, but at other times the relationships are far less evident. With regard to foreign language learning, the associations are even less clear as Macaro (2003) has pointed out. We have thus conducted an empirical study aiming to contribute to the understanding of this issue by investigating the correlationship between them, or the lack of it, in the Shanghai context.

Research Objectives

This study aims at investigating how social, cultural and economic background influences a pupil's English learning as a foreign language at the compulsory stage in Shanghai. Under this general aim, the research intends to answer two questions:

(1) Whether and how do families' social, cultural and financial factors relate to the outcomes of English language learning?
(2) Why is English language learning subjected to the influences of the social and economic status (SES) of families?

Research Methods

The study adopted a quantitative method in the investigation complemented by qualitative inquiries of interviews with students and teachers. Two questionnaires were designed for students and their parents, who were requested to provide quantitative information. This information was used in our correlation analysis in conjunction with the scores of a proficiency test administered to the students. Finally, the interviews were conducted to elicit in-depth data to explain the results from quantitative analysis.

Two questionnaires were distributed to 2034 students at grade nine, the exit grade of compulsory education[7] and 1460 of their families in April 2005. The questionnaire for the students required that they provide answers to questions under the broad categories of teaching in their schools, including the class size, their teaching style, their self-evaluation of English learning and their participation in various learning programmes inside or outside school and their reasons for participation in these programmes. The questionnaires were usually administered by the class teacher before a teaching session and were collected immediately after the students had completed them. In this way, 100% questionnaires were returned.

The questionnaires for parents were distributed through the students to their families and required their parents or guardians to provide answers to questions under the broad categories of parents' profession, educational background, household income range, starting age of their children to receive (or not) private or commercial teaching of English, and the types of commercial course their children attend and expenses; expenses on extra teaching materials or equipment related to English learning; and reasons for (not) outsourcing commercial teaching. Out of 2034 questionnaires issued, 1460 were returned.

One English proficiency test ($\alpha = 0.8783$) was administered in all the selected schools to gauge the students' English proficiency. The test was designed on the basis of the textbooks designated by the government for all schools in Shanghai; it followed the general syllabus of the examinations sponsored by the Examination Authorities of Shanghai Municipal Education Commission for streamlining purposes. The test was administered in this way because almost all schools use this syllabus in their classroom teaching and preparatory courses for high school entrance examinations.

About one month after the test, seminars were held in each selected school, followed by telephone interviews with 11 former and current students, three current veteran teachers in commercial language teaching business and one marketing researcher in a language teaching business. The purpose of both the seminars and interviews was to confirm whether the interpretation of the quantitative data could be confirmed with the data collected from the teachers and students.

Results

The data from the investigation are presented in Table 10.1, which reflects the information gathered from (1) the English proficiency tests that all the students wrote in the study, (2) the students' and (3) their parents' answers to the questions in the two questionnaires. The table first correlates the students' mean scores in the proficiency test with the SES of their families.

The family background is defined in terms of family social status,[8] parent's educational level and family economic status, which represent the family's social, economic and cultural power, respectively. The social status is determined according to the highest social position of one of the two parents. The economic status is determined according to the household monthly income at one of four ranges: High (over 5000 RMB), Mid-High (4999–2500 RMB), Mid-Low (2499–1001 RMB) and Low (below 1000 RMB).[9] The family educational level is defined in terms of three levels that roughly fall into High (university or more advanced degrees), Middle (diplomas from vocational schools/senior high schools) and Low (diplomas from junior high schools or lower).

As shown in Table 10.1, students' performance in the proficiency test is positively related to the social status of their families between High and Middle (62.68 for High and 65.43 for Middle) and Low (57.51). Although the differences between the three groups have reached the significant level ($F = 15.72$; $p = 0.000$), the Post Hoc Multiple Comparison

Table 10.1 The results of one-way variance analysis of the relationship between SES and English proficiency test scores

Family background	Rank	n	Mean test scores	SD	F-value	Sig.	Post Hoc Multiple Comparison
Family social status	High	76	62.68	19.99	15.72	$p = 0.000$	Tamhane's T2: L-M: $p = 0.001$ L-H: $p = 0.070$ M-H: $p = 0.610$
	Middle	193	65.43	16.48			
	Low	1191	57.51	19.64			
Parents education level	High	130	65.63	17.09	17.522	$p = 0.000$	LSD: L-M: $p = 0.000$ L-H: $p = 0.000$ M-H: $p = 0.002$
	Middle	804	59.93	19.22			
	Low	526	55.47	19.66			
Family economic status	High	158	63.79	19.85	26.708	$p = 0.000$	LSD: L-ML: $p = 0.000$ L-MH: $p = 0.000$ L-H: $p = 0.000$ ML-MH: $p = 0.000$ ML-H: $p = 0.000$ MH-H: $p = 0.701$
	Mid-High	433	63.12	17.70			
	Mid-Low	638	57.70	19.34			
	Low	231	50.50	19.31			

L: Low; M: Middle; H: High; ML: Mid-Low; MH: Mid-High.

indicates a strong co-efficiency only for the Low-Middle pair. In other words, such co-efficiency does not exist between Low-High and Middle-High pairs. The lack of co-efficiency in these two pairs may be caused by two reasons. It may be due to changes in the social structures of modern China in the past two decades. The 20-year long opening-up reform has allowed many people to be successful in business and to go straight into the top management of big businesses even without much advanced educational experience, such as university degrees or a strong political background, as modern China is moving towards an economic power sensitive society rather than a social position sensitive society (Zhang, 2004: 207). This is especially true for Shanghai in recent years. Economic power gained through private businesses can be translated into social power. However, it may not be so easily turned into outstanding performances of the next generation. In relation to this, the second reason is that the Middle rank is mostly composed of professional people, such as doctors, lawyers and people in management, with special skills and knowledge. The performance of their children in the test is clearly stronger and more uniform (mean test scores = 65.43, SD = 16.48) than the other two groups (mean test scores = 62.68 for High, 57.51 for Low, SD = 19.99 for High and 19.64 for Low). This also suggests the dynamic nature of the social positions, and their related powers in modern cities in China that are constantly undergoing dramatic changes.

The second dimension shows that the parents' educational levels are significantly related to student's achievement ($F = 17.522, p = 0.000$). The group High achieved 65.63, the group Middle achieved 59.93, and the group Low achieved 55.47 in the proficiency tests. Co-efficiency can be found in the comparison of almost any two pairs with $p = 0.000$ for L-M and L-H, and $p = 0.002$ for M-H.

Support in the process of learning seems to vary with different backgrounds of parental educational levels. Table 10.2 reports another set of data in terms of parental help in different types of families.

The data in Table 10.2 show that there are parents (or guardians) from all three levels of educational background trying to offer help to their children in English learning. However, the parents at the High level are significantly more likely to support their children in learning (33.1 vs. 16.1 and 15.4%) than the parents at the other two levels (Cramer's $V = 0.130$).

The data in the third dimension of the family economic status reveal a more complicated picture than the family educational dimension. As the data show, there are correlations between income levels and test achievements ($F = 26.708; p = 0.000$). The test scores are in a descending

Table 10.2 The help from parents of different educational levels (cross tabulation)

			Parental education level (PEL)			Chi-square test
			High	Middle	Low	
Are either of your parents (or others) from your family helping you in your English learning?	No	Count	87	674	445	$\chi^2 = 24.754$ df = 2 p = 0.000
		% within PEL	66.9	83.9	84.6	
	Yes	Count	43	129	81	
		% within PEL	33.1	16.1	15.4	
Total		Count	130	803	526	

order from 63.79, 63.12, 57.50 to 50.50, respectively, for the ranges from High, Mid-High, Mid-Low, to Low. However, the Post Hoc Multiple Comparison shows correlations between all six pairs except for the last pair MH-H with $p = 0.701$. The small difference in testing scores between the Mid-High and High groups suggests that while financial conditions are important for learning a foreign language, this influence may be limited. With this difference in view, it is perhaps interesting to take a look at another set of data that show how much each category spends on learning English when paying beyond normal school cost, as given in Table 10.3.

The data in Table 10.3 show that the families of High economic status spend over 12,132 yuan RMB per student, significantly more than that of the students from the other three groups, and over five times that of the students from the low level.

Comparing the students' English score in Table 10.1 and the family expenditure on their English learning in Table 10.3, we can see the limitation of the notion that one can learn a foreign language better with more expenditure. Although High SES families have spent significantly more money on their children's English learning than MH SES families ($p = 0.000$), there is no significant difference in the English scores between the students in these two groups ($p = 0.701$). This result suggests that the great economic power of the family may not lead directly to a better performance in the test. High education background of parents can sometimes offset the disadvantage of lower expenditure on children's English learning, in that there is a high percentage (80%) of parents in the Mid-High SES level with a college education. Of course,

Table 10.3 Expenditures of the four levels of family economic status

Dimension	Rank	n	Expenditure per student (yuan RMB)	F-value	Sig.	Post Hoc Multiple Comparison
Family economic status	High	158	12,132	140.77	$p = 0.000$	Tamhane: H-MH: $p = 0.000$ MH-ML: $p = 0.000$ ML-L: $p = 0.000$
	Mid-High	433	9,606			
	Mid-Low	638	6,071			
	Low	231	2275			

other factors such as quality of instruction, motivation and cognition are also important, as commented by the teachers from the schools investigated.

Although economic factors seem to play only a secondary role in affecting the testing scores of the learners, its power should not be ignored because economic conditions could be related to both quantity and quality of language exposure for a learner through outsourcing extracurricular opportunities of language tuition in commercial programmes. This relationship can be found in Table 10.4.

The data in Table 10.4 show the relationship between the level of the family economic status and the quantity of outsourcing. The questionnaire lists eight types of English language extracurricular tuition popular in Shanghai, ranging from the cheapest programmes offered by the public schools to the most expensive ones provided by English-speaking native speakers in commercial language schools.[10] The results show that the majority of the students from the low income group participate in only one type of commercial programme. And they have the highest percentage of None-participation (18.2%) in contrast to that of the groups High (3.2%), Mid-High (1.8%) and Mid-Low (6.4%). Their high concentration in one type of commercial programme (52.4%) differs qualitatively from the students in the groups Mid-Low, Mid-High and High, in that most of them only participate in the remedial programmes offered by their own schools that focus on the school examinations, according to the interviewed teachers. As teachers reported, most of these students, in fact, were forced by their parents to stay in these programmes after school, often repeatedly throughout the year. When asked to explain the reasons for participating in none or one type only in the questionnaire,

Table 10.4 Variety of outsourced opportunities for families of different economic status

Rank	None	One type	Two types	Three or more types	Total	
High	5 (3.2%)	52 (32.9%)	55 (34.8%)	46 (29.1%)	158	$\chi^2 = 114.95$
Mid-High	8 (1.8%)	149 (34.4%)	151 (34.9%)	125 (28.9%)	433	df = 9 p = 0.000
Mid-Low	41 (6.4%)	273 (42.8%)	203 (31.8%)	121 (19.0%)	638	
Low	42 (18.2%)	121 (52.4%)	54 (23.4%)	14 (6%)	231	
E/per student (yuan RMB)	1830	4387	7006	8978	$F = 96.735$	$p = 0.000$
Test scores	56.55	57.59	59.52	61.02	$F = 2.848$	$p = 0.036$

Note = no participation in commercial language teaching programmes outside school as reported by the students. *One type* = one type of commercial programme taken by the students, etc. E/per student = expenditure per student for outsourcing English language instruction.

not surprisingly, most parents responded that the cost of the programme was their major consideration.[11]

The data in Table 10.4 also present a general picture of the cost and the number of language programmes taken by the students. The more programmes one takes, the more it will cost one to learn English in Shanghai. Even for the students in the none participation category, they still need to spend 1830 yuan RMB per person on things like extra reading and listening materials or test preparation materials.

In this study, we also investigated how the types of schools correlate with such factors as family expenditures on English learning, students' English test scores and their interest in English. And the answers we found are presented in Table 10.5.

As Table 10.5 shows, the students from MBSs featuring FLT made the best achievements in the language test. This is attributable to the fact that they are already the best students in terms of foreign language learning as they enter this type of school through competition. They are also unique with the biggest expenditure (19,028 yuan RMB per person on average). However, it is interesting to note that this group has a lower rate of students expressing an interest in language learning than those in ordinary MBSs and suburban schools, similar to the rate of students from ordinary urban schools. Interviews with their school teachers show that most of them have had strong family support by either helping outsource appropriate language programmes or having an early start at the age of five or six.[12] Although research so far does not fully support the view that 'the earlier the better in language learning' (Stern, 1983: 366;

Table 10.5 Correlations between types of schools, family's financial conditions and interest and achievement

	MBS/schools of foreign languages	Ordinary MBS	Ordinary urban schools	Suburban schools	Inferential statistics
Expenditure per student (yuan RMB)	19,028	10,974	6531	2812	$F = 147.135$; $p = 0.000$
Test scores	75.19	69.64	53.67	60.82	$F = 72.69$; $p = 0.000$
Interest as reported by students (%)	35	48	34	54	$\chi^2 = 43.405$; $p = 0.000$

Long, 2007), an early start does play a role in assisting a child in a competitive environment (Zhao & Zou, 2008). While the early experience of language helps increase one's performance in examinations, the competitive environment in an MBS featuring English provision may reduce their interest or intrinsic motivation in learning English.

Another interesting point worth making regarding Table 10.5 is the relationship between the scores and the interest level of the students in suburban schools. These students are usually from the families of peasants or migrant workers living in the community or villages where the public school is located. They have the lowest expenditure on extracurricular language learning programmes (2812 yuan RMB per person on average). The reason is that there are almost no commercial programmes available in their community, not even the remedial ones that are often found in the urban schools. However, about 54% of them showed an interest in learning English. What is more, their English test scores, on average, are higher than those of urban schools that have the lowest rate of students expressing an interest in learning English. Given the similar family background in economic and educational terms, students from urban and suburban schools present two different levels in terms of test scores and interest. Interviews with teachers show that teachers in suburban or rural schools usually have a closer relationship with their students because the teachers consider themselves part of the local community while the teachers at the urban schools tend to treat teaching less affectively, as a 'nine-to-five job' in their words.[13]

Discussion

This study shows that there are complex relationships between foreign language learning and the influence of the SES of the family. It appears that factors of economic conditions and parent's educational levels play an important role in affecting the learning processes and impacting the learning outcomes of the students. The social power of the family does not seem to be an important factor. With better economic conditions, parents are able to find better resources outside schools, created by market demands. Better quality of instruction, materials, teachers and authentic language practice opportunities can be traded. However, advantage obtained through financial means is limited; parental educational level proves the most important in affecting the learning outcomes. More money does not always guarantee an appropriate choice in outsourcing programmes. It requires some knowledge to select a suitable programme at an appropriate time. It is at this point that parents with a better educational level tend to avoid the market traps. In addition, parents of good educational background can help their children learn English at home at an early age in an informal, often relaxed and friendly environment, which is often more effective and economical.

Empirical data also demonstrate that social power is not a determining factor in affecting the learning processes and outcomes. Some parents have high social power due to their high economic status as successful business people, but have a low educational background. They may hope that their children learn English well, and indeed learn all school subjects well, yet, they may not be knowledgeable enough to make the best decisions, for example, in selecting the right English programmes for their children.

In the study, many of the parents with a good educational background did not belong to the high-income category. They tend to work more in the management or other professional areas that stress the value of academic study, knowledge, independence and hard work. They tend to be more intimately involved with their children's learning through long-term support. This is overwhelmingly evident in many interviews conducted during the study.

According to our data, about 93.42% families ((1460–96)/1460 = 93.42%, as shown in Table 10.4) were involved in one way or another with outsourced language teaching programmes. As the teaching of English has become a highly commercialised business in today's Shanghai, schools and the market are both playing their own roles in promoting English teaching; in many aspects, teaching English has become the concern of the whole society. With such an intensive societal involvement, it is difficult to judge whether the achievement of the students in learning English is the result of school teaching or the teaching by society at large. There appears to be an environment where English can be acquired in this natural setting. For schools, students and their families, the current situation is both a blessing and a curse. It is a blessing because school education itself is not sufficient to train a good bilingual. A good language teaching result should involve a wider social context and environment (Spolsky, 1999: 13), which not only provides a context for language use, but equally importantly, offers multiple opportunities of learning support for the school teaching. Although Shanghai is not a society (not yet) where English is frequently used in any formal or informal domain, the societal involvement, the numerous English programmes accessible to the public as well as to school children, the ever-increasing number of native English speakers and highly proficient non-native speakers have created a *de facto* English as a second language environment. English is found to be used in natural settings as well as in those commercialised programmes. In today's Shanghai, learners who know how to select suitable programmes and make use of the available resources can acquire the language relatively easily.

Just as it is an advantage, the wide range of social involvement in English learning is also a curse for many people. In this sense, we see the complex interaction between the cultural factors, economic conditions and social power of a family. Faced with so many high-stake examinations in the system and with a competitive society, families, whether rich or less privileged, have to make extra investment in their children's learning of English. For some families, this extra investment may be a serious financial burden. As our data show, the highest non-participation rate is with the group of low economic status, in striking contrast to the high rate of participation with the other three groups.

Socioculturally, many people in Shanghai seem to be bewildered about the English craze because English is obviously not in their immediate life. In an interview, one of the students from an ordinary urban school expressed this feeling, 'I did not truly understand the importance of learning English when I was in the middle school because it seemed then so far away from my life'.[14] When commenting on other students' efforts in learning English, the boy replied, 'I thought they were stupid to learn the things that were not part of their lives'. This feeling seems more common among children from low SES families than those from the families with mid-low, mid-high and high incomes. Their motivation level is thus generally lower.

There is an obvious limitation in this study as far as the analytical framework and the methodology are concerned. This study did not take the distinction of spoken and written language proficiency into consideration. Many families, in fact, select speaking classes rather than writing classes, especially parents with higher economic power because they are able to pay the high fees for the expensive classes and even to afford trips for their children to English-speaking countries. Speaking ability is not properly reflected in the written test and quite often a student with good speaking ability may not have a good result in a written test. A more comprehensive testing tool is clearly needed for future research.

Another point worth noting is that this research does not employ either linear or non-linear multiple regression analyses because the influences exerted by family background, such as social power, educational background, economic power and the relevant paid-education choices, are often interactive and even overlapping in many situations, as is clearly indicated by the previous study (Yin, 2004) and by the data collected in this study. Besides, even though the family background and the students' achievements are related in compulsory English education, no obvious causal relationship has been found between the two factors in this research.

Conclusion

Theoretically, this study confirms the view that family background is an important aspect in the conceptual framework of second/foreign language education. More specifically, language learning is not just a matter of a learner's individual endeavour, although it is important. Family involvement and a social support system are equally important in foreign language acquisition, as proposed by Stern (1983). This chapter has answered Macaro's (2003) challenge to enhance studies into social class and its relationship to foreign language learning. Students from different family backgrounds may possess different attitudes to the target language and go through different learning processes. And these differences are the results of the interaction of family conditions, quality of school instruction and the social environment.

Given the current social environment, one's proficiency in English is widely perceived as a vital skill to survive in Shanghai. In the school curriculum, English has equal status with Chinese and mathematics in terms of importance. However, learning English is not only cognitively challenging, but financially demanding. The financial challenge is bound to contribute to inequality in education, which is a potential threat to China's ambition for an equal, harmonious and modern society.

Notes

1. This project was funded by 'China's 985 Project' of Foreign Language Teacher Education of the East China Normal University. The authors would like to thank Mr. Taoyang Shi and Miss Siyi Chen for their valuable assistance in the research.
2. In a more accurate presentation of the document released in the 1996 national syllabus, the requirement should be translated into 'mastering 1200 words of common usage and 740 commonly used set phrases'; 'encouraging teachers to teach through integration of four skills as much as possible, however, the emphasis should be placed on the development of reading ability'. It should also be noted that schools in Shanghai did not follow the syllabus of the local government until after 1997 when the Shanghai Municipal Education Commission was authorised by the MOE to develop its own local standards for English education, which is itself a socio-culturally meaningful change. Shanghai was then the first region in China to develop its own standards for its schools in education as a result of the opening-up and reform movement. The policy was to match the new status

of Shanghai, recognised then as a hotbed for the Chinese economy, and the leader of national movement to modernise education (Wo, 2008).
3. The fees for attending MBSs range from 7000 to 10,000 RMB (approximately US$1029–1470) for a school year. In 2009, the local government approved a new type of MBS, which receives funding from the government. Although bearing the same name, this type of school mostly enrols children of migrant worker's families from rural areas.
4. In order to ease the pressure caused by competition, the state system has been steadily expanding the enrolment of the senior high schools each year. At the same time, the higher education system is also experiencing a rapid increase in the enrolment rate, from around 14% in 2000 to almost 70% in 2010, through many new vocational programmes in newly established colleges. The expansion of colleges has greatly increased the enrolment rate in the country. In 2010, nearly 98% of junior high school graduates could move to senior high schools, according to the announcement posted on the government website in Shanghai (http://www.shmec.gov.cn/html/xxgk/201003/420052010003.php; accessed 20.7.10). This new policy may defer the competition, but it is too early to say if this expansion would effectively reduce the competitive pressure on the students.
5. This information was provided by the students and their parents in interviews and questionnaire surveys (for details of our research, see the Research Methods section).
6. For example, the household system that restricted children from selecting schools with better resources and quality teachers.
7. This number accounts for 1.196% of the total graduating student population in Shanghai in 2005.
8. The division of the social status of Chinese residents was based on Lu's study (2004: 2), which is ranked according to the relative positions in governmental departments, agencies, state businesses, private businesses and free lancers. While this division appears arbitrary, it can be relatively accurate in reflecting the stratification of social classes in a particular society within a certain historical time. The system adopted from Lu (2004) was considered the most comprehensive study in China at the time of its publication, carried out by the China Social Sciences Academy.
9. According to the census reported by the Shanghai Municipal Statistic Bureau, the average disposable annual income per capita for Shanghai residents in 2004 was 16,683 RMB (approximately US$2,034.51 in 2004). On WWW at http://www.stats-sh.gov.cn/2003shtj/tjnj/nj05.htm?d1 = 2005tjnj/C1016.htm. Accessed 31.3.07.
10. The local government imposes strict regulations on charges for services like remedial classes offered by the public schools in Shanghai in order to keep under control the burdensome cost of education on families.
11. As a useful reference, the programme offered by the school, strictly under governmental control in terms of the price and types of teaching, charged 50 yuan RMB for five class hours' instruction a week and 15 weeks per semester for remedial purposes with a class size of about 40 and 50 students in 2004. By contrast, a commercial programme, taught by a trained English-speaking native professional, typically charged about 1400 yuan RMB for 25 class hours' instruction with a class size below 20 students.

12. From the interview with the head teacher of a school in Type 1 on 10 May 2005.
13. Based on interviews with teachers from field trips to these schools on 12 and 19 April 2005.
14. From an interview with a former middle school student on 9 June 2005.

References

Burstall, C., Jamieson, M., Cohen, S. and Hargreaves, M. (1974) *Primary French in the Balance*. Windsor: NFER Publishing Company.

Fang, C.Y. and Ruan, M. (2005) You Yizhong Ai, Bu Neng Cong Lai: Zai Xiao Xuesheng Xinli Yali Ji Duice (There is a kind of care that parents can't afford to fail to give: An investigation on the psychological pressure on the students and some suggestions). *Hunan Jiaoyu* 1, 9–11. (In Chinese)

Lambert, R.D. (1999) National language policy and education. In B. Spolsky (ed.) *Concise Encyclopedia of Educational Linguistics* (pp. 151–157). Amsterdam: Elsevier.

Li, C. (2003) Social and political shifts of the system and educational inequalities. *Social Sciences in China* 3, 86–98.

Li, L.Y. and Liu, L. (eds) (1988) *Waiyu Jiaoyu Wangshi Tan – Jiaoshoumen De Huiyi (Talks about Foreign Language Learning and Teaching: Memories from Professors)*. Shanghai: Shanghai Foreign Language Education Press. (In Chinese)

Li, Q.D. (2003) Yingyu Gaibianle Wode Mingyun (English has changed my fate). (In Chinese) On WWW at http://www.people.com.cn. Accessed 22.3.03.

Long, M.H. (2007) *Problems in SLA*. New York and London: Lawrence Erlbaum.

Lu, X.Y. (2004) *Dangdai Zhongguo Shehui Liudong (Social Mobility in Contemporary China)*. Beijing: Social Sciences Documentation Publishing House. (In Chinese)

Macaro, E. (2003) *Teaching and Learning a Second Language – A Review of Recent Research*. London: Continuum.

MOE (Ministry of Education of China) (1996) Quanrizhi Putong Gaoji Zhongxue Yingyu Jiaoxue Dagang (Gong Shiyan Yong) (The national syllabus of high school English education) (trial-out version). In J. Tang and Y.Z. Gao (eds) *A Collection of K-12 English Curricula of China in the 20th Century* (pp. 150–182). Published in 2001 in Beijing: People's Education Press. (In Chinese)

Musgrove, F. (1979) *The Family, Education and Society*. London: Routledge & Kegan Paul.

O'Connor, C., Hill, D.L. and Robinson, S. (2009). Who's at risk in school and what race got to do with it? *Review of Research in Education: Risk, Schooling, and Equity* 33(1), 1–34.

Okano, K. and Truschiya, M. (1999) *Education in Contemporary Japan*. Cambridge: Cambridge University Press.

Shanghai Times (2003, 18 March) Yingyu Shi Gaoxin Tongxingzheng (English is a Passport to a High Salary). *Shanghai Times*. (In Chinese)

SHMEC (Shanghai Municipal Education Commission) (2005) Shanghai Gaozhong Yingyu Kecheng Biaozhun (Curriculum standards of English teaching for high schools of Shanghai). (In Chinese) On WWW at http://www.shmec.gov.cn/attach/article/134.doc. Accessed 30.3.07.

Spolsky, B. (1999) Linguistics and language learning. In B. Spolsky (ed.) *Concise Encyclopedia of Educational Linguistics* (pp. 26–29). Amsterdam: Elsevier.

Stern, H.H. (1983) *Fundamental Concepts of Language Teaching*. Shanghai: Shanghai Foreign Language Education Press.
Wang, W.H. (2004) A study of high school students' English achievements and their family backgrounds – A Chinese cultural perspective. Unpublished MA thesis. Shandong Normal University. (In Chinese)
Wo, Z.H. (2008, 20 June) Interview with one of the authors in Shanghai. (In Chinese)
Yin, J.Z. (2004) *2004 Shanghai Fazhan Lanpi Shu – Xiaokang Shehui: Cong Mubiao Dao Moshi (A Social Development Bluebook of Shanghai, 2004, Well-Off Society: From Goal to Pattern)*. Shanghai: Shanghai Social Sciences Press. (In Chinese)
Zhang, J.Q. (2008, 20 August) Interviews with the officials from the Media and Publication Bureau of Shanghai. (In Chinese)
Zhang, Y. (2004) Dangdai Zhongguo Liudong Jizhi De Fengxi (An analysis of social mobility of contemporary China). In X.Y. Lu (ed.) *Social Mobility in Contemporary China* (pp. 85–96). Beijing: Social Sciences Documentation Publishing House. (In Chinese)
Zhao, F. and Zou, W.C. (2008) Waiyu Xuexi Nianling Wenti de Zhuanjixing Yanjiu (A narrative study of the age of onset and its implications for foreign language teaching). *Modern Foreign Languages* 31 (3), 317–327. (In Chinese)
Zhao, Y.Z. (2000) Jiating Beijing Dui Gaodeng Jiaoyu Ruxue Jihui De Yingxiang (A study of the effects of family background on access to higher education). *Youth Studies* 3, 30–36. (In Chinese)

Chapter 11
Economic Development and the Growing Importance of the English Language in Guangxi

BINLAN HUANG

Introduction

In the last 25 years or so, not only has the English language been regarded as a valuable resource for China's modernisation drive, but it has also had a great impact on many people's lives and personal welfare. The Four Modernisation programme initiated in the late 1970s (see Gil and Adamson in this volume) and the subsequent reforms in political, economic and social domains have brought about rapid economic development and an increase in commercial, technological and cultural exchanges with the rest of the world. English has contributed to these changes and developments by serving as a vital link between China and the outside world (Maley, 1995; Ministry of Education, 2000c). With China's increasing presence in international affairs and growing importance in the global economy, there has been an unprecedented demand for proficiency in English (Wu, 2001). Proficiency in English is perceived as a cornerstone of further development for the nation and is widely seen as a valuable asset for individuals as well (Gao et al., 2002). It is key to a host of opportunities, such as a university education at home and abroad, a desirable job in the public or private sector and eligibility for professional promotion (Cotazzi & Jin, 1996b; Ng & Tang, 1997). Because of the superior social and economic prestige that proficiency in English has accrued, English language teaching (ELT) has received a great deal of attention from the government, the education authorities, students, parents and society at large (Hu, 2002a; Ross, 1993). The country's entry into the WTO and the recent successful bidding and hosting of the Beijing Olympics have further strengthened people's perceived value and social uses of English.

Since the 1980s, differing paces in economic reform and development have resulted in varying demands for English proficiency in different regions. The rapid economic growth in coastal and urban regions, such as Shanghai and Guangzhou, has brought with it an influx of foreign companies, technological transfers, joint business ventures, English-speaking expatriates, overseas tourists, and cultural and commercial imports (Maley, 1995). All these changes have contributed to an escalating demand for proficiency in English from a whole range of professions, businesses, workplaces and enterprises. As a result, there has been a growing awareness of the importance and utility of English among people in these economically developed places. English has acquired high social and economic value, and ELT has drawn attention not only from individuals, but also considerable investment from local governments and various sectors of the economy. The increasing opportunity to use English for social and vocational purposes has resulted in a growing recognition of the importance of communicative competence in the language. Accordingly, communicative language learning activities and pedagogical efforts directed at enhancing language skills have begun to feature in classroom teaching and learning.

In developing minority regions in China, English has also been gaining in popularity and acquiring more social and economic value in the past few years, though at a slower pace. This chapter will give a critical account of people's changing perception and the growing importance of the English language in Guangxi Zhuang Autonomous Region, a developing minority region in southwest China. The causal factors for the growing importance of English and the socio-economic significance of English-knowing bilingualism for individuals and society will be analysed based on the figures and empirical quantitative and qualitative data collected.

The Historical Context of Guangxi

Guangxi Zhuang Autonomous Region has the largest population of Zhuang-speaking people, accounting for over 38% of the total population of 46.55 millions in the region (Party Committee of Guangxi, 2005). It is one of the five regions granted by the central government with some sort of special right or autonomy to make or adjust their policies appropriate for their local socio-economic development. It has a borderline of 1020 km with Vietnam. Before the 1980s, frequent border conflicts occurred between China and Vietnam and war finally broke out in the late 1970s.

Such historical reasons greatly affected Guangxi's social, economic, cultural and education development. It took Guangxi a long time to recover from the border conflicts and the war with Vietnam. Its economy was lagging far behind that of the developed provinces and cities, such as Guangdong, Shanghai and Beijing. Actually, it was one of the last five least economically developed provinces or autonomous regions among China's 31 provinces, autonomous regions and administrative cities. Because of the backwardness of its economy, Guangxi's education, including English language education, developed exceptionally slowly. Professional talent competent in specialised knowledge and proficient in foreign languages was in short supply and could hardly meet the requirements of the region's socio-economic development, according to reports issued by the local government (The People's Government of Guangxi, 2005). This further hindered Guangxi's participation in and integration into the global economy.

However, great changes have occurred in Guangxi in the last few years, especially since the first China-ASEAN Exposition was held in 2004. People now seem to be increasingly aware of the importance of integrating into the global economy for development. Both the government and individuals are trying to engage themselves in this fast developing world. Policies to promote the English language education have been enthusiastically implemented. For example, almost all primary schools, including those in rural areas, are required to teach English from primary one or at least from primary three onwards. Besides, students at colleges and universities are required to pass the national College English Test of Band 4 after two years' study of English, and bilingual teaching for 5–10% content subjects to be instructed in English, as specified in a Ministry of Education document issued in 2001 (see Huang, 2007), has been implemented (Guangxi Education Commission, 2000; The People's Government of Guangxi, 2005). These measures aim to enhance students' overall English competence. Meanwhile, people's awareness of improving their own and their children's English to meet the growing needs of the globalised economy has been raised gradually. It is now common to see parents sending their children to various tutoring centres or private-school English courses. English corners are no longer found only on the campus of universities and colleges, but also in city centres, or even in some small towns and counties. English has increasingly been perceived as the key to success both in academic studies and careers.

Causal factors for the growing importance of English in Guangxi

To understand how the English language has acquired such high status and popularity in Guangxi today, it is important to give a detailed account of several key developments in the region, including the big international event, the China-ASEAN (Association of Southeast Asian Nations) Exposition, the Beibu Gulf Economic Zone, the booming multinational enterprises established recently in the region, tourism and the expectations of today's employers.

The China-ASEAN Exposition

The China-ASEAN Exposition (Expo in short) has been held annually since 2004 in Nanning, the capital city of Guangxi. Along with this event are the China-ASEAN Business and Investment Summits and the Nanning International Folk Song and Arts Festivals. To successfully host these yearly international events, Guangxi has opened its doors wide and made great efforts to attract international exhibitors and purchasers as well as home participants in order to bring about more business opportunities for business people and enterprises to the region from both China and ASEAN countries. Table 11.1 provides the scale of the Expo.

The Expo is a high-profile one, both economically and politically. Six state leaders from China and the ASEAN countries were present at the 1st Expo, including three Prime Ministers. Besides, 166 ministerial-level government officials were present, including the trade and economic ministers of China and the 10 ASEAN countries, as well as the Secretary-General of the ASEAN Secretariat. On average, about 180 ministerial-level government officials attend the Expo each year. China's Premier Wen Jiabao was present at the 4th Expo.

The Expo has remained large scale since its opening. The standard booth number furnished increased from 2506 booths at the first Expo to between 3300 and 3600 at the following four expositions, with approximately 50,000 m^2 of area for exhibition. The number of enterprises as exhibitors has gone up readily to 2100 at the 5th Expo. These enterprises are from all over the world, including the Global 500 Top Companies such as Ericsson, Electronic de France, ABB, Siemens, Mitsubishi, Panasonic, National and Canon, with approximately 100 exhibiting companies listed in mainland China. The exhibits cover as many as 210 categories of commodities, involving 11 sectors. The number of exhibitors and purchasers has risen sharply from 18,000 at the 1st Expo to

Table 11.1 Scale of the China-ASEAN Exposition (Expo)*

Expo	Exhibitors	Purchasers/ visitors	Booths	Enterprises	Volunteers	Trade volume (US$ billions)	Contracted international trade volume (US$ billions)
1st (2004)	18,000	350,000	2506	1505	12,000	1.084	5.01
2nd (2005)	25,000	>350,000	3300	2000	>16,000	1.151	5.0175
3rd (2006)	49,710	>350,000	3663	2500	18,000	1.27	5.85
4th (2007)	>42,000	>350,000	3400	1908	>38,000	1.42	6.154
5th (2008)	>42,000	>400,000	3300	2100	>38,000	1.597	6.364

*Data were collated by the author[1] based on the figures released in various sources by the local government and mass media.

42,000 at the 5th Expo, and that of visitors to the Expo reached 400,000 in the latest Expo in 2008.

Remarkable economic and trade achievements have been made during the expositions. The trade volume of the 1st Expo hit US$1.084 billion in total; it rose to US$1.597 billion at the 5th Expo, an increase of 12.18%. The contracted international trade volume has also gone up rapidly, from US$5.01 billion at the 1st Expo to US$6.364 billion at the 5th Expo.

Meanwhile, on average, as many as 30 investment promotion meetings and 10 cooperation projects signing ceremonies were held at each Expo. At the 1st Expo alone, 129 bilateral cooperation projects were signed (please note that many projects could be signed in each signing ceremony), involving eight ASEAN countries, namely, the Philippines, Malaysia, Cambodia, Indonesia, Myanmar, Singapore, Thailand and Vietnam.

The success of the Expo has had a tremendous influence on the country's and region's development in almost all aspects. With the success of this Expo, the construction of the China-ASEAN Free Trade Area has turned into a reality from a shared concept. And the success proves that China and the ASEAN countries are more than close neighbours due to their geographic proximity. They have become partners because of the conveniences they have benefited from free trade. It also shows strong interdependence between China and the ASEAN countries. The significance of the Expo also lies in the official meetings of political leaders and the speeches delivered at China-ASEAN Business and Investment Summits, where Chinese and the ASEAN leaders go further with their dialogs and exchange opinions, thereby enhancing political and diplomatic ties on all sides.

It is important to note that Chinese and English are the two major working languages of the Expo. It is well known that English in the ASEAN countries enjoys a high status. As shown in Table 11.2, English is spoken as an official language in half the ASEAN countries. Though it is a foreign language in the other half, 90% of the business people, purchasers and officials attending the Expo are proficient in communicating fluently in English, according to an early study conducted at the second China-ASEAN Expo in October 2005 (Huang, 2006). The English proficiency of the business partners from ASEAN countries has drawn great attention from Guangxi local officials, business people and people in general. They have begun to reflect on and even question the teaching and learning effectiveness of English education in China.

Table 11.2 The status of English in ASEAN countries*

Brunei	Official language
Cambodia	Foreign language
Indonesia	Official/second language
Laos	Foreign language
Malaysia	Official/second language
Myanmar	Foreign language
The Philippines	Official language
Singapore	Official language
Thailand	Foreign language
Vietnam	Foreign language

*Data were collected by the author[1] based on the figures or information released by the local government and media.

Many local officials and business people have realised that, indeed, international personnel with strong English competence are in short supply, as many of them find it hard to communicate directly with their ASEAN counterparts in English after having learnt the language at school and university for many years. Experiencing such big and high-level international events has resulted in an increasing awareness of the importance of English in this ever globalising world.

Meanwhile, university students have also been experiencing the impact of English as an international language through such events. Each year, over 20,000 students are involved in working as volunteers at the Expo, the Summit, and the other events held alongside; approximately half of them work side by side with foreign business people or visitors. They find themselves directly exposed to speakers of English of various accents from the ASEAN countries and some from the other parts of the world. Such experience makes most of them realise the importance of the language and motivates them to work hard on English. Furthermore, on returning to their universities, these volunteers spread words. Empirical evidence shows that the learning attitude towards English learning among the volunteers has changed dramatically and their motivation for learning the language is much higher. This, in turn, influences other students positively (Huang, 2006). The following

Economic Development and the Growing Importance   219

comment made by a junior student represents the overall opinions and feelings of the Expo volunteers:

> I was lucky enough to work as volunteer at the 3rd and 4th Expo. I found most people were not from those English-speaking countries, but they could all speak the language so well and so fluently. When they had business talks or attended the meetings, they seemed to have no language obstacles. This is very impressive. I told myself, my classmates and my friends that English is such a useful tool that we should all learn it well to make us more competitive in the future.

The Beibu Gulf Economic Zone

The Beibu Gulf sits south of Guangxi, China. In late February 2008, China's State Council officially designated this area as the Beibu Gulf Economic Zone, China's first international and regional economic cooperation zone. The construction of the Beibu Gulf Economic Zone began in 2006. It covers six coastal cities along the Beibu Gulf, integrating the cities of Nanning, the region's capital, Beihai, Qinzhou, Fangchenggang, Chongzuo and Yulin. Pan-Beibu economic cooperation involves seven countries: China, Vietnam, Malaysia, Singapore, Indonesia, the Philippines and Brunei. 'The state will adopt policies and measures to support mechanism innovation, rational industry layout and infrastructure construction in the Beibu Gulf Economic Zone', Qinglin Jia, China's top political advisor said in a statement (Beibu Gulf Developmental Plan, 2008). In response, Guangxi has pledged a 100 billion yuan (US$14 billion) investment over the next five years for building and repairing 2500 km of railways to form a network hub in the area. The Zone will serve as the logistics base, business base, processing and manufacturing base and information exchange centre for China-ASEAN cooperation.

Chinese economic experts are optimistic about the future of the Zone. The Beibu Gulf Economic Zone may turn out to be a new economic lead in driving China's coastal economy because Guangxi boasts so many advantages. For one thing, as the only land and sea link between China and ASEAN, the Beibu Zone will benefit from the rapid economic development of both geographical advantages and the improved China-ASEAN relationship. For another, Guangxi connects China's east, central and west. China's sustainable economic development entails 'industries complementing each other' and 'traffic connectivity', which will bring tremendous opportunities to Guangxi (Yun, 2008).

'The Beibu Gulf Economic Zone promises broad prospects for further development and its growth potential is rapidly released', said Xuequan

Huang, director of the Guangxi Personnel Bureau, 'but the shortage of talents and professionals in petrochemicals, iron and steel, electricity, finance, tourism, port planning, logistics and marine industries is our bottleneck'. In addition, he expresses his concern about the professionals' English competence, to which, he states, due attention needs to be paid (Beibu Gulf Personnel Development, 2008). Official documents of the local government are promulgated to urge universities to reform their English teaching. People of all walks of life are encouraged to learn foreign languages to keep up with the local economic development.

Rapid growth of foreign investment enterprises and local tourism

Both the China-ASEAN Expo and the prospects of the Beibu Gulf Economic Zone have made Guangxi one of the most attractive regions in China for foreign investment. Its expansion potential has attracted large numbers of foreign investment enterprises. By the end of 2004, the total number of foreign investment enterprises in Guangxi was only 1300. However, the number rose to approximately 10,000 by the end of 2007. This has greatly increased the demand for international personnel competent in both English and specialised knowledge and further enhanced the local people's strong belief in the importance of English and English education (Huang, 2006).

Tourism, on the other hand, is also propelled by the China-ASEAN Expo and other international events described above. As can be seen from Table 11.3, the number of overseas foreign tourists rose sharply from 1.12 million in 2004 to more than 2 million in 2007. The annual income from tourism reached US$0.424 billion in 2007. Tourism has become another stimulus for the region's economic development. It is predicted that by 2010 the number of foreign tourists to the region may reach 2.8 million while that of the domestic tourists may amount to 95.50 million (Prospect of Guangxi Tourism, 2008). With such a vast

Table 11.3 Number of foreign tourists and annual income from tourism

Year	Foreign tourists (millions)	Income volume (US$ billions)
2004	1.12	
2005	1.462	0.32
2006	1.7077	0.423
2007	>2	>0.424

Note: Figures are cited in internal official documents of Guangxi.

number of overseas tourists visiting the region, exposure to the English language for the local population is much greater and more frequent. Huang (2006) quotes one interviewee from the world famous tourist attraction, Guilin, as saying:

> The rapid development of Guilin's tourism has benefited much from people's English proficiency in the city. We have many people (though the number is still small, he added) who have rich knowledge of tourism and certain proficiency in English. When foreign tourists, particularly those from Europe, Latin America come to visit Guilin, they will find that Guilin is such a language-friendly city that even some old grannies can communicate with them when they need help. As a result, Guilin has become one of the tourist cities with which foreign tourists are the most satisfied. Last year, the number of foreign tourists in Guilin exceeded one million, the highest in history. The development of tourism has helped other industries in the city to grow at greater pace.

Selection criteria of public servants and employees

Data from a survey conducted by the author in late June 2008 show that from 2007 new demands for English have been set for over 60% of the posts for civil servants in Guangxi: candidates for these posts are required to have a CET4 or CET6 certificate[2]; and candidates who apply for posts related to banking, trade, tourism, diplomacy, foreign affairs, hi-tech, information etc. are required to take an additional English speaking test. The message this new policy sends to the public is clear: proficiency in English has become valuable for young people to access life opportunities. A government official interviewed by the author made the following comment in this regard:

> The main reason for setting such new selection criteria is because our contact with the foreign countries has become more frequent. English is such a useful tool that we need personnel in some posts who are proficient in their specialities and English so as to communicate with the outside world, to exchange views and information,... English-knowing bilinguals are important in that they may improve our image and our working efficiency, and bring us many other benefits.

Among the informants interviewed, five are employers: two are from the state-owned factory/company, another two from joint ventures and one from a private company. They were asked how they selected employees and whether or not they thought English proficiency is an important variable in their selection. EM1 is the president of a big state-owned factory that has experienced many ups and downs in the past decades and has managed to survive the fierce competitive market. Its products sell mostly in the home market, with only about 10% exported to the southeast Asian countries or regions. However, he said:

> I tend to employ those armed with both rich specialised knowledge and strong English competence for most of the posts, especially the posts in the marketing department, because such talents are really good to the development of the factory.

EM2 is the president of a state-owned factory, too. The products of his factory are export orientated, and the production of the factory has been going up smoothly, so his factory has made steady profits in the past few years. Here is what he said:

> Yes. I consider that English competence of the technical personnel is very important for the development of this factory. In the past few years, we have established strict criteria in selecting new employees. For example, prospective applicants are required to have passed the National CET4 and the National College Computer Test Level 1. Those who have passed CET6 and Computer Test Level 2 will have more chances of being employed if they possess at the same time rich specialised knowledge in their fields.

As employers of joint ventures, EM3 and EM4 shared the same opinions with regard to their selection criteria of employees.

> EM3: English is the language of international cooperation. Most foreign enterprises in China and other regions of the world prefer English as a communication tool, which has become associated with the prosperity of a company or factory. If our employees have proficiency in English, they will be able to participate in all decision-making about the company's economic development future. However, I think, to be successful in business, proficiency in English language per se is not enough. You know, language is only a carrier. We need employees who are not only proficient in English but have a wide store of specialist and cross-cultural knowledge and communication skills.

> EM4: We are running this enterprise with a foreign company, so we demand that our employees' English is good enough to qualify themselves for their positions. When we employ new technical personnel, we consider that both their specialised knowledge and

English competence are equally important. Only when they are armed with both, will they be able to update their specialised knowledge frequently and be creative. They will be able to exchange opinions directly with their foreign colleagues and communicate with experts from both home and abroad.

These employers all agreed that the more high-quality personnel they have, the more competitive their companies/factories will be. Their perception of the market and economic value of English in employment favour employees proficient in English. Clayton (2002: 25) stated that 'On one side stand individuals who control English and who, as a result, have access to virtually all conversations about the country's political, economic, or development future. On the other side stand those who do not speak English and who thus are denied participation'. Language choice is market driven and the market favours English. It looks certain that English is gradually becoming an inevitable linguistic capital for the regional economy. However, what also looks certain is the fact that, currently, high-quality talent is still in short supply in Guangxi.

Regional Policy Changes in English Language Education

The growing importance of English in the local social and economic development has posed a great challenge to the region's English language education. Consequently, major adjustments and amendments in policies concerning English education have been implemented at the regional level. Huang (2006, 2007) summarises the changing landscape of English language education in the region as follows:

(1) Publicity has been initiated through such media as the Internet, radio, television and newspapers to further raise people's awareness of the importance and necessity of English language education.
(2) English has been made a compulsory subject for all university students, secondary school students and primary school pupils in cities and better developed areas in the countryside in order to produce more high-quality talent for the ever-increasing needs of the people and society.
(3) English has been one of the three most important subjects for the College Entrance Examinations in the region.
(4) Guiding policies have been made to direct schools and universities to reform their teaching curriculum and methods to guarantee the teaching and learning effectiveness of English.

(5) Universities have been required to implement bilingual teaching of 8–10% content subjects to produce more international personnel for the region's economic development.
(6) Doctoral students are required to use and cite authentic academic English books, journal articles or other materials for their thesis in order to make them improve their English competence further.
(7) Trilingual teaching (Chinese, Zhuang language and English) is encouraged and supported in some primary schools in underdeveloped minority areas.
(8) Professional people are required to take a foreign language (usually English) test for higher academic promotion.

In the summer of 2008, the author surveyed 3 out of the 14 cities in Guangxi on their policies and practice of English language education. Six officials from the city education departments were interviewed and asked to fill out a questionnaire. Data from the survey and the interviews show that English instruction has started earlier than ever before, from primary three rather than from junior secondary schools, since 2005 in these cities on the request of the government and pressure from society. According to the data collected, on average, teaching hours devoted to English each week amount to three at primary schools, four at junior secondary schools and five at senior secondary schools. Extra lessons, termed 'lessons of interest' and charged at RMB 80–150 yuan on average for each pupil or student each term, are offered in over 60% of the primary and secondary schools in the three cities surveyed. And at least 15% of the primary pupils and junior secondary students in the city or town residential areas take about one and a half hours of private tutoring English lessons after school. As English is one of the three major subjects tested in the entrance examinations for junior and senior secondary schools and for colleges/universities, all the interviewees believe that early learning of the English language could lay a better foundation for the students' promotion to key junior and senior secondary schools and later for key colleges/universities, and eventually better job opportunities.

When asked about the biggest change in English education practice, the officials agreed unanimously that it is people's changing conception and attitude towards English that has made English a school subject at the primary level. With regard to the major reasons for the growing importance of English in their cities, the informants gave similar answers: people are more aware of the usefulness of English; students themselves long for better English examination scores for higher education advancement; the learning environment is more favourable;

strong English competence helps students become more competitive in the job market.

Meanwhile, colleges and universities have initiated more pragmatic policies to keep up with the regional socio-economic needs. For example, a policy (Cited in an official document of Guangxi, internal document accessible on request) that all first- and second-year students take an English speaking test has been implemented in almost all the colleges and universities in the region with the intention to push up students' communicative competence in English. The speaking test accounts for 10–30% of the final aggregate.

While English is enthusiastically promoted, a set-back is also evident. The popularity of English has resulted in more difficulty in implementing mother tongue Zhuang language education in minority areas despite the regional government's constant encouragement and increased funding (Huang, 2007). According to the interview data, the Zhuang language was taught as an experimental subject in some rural primary schools five years ago, but now it has mostly been cancelled. The Zhuang language is actually used only as an instruction medium for some bilingual or trilingual subjects at an early stage in some rural schools. 'The harsh reality for many of the world's bilinguals is that their minority language has little or no economic value' (Baker, 2006: 434). This seems to be the case for the Zhuang language.

Conclusion

The empirical study was conducted to explore and evaluate the driving forces for the growing importance of the English language in the Zhuang Autonomous Region of Guangxi, China. The empirical evidence from both the quantitative and qualitative data indicates that English has indeed been acknowledged as an important and prestigious language in Guangxi in the past five years, thus many people believe that access to it means access to valued forms of knowledge and access to affluent and prestigious social and professional positions.

However, though English has assumed such importance in the region, there still exist many challenges. Clearly, instrumental motivation prevails among most people who learn the language. Students learn it mainly for passing examinations at school and universities; graduates learn it for passing examinations for civil servant vacancies or for further study abroad. This examination-orientated mentality has thus affected teaching quality and effectiveness (Huang, 2007). Evidence from the survey conducted by the author in Guangxi's three cities in late June 2008 also shows that nearly 80% of primary English teachers in the three cities surveyed are graduates who majored in various disciplines other than English. Of the 292 primary English teachers in Chongzuo City, for example, only 60 are graduates of an English major, while the others are either high school graduates or non-English major graduates who have learnt very limited English. These teachers have had little preservice training, not to mention systematic knowledge of how to teach. Furthermore, there is still a shortage of government funding and investment, leading to inadequate research on English education. Above all, as mentioned before, in a region that is dominated by the Zhuang nationality, how to maintain the local Zhuang language in an increasingly global world presents a bigger challenge to the local government and people in general (Huang, 2006). How these issues can be addressed in a fast developing Zhuang Autonomous Region remains to be seen.[2]

Notes

1. The author worked as deputy director of the Liaison Department of the China-ASEAN Secretariat as well as chief translator for the Expo. Thus, she witnessed the impact of the international events on the local economic development and the growing importance of English in the region.
2. CET4, short for College English Test 4, is a nationwide proficiency English test held twice a year for college students in China. Almost all the students are supposed to take and pass it at college.

References

Baker, C. (2006) *Foundations of Bilingual Education and Bilingualism*. Clevedon: Multilingual Matters.
Bamgbose, A. (2000) *Language and Exclusion*. Hambury/London: LIT Verlag.
Burchfield, R. (1985) *The English Language*. Toronto: University of Toronto Press.
Beibu Gulf Developmental Plan (2008). (In Chinese) On WWW at http://www.gxtj.gov.cn/list0.asp?typid=33. Accessed 18.3.08.
Beibu Gulf Personnel Development. (2008) (In Chinese) On WWW at http://www.gx.xinhuanet.com. Accessed 26.6.08.
Clayton, T. (2002) Language choice in a nation under transition: The structure between English and French in Cambodia. *Language Policy* 1, 3–25.
Gao, Y.H., Li, Y.X. and Li, W.N. (2002) EFL learning and self-identity construction: Three cases of Chinese college English majors. *Asian Journal of English Language Teaching* 12, 95–119.
Guangxi Education Commission (2000) Opinions on improving the overall quality of undergraduate teaching. No. 15 document issued by Guangxi Education Commission on 16 October 2000. (In Chinese.)
Hu, G.W. (2002a) Recent important developments in secondary English-language teaching in the People's Republic of China. *Language, Culture and Curriculum* 15, 30–49.

Huang, B.L. (2006a) An empirical study on the translation quality of the 2nd China-ASEAN Exposition. *Guangxi University for Nationalities Press* 2, 189–192. (In Chinese)

Huang, B.L. (2006b) An evaluative analysis of the opinions of policy-makers, employers, teachers students on college English education in improving the regional economic development of Guangxi, China. Unpublished EdD thesis, University of Hull.

Huang, B.L. (2007) Teachers' perceptions of Chinese-English bilingual teaching in Guangxi. In A.W. Feng (ed.) *Bilingual Education in China—Practice, Policies and Concepts* (pp. 219–239). Clevedon: Multilingual Matters.

Maley, A. (1995) *English 2000: The Landmark Review of the Use, Teaching and Learning of English in the People's Republic of China*. Manchester: The British Council.

Ministry of Education (2000c) *Quanrizhi Gaoji Zhongxue Yingyu Jiaoxue Dagang [English Syllabus for Fulltime Senior Secondary Schools]*. Beijing: People's Education Press. (In Chinese)

Ng, C. and Tang, E. (1997) Teachers' needs in the process of EFL reform in China – a report from Shanghai. *Perspectives: Working Papers* 9 (1), 63–85.

Party Committee of Guangxi (2005) A brief introduction to Guangxi Zhuang Autonomous Region. Internal document accessible on request. (In Chinese)

Prospect of Guangxi Tourism (2008) (In Chinese) On WWW at http://www.gxtj.gov.cn/list0.asp?typid=33. Accessed 20.12.08.

The People's Government of Guangxi (2005) Work Report of the Government 2005. Internal document accessible on request. (In Chinese)

Ross, H.A. (1993) *China Learns English: Language Teaching and Social Change in the People's Republic*. London: Yale University Press.

Wu, Y.A. (2001) English language teaching in China: Trends and challenges. *TESOL Quarterly* 35, 191–194.

Yano, Y. (2001) World Englishes in 2000 and beyond. *World Englishes* 20, 119–131.

Yun, M. (2008) Guangxi to build China's first regional economic zone. (In Chinese) On WWW at http://www.emerging-china.com/articles/717507.html. Accessed 14.3.08.

Chapter 12
Trilingual Education Policy Ideals and Realities for the Naxi in Rural Yunnan

DONGYAN RU BLACHFORD and MARION JONES

Introduction

In the face of increased globalisation, and therefore an ever greater emphasis on functionality in the universal language of commerce, minority people worldwide are facing a greater challenge, one that is brought closer each day by advancements in international communications technology (Hicks *et al.*, 2008). These pose both a threat to socio-cultural identities among already marginalised people, and an opportunity for new socio-economic integration and well-being – assuming that these minority people have access to quality English language education. There are many locations around the world where bilingual education and bilingualism is the social, cultural and legal norm. Much more unusual are locations where three or more languages are at play in a formalised education setting, as is the case for China's ethnic minorities. In 2001, the government promulgated an education policy stating that English is to be introduced into elementary school classrooms no later than grade three (Ministry of Education of the People's Republic of China, 2001). As a result, from the big metropolitan centres of Beijing and Shanghai to remote villages such as Wenhai in Yunnan, children of extremely varied linguistic, cultural and socio-economic backgrounds are learning English, and need English to compete for places in senior high school and university entrance and graduation. This means that there is an enormous range of socio-economic conditions, from Han children of Shanghai and Beijing millionaires who can afford private tutors in English and summer vacations in English-speaking countries at one extreme, to minority children whose parents can barely afford a trip to the county town and a nutritious meal at the other. To compound the problem, in its bid to create an educational utopia, the government has mandated, in many cases, that national minority children should receive education in their own language. So these minority children are learning Mandarin as a second language (MSL) and English as a third language (ETL), but for many minority groups, proficiency in their own language does not count towards school entry and exit qualifications. The reality is a highly uneven playing field, far divorced from the policy ideal passed in Beijing, where rising income inequality and rising educational inequality – in both inputs and outcomes – creates a self-reinforcing cycle. In this chapter, we discuss findings from qualitative ethnographic data examining the reality of trilingualism for Naxi minority children and adults in rural Yunnan as a case study. We will examine how English use and education, particularly the economic and language environments, curriculum, teachers, school and teaching resources impact the lives of the Naxi. Ultimately, we are interested in how the gap between language and education policy ideals and reality impacts their lives as a whole.

Naxi Ethnic Minority in Yunnan, and the Wenhai Case Study

The multi-ethnic Province of Yunnan is home to 25 out of 56 ethnic groups, excluding Han Chinese. This is the most ethnically diversified province or region in China, although national minorities constitute only 33.6% of the provincial population, the remainder being Han Chinese (Yang, 2008). As a result, this south-western province has been fertile ground for anthropologists and ethnographers, policy makers, researchers and government for the study and implementation of a variety of bilingual and lately trilingual programmes at various levels of schooling, and other ethnically related policies.

According to recent data, about 11% of current total minority elementary school enrolments, or 158,000 out of 1.44 million minority students in Yunnan, are receiving education in both their mother tongue and Mandarin (Yang, 2008). The same source also reveals that currently about 6.5 out of 15.3 million minority people (42.5%) in Yunnan do not understand or use Mandarin, especially in rural areas of concentrated monolithic minority occupation. Given this, the new policy of starting English language instruction from grade three for all school children poses new challenges and complications for the education of minority children, and the prospects for their continued advancement to higher education. It is common knowledge that the teaching resources in many rural areas in China fall far behind those available to urban residents – as is often true worldwide. However, the necessity of trilingual proficiency imposes a new and formidable barrier to the future success of rural minority students.

The Naxi are one of the 25 non-Han ethnic minorities in Yunnan with a population of 308,839, with approximately 90% of them living in compact communities in the Lijiang Naxi Autonomous County in the north-west part of Yunnan province (Hao, 2002),[1,2]djoining the western border of Burma, the south-eastern border of Tibet and the south-western border of Sichuan province. The Naxi are well known for their rich cultural heritage, especially their unique pictographic written script, called Dongbawen, which was created over 1000 years ago. The Naxi have a bifurcated language system, with a vibrant and widely used oral language – Naxiyu – and two written language systems, one called Gebawen that relates directly to Naxiyu, and Dongbawen, largely reserved for religious practice. It is safe to say that until 50 years ago, most Naxi people were illiterate regardless of the form of script considered due to a lack of schooling outside the monastic/religious system.

We present an ethnographically rich case study to illustrate the multi-faceted reality of English teaching and trilingualism in rural China for minority children and their community. This case study illuminates the following issues: the performance of minority students in primary school English classes; the relevance of teaching materials to rural minority children; the quality and adequacy of English teaching resources in rural minority schools; what English language learning means for the current and future socio-economic well-being of minority children, their families and their communities; the attitudes of students, parents, educators and villagers to primary school English classes in rural minority schools; and the challenges posed by teaching English in rural minority schools with limited resources and supports and a challenging language learning environment.

The case is a small rural Naxi community in Lijiang County. Wenhai is a small Naxi village composed of 64 households, plus a primary school and an eco-tourism lodge, which is run cooperatively by 56 of the village's families. Wenhai is only recently accessible by road and, through the collective ecotourist lodge, is following a bumpy path to integration into the Han and global economy. Although it is only about 30 km from Lijiang city to Wenhai, the paved road runs out at a new temple part way up the ridge from Baisha – a larger village down on the plain (2600 m) and closer to Lijiang city where students from Wenhai attend middle school – and deteriorates into a terribly rutted muddy track, so that it takes between 1.5 and 2 hours by Jeep, or intrepid

Chinese minivan. The entire territory around Wenhai is at an altitude of more than 3100 m, making agriculture very limited despite the southern latitude, and winter daytime temperatures modestly above freezing and nighttime temperatures below freezing, while summers are temperate and humid. There is a large seasonal bathtub lake in the valley bottom providing seasonal pasture, which is surrounded by high hills culminating in *Yulongxueshan* (Jade Dragon Snowy Mountain 5600 m) to the north-east. The dominant cultivation is fodder crops for the wide variety of livestock – yaks, goats, sheep, pigs, mules and cattle – that are raised in the area, although all but the pigs show obvious signs of food and nutrient shortages; a good example of the tragedy of the commons. The higher pork prices of 2007–2008 have been a great boon to the welfare of families here, which is manifest in new clothes and greater savings towards further education for the village's children. Potatoes are the staple food for humans in the region, supplemented in the summer with some green vegetables, wild berries, mushrooms and pine nuts, and in the fall and winter with meat from their livestock. The government provides wheat and rice to the village for social welfare reasons, and to ensure social, political and environmental stability, with limited success on the environmental front.

The Naxi are a particularly good case study, because despite being a small and geographically concentrated ethnic minority group, they have, arguably, one of the most strongly and readily identifiable cultures in China – on par with much larger and more extensive groups such as the Uigurs of Xinjiang, the Tibetans or the Mongolians. Further, the Naxi have been particularly aggressive in marketing their cultural capital as both a tourism resource and as commodities available from Beijing and Shanghai to London and New York, and have been doing so since the late 1980s (Jones, 1994; Jones & Ambrosi, 2003). However, this integration is limited to a small number of communities within the Naxi region. Many other locations, such as Wenhai, remain relatively isolated with only limited exposure to Han or international influences. As a result, in a culturally homogenous and geographically concentrated location, we can capture a microcosm of the Chinese national minority milieu. Further, if there are strong signs of cultural vulnerability and cultural pollution among the Naxi, then smaller groups and groups with a less strong and distinct cultural identity are likely to be even more vulnerable to these external influences. To this end, we see some scope for generalisations in educational practice to the national level and certainly to the provincial level in Yunnan, home to the widest cultural diversity in all China.

Literature Review

For the past 50 years, China's minority language policy has gone through several phases when minority languages have suffered various fates, ranging from extreme encouragement backed by large-scale government assistance to virtual elimination through totally forbidden usage. Blachford (2004a, 2004b) identified four major factors that contributed to such policy changes: the characteristics of China's national minorities; Communist ideologies on ethnicity and ethnic languages; deeply rooted Chinese traditions in nationality relations; and the political and economic agendas of the Party in power. Although this combination of elements provides a context for an understanding of the minority language and education policies and practice and their development in contemporary China, we posit that the added third language, English, has brought strong international and economic aspects to the already complex issue of education and minority policy making in China.

Since the communist party of China took power in 1949, minority language and education policy has largely focused on either Mandarin monolingual education or bilingualism and bilingual schooling for China's ethnic minorities, meaning Mandarin Chinese and minority languages, depending on the time period (Blachford, 2004a; Zhou M.L., 2004, Zhou Q.S., 2004). Inspired by the opening up of the country, starting in 1978, and accelerated by China's global trade dominance and accession into the WTO, the introduction of English into the school system poses a new challenge for minority language education and policy in the form of Han bilingualism versus minority trilingualism and the full and fair participation of minority groups within both society and the economy. Yet very little is known of the impact this challenge poses on minority language and culture, as well as their overall well-being. Even less is known about the impact the necessity of trilingualism might have on many other minority languages and cultures in other parts of the world.

An examination of the extensive literature in both Chinese and English on language education for Chinese minorities, reveals that most publications, even the most recent ones, are focused on bilingual issues, as in the collections in Feng (2007) and M.L. Zhou (2004). Almost all studies, including a bilingual education study for Naxi children (Feurer, 1996), emphasise the lack of resources and the threat of losing their minority language and culture as preeminent among numerous challenges and obstacles facing minority peoples (Geary & Pan, 2003; Lin, 1997). When English is introduced to minority school children, issues become much more complicated. A handful of publications looking into this area, mostly by Chinese scholars, have presented preliminary studies and arguments for trilingual education (Ajiarehamo, 2006; Bai, 2007; Gai, 2003; Hou, 2006; Krashen, 1996; Li S.Q., 2002; Liu, 2006; Wu, 2005).

Some have argued that trilingual education for minority children is theoretically plausible and a necessary reality in modern China for the following reasons.

First, trilingual education will improve the economic development of the areas where minority people live (Gai, 2003; Li S.Q., 2002; Liu, 2006; Wu, 2005). For example, tourism plays an important part in the economic development of Yunnan. Li (2002) discusses the need to have a greater number of people proficient in foreign languages so as to build Yunnan into a prosperous tourist destination. Hou (2006) presents two cases showing that village tourism plays a positive role in eradicating poverty. The Naxi farmers at Lashi Lake of Lijiang have developed the local economy by organising tourism cooperatives, serving tourists travelling to Lijiang. This study has provided important data to show the difference in farmers' income before and after their starting the tourism cooperatives. Take Enzhong community for example, before 2005 when the farmers organised the cooperatives, the average annual income per person was 800 yuan; after 2005, the average annual income per person was about 10,000 yuan (Hou, 2006: 68). Some researchers believe that learning English is associated with the economic development of Yunnan, since both Mandarin and English are essential tools for a flourishing tourism industry. In the Lijiang area, as in China as a whole, about 80% of tourism receipts come from domestic tourists (90% of all tourists) and 20% come from international tourists (10% of all tourists) (YNTJNJ, 2010). Tourism accounts for 6% of Yunnan's GDP, and an even larger proportion of GDP for Lijiang County, making it a leading industry in the region (Jones & Ambrosi, 2003).

Second, according to many Chinese scholars, globalisation makes it imperative for all Chinese citizens to learn English (Ajiarehamo, 2006; Gai, 2003; Liu, 2006; Wu, 2005). For example, when examining the feasibility of trilingual education among the Yi ethnic group in Sichuan province, Ajiarehamo (2006) indicates that ethnic minority children there are able to participate in trilingual education programmes. It is imperative that they learn English because of the effects of globalisation, while Mandarin is fundamental to participation in all aspects of Chinese society, and Yi language and cultural education will maintain their own Yi traditions. Wu (2005) demonstrates that multi-language education is of great importance in a multi-ethnic society, especially in the modern world, as people have to transcend cultural barriers to develop their local economy. Wu indicates that the use of multiple languages is a symbol of the enhancement of modern civilisation, and accepting and learning a foreign language is to open to the outside world, and consequently, trilingual education will be of great help in the economic development of a multi-ethnic country like China.

Third, trilingual education will help pass on and spread minority groups' traditional ethnic culture (Ajiarehamo, 2006; Bai, 2007; Gai, 2003). In response to the concern that tourism may weaken minority people's ethnic identity, Bai (2007) argues that the tourist industry has not weakened Bai people's ethnic identity in Dali Prefecture in Yunnan; on the contrary, it has become a daily reminder of ethnicity to both themselves and the tourists. In Dali it is tourism, both domestic and international, and scholarship that has been crucial in the assembly of the Bai orchestra and its continued success, following the model of Xuan Ke and the Naxi orchestra in Lijiang. Cultural tourism can be an important means of preserving local culture. Indeed, it is arguable that cultural and botanical tourism was at the root of the preservation of Naxi culture in the first place through the efforts of Joseph Rock, who himself was quadrilingual and published his work in English, Mandarin and Dongbawen/Naxiyu.

Fourth, the minority student's bilingual educational experience can help them to acquire a third language. Previous studies have confirmed the positive role played by prior linguistic experience in third language learning (Bardel & Falk, 2007; Genoz, 2001; Hufeisn & Marx, 2007; Krashen, 1996; Mißler, 2000; Ringbom, 1987). Ringbom (1987) compares the performance of bilingual and monolingual learners in Finland learning English as their third or second language, respectively, and found that the former outperformed the latter. Hufeisn and Marx (2007) identify five major factors that affect the language learning process: neurophysiologic factors, learners' external factors, emotional factors, cognitive factors and linguistic factors, and they argue that the third language learners have stronger cognitive ability in learning a third language than second language learners in learning a second language, because previous foreign language learning experience has familiarised the third language learner with the foreign language learning process and may help them to develop more effective learning strategies and styles. The study of Bardel and Falk (2007: 479) further indicates that 'the positive influence of all previous languages' would 'facilitate the learning task' for the foreign language learners.

Fifth, through discussions with government scholars and experts on ethnic issues in Beijing, whose research often influences government policies, we get the sense that providing minority children with access to English language learning is done with a view to creating equality of educational opportunities with Han children. However, our study demonstrates that this equal access policy is far from achieving equality of opportunity and farther still from equality of outcomes. The reality is quite the opposite. A robust scholarly literature argues against trilingual education due to non-feasibility, essentially through a lack of resources (both financial and human capital) and a fundamental inequality of opportunity echoed in some of our findings, as indicated by the above-mentioned scholars who support the idea of trilingual education in principle. Cobbey (2007) noted that a lack of resources makes it impossible to launch successful trilingual programmes and the learning results are unsatisfactory. Finally, Long (2006) asserts that mandatory trilingual education is unconstitutional.

Others have argued that trilingual education is problematic for minority peoples in China as a result of practical difficulties in realizing, on the ground, the policy ideal, particularly the shortage of qualified teachers of English from within the minority community, and the lack of ESL teaching materials based in the minority language.

First, in practice, trilingual education in China inevitably faces numerous problems. Ajiarehamo (2006) points out that since there are so many ethnic groups in China, and the circumstance of trilingual education is highly complex, as a result, there is no existing single theory that can provide a framework for Chinese trilingual education. As Wei (2005: 2) asserts, trilingual education goes beyond merely the teaching of three languages; it involves not only curriculum design and the development of instructional methodology, but also includes other elements regarding trilingual programme design within the whole educational system, so as 'to improve the students' multi-language learning ability through learning three languages'. That is to say, the lack of a theoretical framework is not only a challenge for school teachers, but also a challenge for Chinese educational agencies at all levels.

Second, most ethnic minority students have experienced English learning anxiety (Guo, 2004; Li, 2003) for a variety of reasons, such as unsatisfactory academic performance, insufficient learning motivation and poor material learning conditions. Some studies have investigated in detail the problems that teachers and students have encountered in English teaching and learning processes across various academic levels, and have found that ethnic minority students have to overcome more difficulties than Han students, and the average academic performance of Han students is better (Li, 2003).

Third, due to historical, geographical and political reasons, the majority of ethnic minority communities are located in some of the most undeveloped areas in China. As a result, most studies indicate that the level of economic development in minority areas varies greatly, and therefore, trilingual education has to be designed differently to meet these different conditions, which makes things more difficult for both students and teachers. Moreover, living in remote places makes many minority children unfamiliar with the outside world, especially western culture, and consequently makes learning English seem irrelevant (Li, 2003; Liu, 2006).

Fourth – and here we come to the arguments of principle – while it is true that bilingual and trilingual education may help promote regional economic development in minority areas, the province and the country as a whole, nonetheless there is a question about the extent to which this will improve the lives of minority students. Is it enough to justify them learning a second or even a third language? While learning foreign languages, how do they protect their own culture and language? Zhang and Long (2000) indicate that some people have neglected the importance of protecting ethnic and cultural resources and instead have over-emphasised the economic development of the province. They predict that the well-known Naxi Dongba Culture will no longer exist in less than 20 years, outside its shallow commercialised veneer or pastiche.

Fifth, Long (2006) examines current foreign language education in China from a legal perspective, and concludes that the current foreign language education system violates several laws and regulations, such as: the Constitution; the Education Act; the Compulsory Education Law; the Law of National Regional Administration; the Law of National Commonly Used Spoken and Written Language; and the Regulations of Kindergarten Management. Long says that the drawbacks of this system have become serious. First, the compulsory foreign language education system has deprived Chinese citizens who cannot learn a foreign language well of the opportunities to receive further education or to be promoted. Second, some universities and colleges have stipulated that a CET4 certificate (College English Test Band 4) is mandatory to obtain a Bachelor's degree, which is actually a violation of the Regulations of the People's Republic of China on Academic Degrees, because the Regulations say that a student should be granted the degree as long as she/he has passed all of the courses, finished their thesis and attained certain academic achievements. Obviously, English proficiency is not required.

Finally, making a foreign language a degree requirement through national legislation does not conform to established international practice, since no other country has followed a similar policy. This would violate the principles of academic freedom and University autonomy in most OECD countries for example. Long indicated that foreign language learning should be encouraged but not required.

This State-mandated shift towards the principles of liberal arts education is as remarkable as it is unprecedented. Although this policy ideal aims to create equality of opportunity, the reality is that it has succeeded in making an even more uneven situation. Here we need to make it clear that even though in the documents of the Ministry of Education (2001, January 18) it is stipulated that 'where conditions allow, English teaching can be started from the third grade....Each week one hour of language class (not clear whether it refers to Mandarin or minority language class) will be replaced by an English class', it has not been formally mandated in law. However, it has been a long tradition in China that any document from the Center is treated as policy and an order to be carried out. One may also notice that it said that to permit English education, one hour of Mandarin or minority language instruction will be cut. This is a recipe for not only low-quality English teaching, but weakening the already poor results in Mandarin or the minority language.

Just as Ajiarehamo (2006) indicates, trilingual education is theoretically perfect but it is feasible only in areas where the material conditions are good and both the teachers and students are ready.

With respect to the Naxi in particular, there is essentially no literature in either English or Chinese making the case for the necessity of trilingual education, let alone any study that discusses the outcomes of these competing policies. As a multi-ethnic province, Yunnan has 25 non-Han ethnic minority groups, many of which are not geographically isolated, but instead are overlapping, making trilingual education in Yunnan very complicated. For example, the Wenhai school educates both local Naxi children and Yi children from a neighbouring village that no longer has its own school. Therefore, the Yi children receive education in Naxi and not Yi, and have teachers who have no proficiency in their mother tongue. It is through Naxi that they learn Mandarin, and through Mandarin that they learn English. In one study examining the quality of English education in the elementary schools of Yunnan province, Wu (2004: 9) found that by December 2003, among all the elementary school English teachers, only 89 (3%) had a university education, 1385 (47%) had a post-secondary specialised college education, 1349 (46%) had secondary education and 138 (5%) did not finish high school. This study found that a large number of the elementary school English teachers encountered various problems in teaching: some had pronunciation/intonation problems; some were unable to employ proper teaching methods that met the students' needs; and some could not understand the teaching objectives clearly (Wu, 2004). Our case study findings match Wu's findings. To make it worse, teaching equipment and materials were sadly absent, and the textbooks used in the school, although new were either too difficult or irrelevant for children in undeveloped rural areas. Wu indicated that imitation played an important role in learning to speak, and children had strong imitation skills, so it was very important for the English teachers at the elementary level to be able to speak fluent and good English, but obviously by 2004 the English learning conditions in Yunnan elementary schools remained far below the desired level. As related to us by an English teacher at one of the elementary schools in Lijiang city: 'The English level in Yunnan provinces as a whole is below the national average' (Experimental School, interview 1). These problems were not limited to Yunnan.

Under such learning conditions, it is understandable that the average proficiency in English among minority students in Yunnan is low. In his paper examining English acquisition by minority students, Li, D.H. (2002) finds that Yunnan University for Minorities annually enrols some students whose English scores in the National College Entrance Examination are 20–30 (out of 150, while the passing grade for university entrance stipulated by the central government is 90). Even the Department of English enrols some students with a score of only 60–70. The score in English among most new students at this college is 50–90, and among new students in the English department is 80–100. Only about 1% of the new students have scores higher than 100 (Li, D.H., 2002: 119). Li points out that an important factor causing the serious backwardness of English teaching among minority students is that there has been an inadequate study of English teaching to minority groups. Li suggests that more research is needed comparing minority language and culture to English language and culture. Meanwhile, Li argues that more ethnically sensitive teaching approaches should be developed, such as textbooks specially designed for minority students with relevant content.

Most of the previous studies were empirical studies based on surveys or test scores. Our study provides a picture of the lived experience of the Naxi people including children, so as to explore what English means for their education and lives. Not only is the school examined in detail, but the scope is widened to include parents and villagers, and the framing socio-economic, geographic and political contexts.

Methodology

This study employed multiple methods (Creswell, 1998), including document analysis, participant and non-participant observation and in-depth interviews in line with standard practices in such qualitative methodologies (Glasser & Strauss, 1967; Charnaz, 2000). In-depth interviews were conducted with the administrators and teachers at the school, and also with parents and villagers to the point of theoretical saturation (Holstein & Gubrium, 1995; Dale *et al.*, 1988). Additionally, focus group interviews were conducted with several constituencies within the village, also to theoretical saturation (Holstein & Gubrium, 1995). We engaged in participant observation in grades 3, 4, 5 and 6 English classes at the Wenhai school, all the classes they have. Additionally, we conducted both participant and non-participant observation in the village and in other school activities. In 2009, we made our fourth visit to the community, and our third visit to the school between 2005 and 2009. We have seen many changes in the community and the school, and have conducted multiple interviews with key informants. This includes two different principals, and changing teaching personnel. Most key informants we have interviewed three or more times over the years, and we spent two whole days with the English teacher in 2008, between interviews and participating in classes. Beyond this, we have become integrated into village life to better inform our research and to seek ethnographically rich data on livelihoods and attitudes towards Mandarin and English. These activities included helping with the harvest of turnips used for pig feed, attending the annual fall pig slaughtering parties in various villagers' homes, and hosting evening parties for various community groups or constituencies to learn more about their lives and the role of language and culture in them. Over many evenings, wreathed in smoke from a charcoal brazier and cigarettes, we shared laughter and stories over cups of tea, snacks and local moonshine, and through these exchanges we became accepted by the community and accessed a greater depth of information.

Findings and Analysis: Wenhai School and Village

The school

The Wenhai school is composed of several small single or two-storey buildings, of traditional post and beam construction with stone foundations and adobe brick walls. There are seven classrooms, divided between two buildings, all measuring about 10×5 m. The classrooms are very basic, with only two blackboards, one at the front of the room for instruction, and one at the back of the room for class notices, with no other decorations or materials on the walls. A single electric bulb lights the space when necessary. Often, the teacher has no desk in the classroom, and if the teacher does have a desk, it is the same small desk that the students have. The desks are about 40×90 cm, and seat two to three students on their accompanying bench. Students barely have room on the desk for their textbook and a pencil case. One long side of the classroom is almost entirely windows, facing onto the hallway that is under the eaves. The other long side on the exterior wall has a couple of windows – often with broken or missing glass. Either side of the blackboard at the back of the classroom there are open spaces with only wooden grillwork over them. Often, much of the ceiling is missing in the classrooms, so leaves and twigs rain down on students and teachers alike on a windy day. There is obvious evidence of rain entering during the wet season and rainstorms. The entirety of the school is in dire need of cleaning and painting, making for a dingy and depressing learning space. The school compound is made up of two adjoining small courtyards. The largest is about 25–30 m on each side, with some garden beds and a large cistern for water, in addition to a concrete pad where the children can play. The smaller courtyard is about 25×12 m, and is entirely covered in concrete with a couple of trees. It is off this courtyard that there is the small building with a kitchen that, in the cold weather, is home to all 47 teacher and student residents when they are not in class or in bed.

> There are 74 students at the school from grades kindergarten -6, half are Naxi, half are Yi. The Yi who come from Xuehua and other surrounding Yi villages (about 8 km/2 hours walk away). (Administrator 2, 19.11.08)

The school has 6 students in grade 6, 6 students in grade 5, 21 students in grade 4, 8 students in grade 3, and 13 students in kindergarten, with the remaining 20 students divided between grades 1 and 2.

> The 37 Yi students live at the school during the week, along with all 10 teachers. We also have a cook from the local village who prepares food for us. The Yi students all walk home on Friday afternoon to their homes, returning on Sunday afternoon or evening. (Administrator 2, 20.11.08)

> The government supplies the funding for the students' meals for the most part. The students also provide some potatoes and charcoal as a contribution in kind. (Administrator 1, 20.11.08)

There is one dorm room with 14 beds for girls, and one dorm room with 11 beds for boys. There are many more students than this of each gender, so the younger students double up. In the boy's dorm, four beds have been placed next to each other, filling the full width of the room, sleeping six to eight children on each of the top and bottom levels.

According to the two administrators that we interviewed:

> The school gets most of its funding from the county government – who are responsible for providing the salaries for teachers. Additionally the government contributes 250 yuan [ca. $35 USD] per student to the school for maintenance and equipment and to subsidize food for the resident students. (Administrator 1, 20.11.08)

> The two TVs, located in the teachers' office and therefore difficult to use for lessons, are gifts from the national Ministry of Education. The textbooks are provided by the county government. School supplies are the responsibility of the students' families. Visitors to Wenhai are good at providing school supplies for the poorer students. (Administrator 2, 19.11.08)

The televisions have no satellite connection, and so receive no television stations; therefore, they are not readily available for either teaching or entertainment during the day or evenings. This limits the exposure of students to outside events, realities and popular culture, or the wider world, which has detrimental impacts on their motivation, their integration at junior middle school in the larger centres closer to the major urban centres.

Teaching resources and curriculum

> The curriculum at the Wenhai school conforms to the provincial and national standards, as much as the teaching staff allows. The standardized textbooks are all provided by the government. (Administrator 2, 19.11.08)

However, there are two issues with respect to the teaching staff that challenge the quality of educational experience at the school. The first is that they are short staffed.

> The usual teaching complement for the school is 12 teachers, but we only have 9, plus one volunteer teacher. We are particularly short of English teachers, with only one of two that are supposed to be at the school. (Administrator 2, 19.11.08)– which means that the grade 5

and 6 students receive only 2 classes per week of English instead of the prescribed 3 periods. (Teacher 1, 19.11.08)

Second, the level of qualifications among the teaching staff is poor. There are only two teachers with bachelor degrees, but from outside teaching. Not only are they not trained teachers, but they are teaching subjects outside their area of expertise. For example, the English teacher has a BA in transportation from Kunming Ligong Daxue (Kunming University of Science and Technology), only the first two years of which included English classes.

The entire school curriculum is based on the standard for the province as a whole. According to Teacher 1:

> Mandarin and Math are taught 5 days a week, 2 classes every day. Grade 3-6 attend two 45 minute classes of English each week. The remaining classes (7 per day, 35 per week) are made up with 2 classes each of science, labour skills (which is biased towards agriculture), moral studies, fine art and music, and physical education. Both the Mandarin and English curricula are the provincial standardized material, with the same textbook and the same exam. (Teacher 1, 19.11.08)

These facts were corroborated by the administrators.

To give a sense of the rate of change in teaching resources at the school, we contrast the description of the school teaching staff by school administrators on two consecutive years.

> At the school, two of the teachers have 4 year BAs, 2 have a 2 year teaching certificate, and the rest all have 3 year teaching certificates. One teaches English from grades 3-6, teaching 2 periods per week per grade. The rest of the 20 periods he teaches Mandarin. A period is 45 minutes. They follow the standard Chinese Government curriculum. Most of the teachers live in the school compound, the only exceptions are the local teachers who live at their homes in the village. Two of the teachers are Yi, the remaining teachers are Naxi. They used to have one Naxi teacher who could teach dongbawen, but since the teacher's departure for another school, there are no more classes in Dongbawen. Chinese classes and other classes ostensibly follow the national/provincial standards (cf. Administrator 1, 15.11.07)

> There are 9 teachers at the school, although the normal compliment is 12. There is also one teacher here as a volunteer for the year. Two of

the full-time teachers and the volunteer teacher are Han. There are 2 Yi teachers, and the remaining 5 are Naxi. Only the two youngest teachers have four year degrees from university – one in transportation and one in fine art. The remainder have 2 years of formal teacher training in specialized subjects, which they supplemented with self-study and challenging exams to obtain teachers certificates and degrees. All of the teachers are from Yunnan. The teachers are provided by the county. They often stay only 1-2 years, and leave for Baisha and other villages down on the plain, after applying for a transfer. This leads to poor educational experiences for the students, through limited familiarity and continuity with the teaching staff. (cf. Administrator 2, 19.11.08)

[Please note that the English teacher is female in 2008, in contrast to the male teacher the year before.]

When asked why the school has only 9 of 12 teachers, which is their State provided allocation, both school administrators indicated that it was due to a fundamental shortage of teachers in the region. One administrator had been there for six years, the other for five years. They were the only long-serving members of the teaching staff. Teacher 2 related with humour that:

> there are so many teachers in city schools that some teachers only teach two periods a day, so that there is no fundamental shortage of teachers. People with connections and money, and people with the best qualifications have an easy time escaping from a posting to villages like Wenhai. (Teacher 2, 20.11.08)

There are actually teachers waiting to be hired in the much favoured city schools, so that these schools have no difficulty in obtaining their full complement of teachers.

Although the teachers appreciate the politeness and enthusiasm for learning so obviously displayed by the Wenhai students, none of them are from the community and none of them really want to be at Wenhai. The reality of their lives is harsh. There is no heating in either the classrooms or the bedrooms for the teachers or the students, even when the temperatures are close to or even below freezing both during the day and at night. They must spend five days out of every week away from their spouses and their children, even having to truncate breast feeding of infants due to their postings. The school is understaffed so they carry a heavier teaching load, often outside their area of expertise, and they live at the school with half of their students, so that they are also surrogate parents for five days a week. No supporting teaching equipment or materials outside the state-provided textbooks are available, and there is absolutely no scope for field trips or other sources of additional stimulation of learning (cf. Teacher 1, 19.11.08 and 20.1.08; and Administrator 2, 20.11.08).

> Exams are set at the county level, based on a provincial standard curriculum (national) by discipline. Sometimes there are external examination monitors who come to the village school. Other times the local schools swap teachers between schools to oversee the exams and their marking. Sometimes the teachers in a given discipline from the local area all come together and mark the exams for all their schools collectively. (Administrator 2, 20.11.08)

According to Administrator 2:

> Schools are ranked based on their performance in the standardized county-wide final exams. The overall exam standards are very low, the school is near bottom in English, while the performance in Mandarin is a little better. (Administrator 2, 19.11.08)

Based on the foregoing material, it is not surprising that the harsh conditions of employment lead to low staffing levels and sub-optimal teaching in the classrooms. From this, it is equally obvious why test results for students from Wenhai are low, and that drop-out rates in junior high school are so high. Based on all of the standard indicators, ranging from family background and community conditions to the teaching resources, the Wenhai students are starting from a highly disadvantageous position. Thus, we see the systematic narrowing of the capability set for these students (Sen, 1992), as poor socio-economic conditions yield poor educational outcomes in a self-reinforcing cycle.

English teaching and learning

The teacher

The teacher is a 28-year-old Han Chinese woman who is married to a Naxi man; they both grew up in Lijiang city, which is where they now live. She has a BA in transportation from Kuming Ligong Daxue (Kunming Science and Technology University). This is her second year at the Wenhai school. During the previous year, she had her new baby with her because she was breast feeding. As a result, she could not devote as much time to her classes as she would have liked. Also, she kept getting sick with colds and the flu, so for part of the year she was back in Lijiang city and someone else taught English. Her baby is at home in Lijiang city with her husband and his parents. She is quite fearful and uncomfortable teaching English, as she herself only had English classes during the first two years of her university studies, and she has no formal teacher training. Regardless of this, she ended up teaching English and Mandarin – 8 English classes per week and 10 Mandarin classes per week. She plans to stay four to five years. Given the fierce competition for teaching positions in the city, this may be her only option. Having spent four or five years in a hardship post like Wenhai may be her best hope of a job in a better school in a bigger community.

Class observation
Grade 4 English class. The grade 4 class was conducted at the end of the school day from 5:00 to 5:45. The students were very keen to start class, running to the classroom as soon as the bell was struck (an engine part from a tractor motor struck with a $\frac{3}{4}'$ machine bolt and nut). Two students were in the classroom during recess, one doing mathematics homework and the other practicing English words. The classroom itself was very dilapidated, with parts of the ceiling missing, broken windows and a cold wind blowing in, on a mid-November day. We did not believe that 21 students would fit into the classroom with three small rows of little desks with narrow benches. However, in high spirits they quickly found their places and were ready to learn. Classroom discipline was exemplary, despite the unexplained distraction of two foreigners sitting on low stools at the back of the classroom.

The young teacher greeted the class with 'good afternoon' in English. The students all answered 'good afternoon' and then sat down when asked to in English. The students seemed to know where they were in their textbooks, and quickly had their books open to start the lesson. The textbook was a letter-sized (A4) paperback with about 100 pages. It was printed in colour and used pictures and cartoons to illustrate the lessons accompanied by various activities. The class started with a review of the vocabulary from the four lessons that they had already studied. The teacher read a word and the students responded, reading as they went. Next, they started a new lesson consisting of four new words and four new sentences all on one page. The teacher seemed to engage the students by asking them to divine the meaning from the picture, and explaining the words in Mandarin. Most of the time was spent explaining and then repeating the four sentences, their meaning and their structure. The four new vocabulary words were fitted into obviously repeated sentences (sentence structures) to create four new sentences. At times the teacher did change certain pieces of the sentences, such as changing 'my' to 'our' and 'home' to 'school' or vice versa, and 'like' to 'love', discussing the differences and expanding their abilities. She also encouraged the students to demonstrate their ability to speak the sentences in the class, both in unison and individually. Students seemed to be shy and nervous when singled out to speak in class. However, we did notice that the students were all very focused, enthusiastic and responsive. When the students were confident of their abilities – such as writing vocabulary on the board – they were very keen to demonstrate their abilities, and rather more reticent when they were not so sure of their abilities. Overall, the students did seem to genuinely enjoy the subject and seemed, for the most part, to be mastering the material being taught. It pains us as much as it pains the teacher to see these enthusiastic students reliant only on this textbook with no other supporting materials. One can only hope that with access to supplemental teaching materials and multimedia support in English, the students might excel. Our final observation is that even though it was the end of the day, the students' focus and enthusiasm remained unwavering, and they cheerfully bid us good-bye in English.

Grade 3 English class. We were fortunate to get to observe an extra English class with the grade 3 students; an extra class was added to replace a cancelled mathematics class. The students all seemed delighted to have an extra English class rather than self-study or play time, which were the alternatives during this cancelled class. The students in the grade 3 class are all very attentive and are excellent at imitating the teacher. Unfortunately, when the teacher makes a mistake in pronunciation, the students all copy her and learn the wrong thing.

When the teacher asked the students what stuffed animal their parents have bought for them – as the lesson was on animals – most were silent. Out of the eight animals in the lesson, other than the farm animals that they have at home, the only image the students have of a monkey, panda, elephant etc., are the images in their textbook. Some children did indicate that they had seen some on television at home.

We also noticed that the teacher was very flexible when she found the students could not answer the questions on what they had learned. She quickly abandoned her plan to teach a new lesson, and instead reviewed the material from the previous lesson.

The classroom is so cold that the five boys and three girls are all sniffling and coughing, and we had trouble holding our pens to write notes. Yet, the students are so keen to learn that the harsh conditions do not seem to bother them. New radiators were installed this summer with a new solar heating system, donated by a group from Australia. However, they have never been used because the system was not properly installed and leaks.

The teacher's teaching style is very much the same as in the grade 4 class that we also observed. She worked hard to relate the material to the students' lives – e.g. for the animals, both domestic and wild, that the students have access to, she suggested that they should practice calling them by their English names when they see them around the village and at home.

The teacher asked us to take over the class, and the children were so keen to learn that they ignored the 'bell' for the end of class and worked with us through recess, only leaving class when the 'bell' for the next lesson called them to another class.

In summary, the teaching style was heavily reliant on rote learning and repetition. Given that the teacher has had no formal teacher training, this is perhaps not surprising. For a self-taught teacher, she does quite well at encouraging the grade 3 and 4 students in the early stages of learning. Greater training in a wider variety of techniques would, of course, improve the learning outcomes.

Grade 5/6. This was a combined class of 12 children, 6 from each grade five and grade six. The classroom was in the same dilapidated condition as the other classrooms, with three students crowded around one textbook because of the combined class. The current English teacher has only started full time this year. The previous year, she was breast feeding a new baby and had to leave due to chronic colds and flu. So this is the first full year of English lessons after a two-year break for these students. Before that time, the English teacher appears to have been unsuccessful in establishing a solid base. As a result, the grade 5 and grade 6 students are working on grade 5 material together.

As the material increased in difficulty, with longer phrases and more grammatical content, the limitations of the teacher's own English ability and her lack of formal teacher training were exposed. For example, the number of incidences of mispronunciation increased significantly, and the explanation of sentence structure was verbatim from the teacher's manual with no amplification or further explanation. It became obvious that the students were lost, and could not follow the teacher. As a result, they became less interested in learning. She repeated rote learning of vocabulary on a lesson that they had previously studied many times. Despite this, she had no success in getting responses to a simple question based on the vocabulary studied. The material and its presentation seemed to be far beyond their capacity, and so they lost interest, or were just lost. Rather than showing signs of frustration, the students were shutting off. After numerous reviews of the vocabulary in unison, the teacher asked the students to read the material on their own. During this exercise, some students fiddled with their pens and pencils and did nothing, while others gave up trying to read after they had exhausted the four to five phrases they had memorised.

Having realised that she had failed to make the material understood, the teacher reminded the students that this vocabulary would be on the standardised test, and that they should memorise them so that they could go from Chinese to English and from English to Chinese – regardless of whether or not they could understand the meaning or how to use them. As the lesson progressed, and its lack of success became increasingly obvious, she resorted to increasing amounts of Mandarin in her teaching. Towards the end of the class, she abandoned English and the lesson entirely, using one vocabulary word 'helpful' as a jumping off point to slide into civics lesson material. The sound of the 'bell' seemed to come as a relief to both the teacher and the students. The disappointed look on the teacher's face, we took to be both an indication of her fear of the poor test results for this class and a poor reflection on her teaching. She also cared deeply about the students and their learning and so she was frustrated at the entire situation.

Based on the evidence from this class, the truth of the teacher's and administrators' comments regarding poor examination performance and low standards is readily apparent. These students will not be in a position to compete favourably with students from larger villages and the city at higher levels of education. The significant potential to undermine their self-esteem – a factor so fundamental to the high drop-out rates at junior high school – is also beyond doubt. The result is truncated access to human capital, which is so vital to improved social inclusion and material well-being (Bourdieu, 1999; Sen, 1992). Given the shortage of women in China, this also means a truncation of prospects for marriage and children by young men in these rural communities, showing the primacy of human capital over other forms of capital in this community (Bourdieu, 1999; Freire, 1994).

Learning results

Based on the information presented above about the school, the teachers and our observations in English classes, it will come as no surprise to learn that the examination results for the students from

Wenhai school are poor. Indeed, the principal and vice-principal are quick to admit that the school is among the bottom decile in the county based on standardised examinations. To reprise, the key factors contributing to the poor learning outcomes for the Wenhai students are: the poor conditions at the school; the poor qualifications of the teachers, which adversely affects their teaching style; the severe lack of teaching resources outside of textbooks; the lack of relevancy of official textbooks to local life; and the lack of an English language environment. On these last two points, Teacher 1 was most eloquent:

> The children in Lijiang [city] have access to cartoons and DVDs in English both at school and at home. Additionally they are exposed to English, as well as Mandarin, in the street and shop signs all around them and in the tourists who visit the city in droves. This creates a rich language learning environment compared to Wenhai. (Teacher 1, 19.11.08)

It should be noted that other than the signs around the gate to the local government compound and the blackboards on the walls in the school compound, there were no signs or writing visible anywhere in Wenhai in Mandarin, and none at all in English.

From this we can see that the school conditions are not alone in creating these poor learning outcomes. Based on our understanding of the factors contributing to good learning outcomes, these students are at a disadvantage on all fronts. There is an almost complete lack of exposure to written language in the homes of the villagers and around the village, mirroring the conditions in the classrooms and the school, where virtually the only text that the students are exposed to is in their textbooks. The teachers clearly blame the low level of educational background on the part of parents, a point that is corroborated by our discussions with the parents themselves. It is clear that these disadvantages are directly a function of Wenhai's rural location, like countless rural communities throughout China. We turn our attention to each of these factors in turn.

Based on our observations, and as expressed by the school staff:

> The primary reason for poor language performance is the poor language environment. Also the significant challenge posed by trilingual or quadrilingual learning is a significant barrier. Even the grade 6 students are still translating in their heads from Naxiyu to Mandarin and then to English. (Teacher 1, 19.11.08)

For the Yi students, for example, they translate from their own language Yiyu into Naxiyu and from there into Mandarin and after that to English. As a result, during four years of elementary English study, 'they only master the alphabet and a few phrases of English' (Teacher 1, 19.11.08).

> All grades (3-6) receive only 2 classes per week in English. There is little interest in learning English, mainly because it has little relevancy to their lives. Mandarin is seen as more useful for communication and in watching TV, etc. Students are very shy about speaking in class, both in Mandarin and English. (Teacher 1, 19.11.08)

Due to a lack of teaching resources, the grade five and six students receive only two of the three classes that are specified in the curriculum. Further, due to the poor foundation from earlier grades and years, the grade 6 students are only working on grade 5 material, graphically illustrating the total effect of all the poor conditions for language learning and retention.

> I feel that it is a wasted effort to try to teach these few years of English, perhaps the time would be better spent on Mandarin or other subjects. I need to go very slowly with the teaching, repeating the material many times. It is particularly hard with the grade 5 & 6 students, because their experience with the previous English teacher was so poor. So now with only 2 classes a week I have to do remedial work on the first 2 years of material plus try to teach the current year's curriculum. The students are badly demoralized by this, and the poor exam results are not surprising. By contrast the grade 3 and 4 students in particular are keen to learn. However, retention of learning is a serious problem due to only 1.5 hours per week of English, and a lack of supplementary materials. The net result is a very limited retention of English and poor exam scores. (Teacher 1, 20.11.08)

> The motivation of the students is poor, particularly those who live at the school during the week. There is no entertainment at the school, no access to TV or teaching support outside of the State textbooks. Yes, motivation is poor in this school. (Teacher 1, 19.11.08)

> The students are keen to learn Mandarin, as they can see that it is useful in everyday life. The teaching of Mandarin is by immersion, very little Naxiyu is employed in teaching beyond the first grade. Some, but not all, teachers can speak Naxiyu. There is no Dongbawen taught here...indeed less than 2% of Naxi people can read and write Dongbawen. (Administrator 2, 19.11.08)

When asked about her own son, who is in grade 7 in the Baisha junior high, and his learning of English – Teacher 2 (20.11.08) commented that 'he does not like it because there is no environment to support learning English'.

Most children come from farming families, and according to Administrator 1, one of his big problems is that the parents do not care about their children's education, and this manifests itself most obviously in that the children do not do their homework.

> Many parents have a very low level of education, with a significant minority who are illiterate or semi-literate. As a result they can provide little assistance to the students in their studies regardless of how much they want to. (Administrator 2, 20.11.09)

The parents do not ask about homework or enforce the completion of homework. The only exceptions are the parents who conduct business in town and can see the value of an education. One strategy is described by a teacher:

> Most of the Yi parents are illiterate, while most of the parents with some education have only grade 3. As a result is it very hard for these parents to help their children no matter how much they wish to – also for the students living at the school they have no access to parental help during the week. So I provide extra tutoring to the students outside of school hours. (Teacher 1, 19.11.08)

Moon, a Naxi mother of two, only attended primary school for half a year, while Mason, their father, completed seven years of schooling, states 'Naxi is the only language used at home. This makes it difficult for us to judge the boys' Mandarin skills' (20.11.08). The same is, of course, true of English. Additionally, we observe that even during the 'low season' for agricultural activities, the parents are extremely busy from sun up to sun down, with little rest for the women of the village even when the sun goes down. As a result, even if the parents are willing to help, they have neither the means nor the opportunity.

All this contributes to a poor performance on provincial examinations compared to Lijiang County on average. This is one of the principal's biggest headaches, because the results are below the regional average. The principal jokingly remarked that:

> I was scolded for the poor quality of my students at regional meetings. As a result, my goal is to improve the quality of teaching and results each year by at least a little bit. (Administrator 1, 15.11.07)

Progress to higher levels of education

By law, all children should receive nine years of education in China – six years of primary education and three years in junior high school, or middle school. The unfortunate reality is that the vast majority of the students from the Wenhai school complete no more than one semester or one year in the middle school in Baisha.

> By policy, 100% of the students progress to junior high school, but many drop out either during grade 7 or in grade 8 due to poor performance. However, most students are keen to learn English because it is a major subject in junior high school and beyond. Only a very small number of students continue to high school. The junior High is in Baisha, and the high schools are in Lijiang City. (Administrator 2, 20.11.08)

Success at this level is most fervently wished for by local parents who make great financial sacrifices to ensure their children have the opportunity for further learning and much better prospects for a life outside the village, the county and even the province. Such an investment is still seen as the means to insure their old age. Mason thinks that it is very important for his two sons to learn Mandarin and English. He wants his children to attend high school, feels it is very important, and despite the very high cost compared to the family income, would support them in secondary education.

> I earn more from guiding tourists for a few hours either hiking or riding mules, than in many days of hard labour in building foundations, so I am adamant that my sons learn Mandarin and English, as this is the key to their future prosperity. (Mason, 16.11.07)

Moon has 2 sons, one is 13 and is in grade 7 at Baisha junior high, and the other is 9 and is in grade 4 at the Wenhai school: 'My older boy has traditionally been the more studious one, but he is now keen to drop out of school, as are most of his friends' (20.11.08). The sad reality is that even the top students from the Wenhai school struggle to meet an average standard at the Baisha junior high school. The parental view is different:

> I feel that Mandarin is important to their having the possibility of a life beyond the village, maybe in Kunming or Beijing. I am happy that my sons are learning English also as it is important for advancement. (Moon, 20.11.08)

As a result, they are happy for any and all extra learning. When asked to prioritise between Mandarin and English learning, Mandarin was the obvious top priority. The lodge manager, who often served as our interpreter from Naxiyu to Mandarin, amplified that this is because of the very limited exposure in the village to foreigners and therefore, the usefulness of English. He observed that among the wealthy in Lijiang city, the attitude was the exact opposite, those who are thinking of sending their children abroad, value English more highly.

The parents are adamant that the older child finishes junior high school, and continues to further studies if possible. This is seen as being crucial for the family's welfare. They are investing in their children now so that they might be cared for in turn later on.

> We are willing to do whatever it takes to provide the necessary financial support. This represents a significant burden to our family – 60-70 yuan per week or 300 yuan per month for food alone. There are additional fees for textbooks and school supplies and other fees. We find these expenses are almost unbearable, but they are worth it. We are putting aside the necessary funds for both of our sons to go as far as possible in their studies.

> I miss my son while he is away in Baisha for the week, and worry about whether he is behaving himself, and also that he is doing well in his studies. My son is happy to be in Baisha with his friends – particularly when playing. He misses home most at meal times. We pay the lowest level of room and board fees while other students pay more and receive better meals.

For her son, cheap staples dominate the meals, with few vegetables and little meat.

> Instant noodles (costing 1-2 yuan) are a rare treat for those days when he just cannot stand the school meals any longer. (Moon, 20.11.08)

The level of sacrifice in terms of both economic resources and emotional well-being, on the part of both parents and children is readily apparent in these statements, as well as the depth of their faith in education as a source of upward mobility and greater financial security.

'I hope that my sons' exposure to tourists will widen their view of their lives and the world' (Moon, 20.11.08). The hope here is obviously one that widened horizons will lead to her sons attaching a greater importance to studying both Mandarin and English.

The good news is that some of the best students do succeed, although there are only 10 high school graduates who started at the Wenhai school, and only two or three of these have managed undergraduate degrees from university.

> There are some Yi students as well as Naxi students, and some girls as well as boys among the 10 students from here who have graduated from high school. There seems to be no socio-economic pattern to those who succeed – everyone starts from the same low point. (Administrator 1, 20.11.08)

Unfortunately, the Wenhai students are at a significant socio-economic and educational disadvantage from day one. They arrive at middle school far behind their peers from larger villages and towns, which severely undermines their self-esteem, and the high drop-out rate in or after grade 7 is a predictable result. The drop-out rate is compounded by their lack of knowledge of popular culture, their unfashionable clothing and their lack of access to transportation, further eroding self-esteem.

> Although all students start junior high in Baisha, the vast majority of the students drop out either in their second semester or in their second year (grade 7 or 8). There have only been 10 students who completed high school from this primary school, and only 2-3 who have gone on to university. The students feel they are far behind their peers from other primary schools, and their test scores are poor. They suffer from low self-esteem, and quickly give up on studying and getting an education. It is going to be a long struggle to change the situation, and it will require a concerted effort on the part of all of the teachers and the parents. Expectations from the education system as a whole are too high for the children from these poor rural schools. They need a modern building and equipment for the school. (Teacher 1, 19.11.08)

> Those students who drop out in grade 7 or 8 end up either helping with the family farm, or finding service sector jobs in the city. (Administrator 1, 20.11.08)

Based on our observation of the English classes, it is clear that poor performance in English is a significant contributing factor to their difficulties in continuing in education.

Conclusions

The conditions in rural and remote schools are far below urban standards, and far below the provincial average. Therefore, a unified national policy on language teaching for millions of children, especially for minority children, does not seem to be reasonable. Based on our findings, in some cases, it is absolutely impossible. Further, it produces an enormous barrier, preventing access to higher education for most minority children outside major urban centres like Lijiang city, denying them the human capital investment that is so crucial to both economic and personal development and improved material well-being (Freire, 1994; Sen, 1992; Bourdieu, 1999).

Given the economic and linguistic realities in Yunnan, not all school children can benefit from learning English, especal at schools like the one in Wenhai, at least not until the language environment and teaching and learning resources are closer to the provincial average for these children. The curriculum requirements for English steal valuable time and resources away from other more attainable pedagogic goals in these remote and rural communities. However, the current education laws put these rural schools and their students in a virtually impossible situation, because the entrance requirements for Mandarin and English proficiency exclude children from garnering further cultural and social capital in a systematic way, i.e. they can neither abandon sub-standard English in favour of strong Mandarin and mathematics performance, nor can they achieve success with such limited resources in both languages.

What has been argued to be theoretically and ideologically sound on the grounds of equality of opportunity, such as trilingual education for minority children, in practice falls far short of these equitable ambitions. Instead it produces systemic cultural, financial and spatial inequality in access to senior high school, college and university education – reinforcing and exacerbating the existing patterns of relative deprivation and inequality (Bourdieu, 1991, 1999; Bourdieu & Passeron, 1977; Freire, 1968, 1985, 1994) and increasing their risk and vulnerability (Beck, 2005).

So far, little is known about the impact of English language teaching for minority children. What does this mean in the long term for their cultural and social capital attainment, and their socio-economic well-being? What will this mean for their learning and retention of their own language and culture? What does this mean for their learning of Mandarin and integration to mainstream Han society? All these questions need to be answered through further research.

Acknowledgements

The authors would like to acknowledge the support of the University of Regina for the seed money to establish this research programme and support for early fieldwork, and the Social Sciences and Humanities

Research Council of Canada for on-going support. We would also like to acknowledge our research assistant, Bailing Zhang, for her efforts on the literature survey. We owe a large debt of gratitude to the people of Wenhai village and the Wenhai school, many who cannot be named specifically to protect their identity. They have warmly welcomed us into their homes, their classrooms and into their lives. This is a gift that we hope to repay some day with an improved understanding of and improved conditions in China's rural schools. All remaining errors are, of course, the responsibility of the authors.

Notes

1. Recently, Lijiang xian was split into Yulongxian (rural) and Gucheng (urban), but between them they remain the epicentre of Naxi settlement and culture.
2. Joseph Rock was Austrian by birth, a botanist working as a researcher for Harvard and a correspondent and photographer for *National Geographic*, who was based in the Lijiang area from 1922 to 1949. He learned both Naxiyu and Dongbawen, and befriended the remaining Dongba shamans to record and translate their scriptures and their religious and cultural ceremonies and practices into Mandarin and English. His first set of materials, shipped to the USA in 1944, was lost at sea due to the war. He then set about recreating all of his scholarship on Naxi ethnography again, before Mao expelled him in 1949. Rock's work has been crucial in the retention of Naxi culture and to scholarship on the same.

References

Ajiarehamo (2006) Liangshan Yizu Diqu Shishi Sanyu Jiaoxue de Kexingxing Yanjiu (The feasibility studies of trilingual education in Liangshan Yi minority). *Xiandai Jiaoyu Kexue* 6, 102–103. (In Chinese)

Bai, Z.H. (2007) Ethnic identities under the tourist gaze. *Asian Ethnicity* 8 (3), 245–259.

Bardel, C. and Falk, Y. (2007) The role of the second language in third language acquisition: the case of Germanic syntax. *Second Language Research* 23 (4), 459–484.

Beck, U. (2005) The silence of words and political dynamics in the world risk society. In S.E. Bronner (ed.) *Planetary Politics: Human Rights, Terror and Global Security* (pp. 3–20). Lanham: Rowman & Littlefield.

Blachford, D. (2004a) Language spread verses language maintenance: Minority language policy making in China. In M.L. Zhou and H.K. Sun (eds) *Language Policy in China: Theory and Practice since 1949* (pp. 99–122). The Netherlands: Kluwer Academic.

Blachford, D. (2004b) The socio-political and economic foundations behind minority language and education policy in China. In R.W. Heber (ed.) *Issues in Aboriginal/Minority Education: Canada, China, Taiwan* (pp. 154–172). Saskatoon: Indigenous Studies Research Centre, First Nation University of Canada.

Bourdieu, P. (1991) *Language and Symbolic Power*. Cambridge, MA: Harvard University Press.

Bourdieu, P. (1999) *The Weight of the World, Social Suffering in Contemporary Society*. Stanford: Stanford University Press.
Bourdieu, P. and Passeron, J.C. (1977) *Reproduction in Education, Society and Culture*. London: Sage.
Cenoz, J. (2001) The effect of linguistic distance, L2 status and age on crosslinguistic influence in third language acquisition. In J. Cenoz, B. Hufeisen and U. Jessner (eds) *Cross-linguistic Influence in Third Language Acquisition: Psycholinguistic Perspectives* (pp. 8–20). Clevedon: Multilingual Matters.
Charmaz, K. (2000) Grounded theory: Objectivist and constructionist methods. In N.K. Denzin and Y.S. Lincoln (eds) *Handbook of Qualitative Research* (pp. 509–535). Thousand Oaks, CA: Sage.
Cobbey, H. (2007) Challenges and prospects of minority bilingual education in China – an analysis of four projects. In A.W. Feng (ed.) *Bilingual Education in China: Practices, Policies and Concepts* (pp. 182–199). North York: Multilingual Matters.
Creswell, J.W. (1998) *Qualitative Inquiry and Research Design: Choosing among Five Traditions*. Thousand Oaks, CA: Sage.
Dale, A., Arber, S. and Procter, M. (1988) *Doing Secondary Analysis*. London: Unwin.
Feng, A.W. (ed.) (2007) *Bilingual Education in China: Practices, Policies and Concepts*. North York: Multilingual Matters.
Feurer, H. (1996) Bilingual education among minority nationalities in China: A study of the Naxi pilot project at Yilong, Yunnan. *RELC Journal* 27 (1), 1–22.
Freire, P. (1968) *Pedagogy of the Oppressed*. New York: Seabury Press.
Freire, P. (1985) *The Politics of Education: Culture, Power and Liberation*. South Hadley, MA: Bergin and Garvey.
Freire, P. (1994) *Pedagogy of Hope*. New York: Continuum.
Gai, X.Z. (2003) Sanyu Jiaoyu Santi (On trilingual education). *Dali Xueyuan Xuebai* 2 (6), 83–88. (In Chinese)
Geary, D.N. and Pan, Y.R. (2003) A bilingual education pilot project among the Kam people in Guizhou province, China. *Journal of Multilingual and Multicultural Development* 24 (4), 274–289.
Glasser, B.G. and Strauss, A.L. (1967) *The Discovery of Grounded Theory: Strategies for Qualitative Research*. New York: Aldine Press.
Guo, X.Z. (2004) Qinghai Shaoshu Minzu Daxuesheng Yingyu Xuexi de Zhang'ai ge Duice (The key problems and the main solutions in the English studying of the minority nationalities students in Qinghai Nationalities Institute). *Qinghai Minzu Yanjiu* 15 (3), 100–102. (In Chinese)
Hao, S.Y. (2002) (ed.) *Atlas of Distribution of National Minorities in China*. Beijing: China Atlas Publishing House.
Hicks, S., Jones, M.E. and Graham, J.R. (eds) (2008) To the digital divide and back: Social welfare, technology and the new economy. *Currents* December 7 (2), 1–13.
Holstein, J.A. and Gubrium, J.F. (1995) *The Active Interview*. Thousand Oaks, CA: Sage Press.
Hou, R.L. (2006) Lijiang Lashi Haixiangcun Lüyou Tuopin Diaocha Anli Fenxi (A case study of the tourism-based poverty eradication at Lashi lake of Lijiang). *Yunnan Minzu Daxue Xuebao* 23 (6), 67–69. (In Chinese)
Hufeisen, B. and Marx, N. (2007) How can DaFnE and EuroComGerm contribute to the concept of receptive multilingualism? Theoretical and practical

considerations. In J. Thije and L. Zeevaert (eds) *Receptive, Multilingualism: Linguistic Analyses, Language Policies and Didactic Concepts* (pp. 307–321). Amsterdam: John Benjamins.

Jones, M.E. (1994) Poverty, inequality and living standards in rural China 1978–90: A comparative study of Anhui and Yunnan. Doctoral dissertation, University of London.

Jones, M.E., Ambrosi, R. and Yang, D.S. (2003) Lüyou Zuowei Quyu Kechixu Fazhan de Gongju–Yiba Shuangrenjian: Yi Zhongguo Xinanbu Diqu Lüyou Fazhan Weili (Using tourism as a tool for regional sustainable development in southwest China: A double edged sword). *Guilin Lüyou Gaodeng Zhuanke Xueyuan Xuebao* 14 (2), 46–51. (In Chinese)

Krashen, S. (1996) *Under Attack: The Case against Bilingual Education*. Culver City, CA: Language Education Associates.

Li, D.H. (2002) Qiantan Shaoshu Minzu Daxuesheng Yingyu Xide (A preliminary study of the minority students' English acquisition). *Yunnan Minzu Xueyuan Xuebao* 19 (2), 119–120. (In Chinese)

Li, Q. (2001) Naxizu Xuesheng Yingyu Xide Yanjiu (On the study of Naxi students' English acquisition). *Yunnan Shifan Daxue Xuebao* 2 (4), 64–69. (In Chinese)

Li, S.Q. (2002) Lüyou Fazhan yu Yingyu Jiaoyu Gaige de Neihan: yi Yunnansheng Lüyouye Wei Li (On tourist development and the connotations of English: Teaching reform—a case study of the tourism of Yunnan province). *Yunnan Minzu Xueyuan Xuebao* 19 (2), 112–114. (In Chinese)

Li, Y.L. (2003) Shaoshu Minzu Xuesheng Xuexi de Teshuxing Yanjiu (A study on the particularity of English learning among the ethnic minority students). *Xi'nan Minzu Daxue Xuebao [Renwen Sheke Ban]* 24 (8), 334–336. (In Chinese)

Lin, J. (1997) Policies and practices of bilingual education for the minorities in China. *Journal of Multilingual and Multicultural Development* 18 (3), 193–205.

Lin, J.P., Zhou, H. and He, Y.H. (2005) Naxi Dongba Minzu Wenhua Chuantong Chuangcheng yu Xiangcun Lüyou Fazhan Yanjiu: Yi Yunnan Lijiang Sanyuancun Xiangcun Lüyou Kaifa Weili (A study on the inheritance and passing on the Naxi Dongba ethnic culture tradition and development of rural tourism). *Renwen Dili* 20 (5), 77–79. (In Chinese)

Liu, M.L. (2006) Cong Jiaoxue Gaige kan Guizhou Gaoxiao Shaoshu Minzu Daxuesheng Yinyu Jiaoyu de Kunnan Yinsu ji Duice (From the reform in education, discuss about difficulties and strategies of English education to the minority students in Guizhou colleges education). *Guizhou Minzu Yanjiu* 26 (111), 178–182. (In Chinese)

Long, Y. (2006, August 25) Woguo Xianxing Waiyu Jiaoyu Zhidu de Falü Sikao (Jural reflection on the current foreign language education in China). *Falü Ribao*. (In Chinese) On WWW at http://fz.qingdao.gov.cn/n2685790/n2685878/257452.html. Accessed 23.7.08.

Ministry of Education of the People's Republic of China (2001, January 18) Jiaoyubu Guanyu Jiji Tuijin Xiaoxue Kaishe Yingyu Kecheng de Zhidao Yijian (Instructions on how to promote the implementation of English curricula in the elementary schools). (In Chinese) On WWW at http://www.moe.gov.cn/edoas/website18/27/info727.htm. Accessed 23.7.08.

Mißler, B. (2000) Previous experience of foreign language learning and its contribution to the development of learning strategies. In S. Dentler,

B. Hufeisen and B. Lindemann (eds) *Tertiär – und Drittsprachen. Projekte und empirische Untersuchungen* (pp. 7–21). (Tertiärsprachen und Mehrsprachigkeit Band 2.) Tübingen: Stauffenburg.
Ringbom, H. (1987) *The Role of L1 in Foreign Language Learning*. Clevedon: Multilingual Matters.
Sen, A.K. (1992) *Inequality Reexamined*. Oxford: Clarendon Press.
Wei, H.J. (2005) Zhongguo Shaoshu Minzu Sanyu Jiaoxue Xingshi Jianxi (A brief analysis on the trilingual teaching forms in the minority areas of China). *Shihezi Daxue Xuebao [Zhexue Shehui Kehui Ban]* 19 (4), 83–84. (In Chinese)
Wu, H.P. (2007) Shaoshu Minzu Yingyu Gaodeng Jiaoyu Yanjiu Shinian Shuping (A brief review of ten years' research on English higher education of minorities in China). *Zhongnan Minzu Daxue Xuebao [Renwen Shehui Kexue Ban]* 27 (2), 174–177. (In Chinese)
Wu, J. (2004) Dui Yunnan Xiaoxue Yingyu Jiaoxue Xianzhuang He Jiaoxue Zhiliang Tigao De Sikao (Thoughts on the present situation of English education in Yunnan elementary schools and the strategies to enhance the teaching qualities). *Gongzuo Zhidao [Xiaojiao Yanjiu]* 5, 9–11. (In Chinese)
Wu, L.J. (2005) Shaoshu Minzu Sanyu Jiaoyu de Zongheng Jiedu (An explanation of trilingual education of ethnics). *Guizhou Minzu Yanjiu* 25 (104), 181–183. (In Chinese)
Wu, W.L. (2002) Lun Ruhe Jifa Shaoshu Minzu Zhongxuesheng Xuexi Yingyu de Xingqu (On stimulating minority high school students' interest in learning English). *Liuzhou Shizhuan Xuebao* 17 (1), 105–107. (In Chinese)
Yang, Y. (2008, June 2) Yunnan shiwu wan baqian ming Xiaoxuesheng Jieshou Hanyu He Shaoshu Minzu Muyu Shuangyu Jiaoxue (158 thousand ethnic minority elementary school students in Yunnan province receive bilingual education). (In Chinese) On WWW at http://www.yn.xinhuanet.com/news center/2008-06/02/content_13434239.htm. Accessed 23.7.08
YNTJNJ (2010) *Yunnan Tongji Nianjian (Yunnan Statistical Yearbook)*. Beijing: China Statistics Press. (In Chinese)
Zhang, J.Y. and Long, M. (2000) Shilun Yunnan Minzu Wenhua Chanye (Ethnic cultural industry in Yunnan). *Yunnan Shifan Daxue Xuebao* 32 (5), 53–55. (In Chinese)
ZGLYNJ (2007) Zhongguo Lüyou Nianjian *(China Tourism Year Book)*. Beijing: China Statistics Press. (In Chinese)
Zhou, M.L. (2004) Minority language policy in China: Equality in theory and inequality in practice. In M.L. Zhou and H.K. Sun (eds) *Language Policy in China: Theory and Practice since 1949* (pp. 71–97). The Netherlands: Kluwer Academic.
Zhou, Q.S. (2004) The creation of writing systems and national establishment: The case of China in the 1950s. In M.L. Zhou and H.K. Sun (eds) *Language Policy in China: Theory and Practice since 1949* (pp. 55–70). The Netherlands: Kluwer Academic.

Chapter 13

Learning English as a Third Language by Uyghur Students in Xinjiang: A Blessing in Disguise?

MAMTIMYN SUNUODULA and ANWEI FENG

Introduction

At the China Central Television (CCTV) Cup English Speaking Contest 2008, hosted by CCTV 9 on 24th November 2008, Tian Wei, a well-known news anchor at the English language CCTV 9 and one of the judges of the contest, asked Faruk Mardan from Xinjiang Uyghur Autonomous Region, a semi-finalist and the winner of Most Energetic Speaker award, the following question:

> Q: I would like to ask this question. China has so many ethnic groups, Xinjiang is, of course, a very exotic and very beautiful place. Many people outside this country may not know it very well. How did you get the chance to participate in a competition like this? What is, you know, English education like in Xinjiang, for example? I am curious. I really like your engaging and passionate speaking style, also your gestures, like a rap singer in a way. (China Central Television, 2008)

Here is Faruk's answer:

> A: I have to tell you that people in Xinjiang [are] really enthusiastic about learning English. Because we have lots of youngsters who are willing to speak English, who are willing to learn English. There are lots of ethnic groups in Xinjiang. They are passionate and enthusiastic. They like new things; English is really new and it is like new blood in their body. (China Central Television, 2008)

Faruk's answer may have only addressed part of the judge's question (multi-questions to be precise), however, the passion and enthusiasm in learning English, which Faruk believes 'the youngsters' in Xinjiang

Uyghur Autonomous Region have, are clearly articulated. Both the question(s) and the answer point towards the general interest of this chapter.

The Context

The Xinjiang Uyghur Autonomous Region is situated in the northwest of the People's Republic of China and occupies one sixth of the country's total land mass. It borders with Russia, Kazakhstan, Kyrgyzstan, Tajikistan, Pakistan, Afghanistan, India and Mongolia and has a complex mixture of ethnic composition and great potential for international exposure, both in socio-cultural terms and economic activities. It is home to a number of officially recognised ethnic groups with a total population of almost 21 million at the end of 2007 (Xinjiang Uyghur Autonomous Region Government, 2009). The largest ethnic group in Xinjiang are the Uyghurs with a population of some nine million, closely followed by China's dominant Han ethnic group, whose population in the region has increased from less than 7% to over 40% in the last half century (Zhongguo Shehui Kexueyuan, 1994: 39–40).

From the end of the 'Cultural Revolution' in the late 1970s till the promulgation of the Xinjiang bilingual education policy in 2004, the education system in Xinjiang was largely divided into two parallel subsystems: minority language medium education for the ethnic minority students with Mandarin Chinese as a second language school subject and Mandarin Chinese language medium education for the Han population with English as the preferred second language school subject. Thus, in this system, the schools were divided along ethnic lines on the basis of the language of instruction and, as Uyghur is one of the two official languages in the Autonomous Region, most Uyghurs were educated in their mother tongue with varying degree of knowledge of the Mandarin Chinese, depending on where they lived and the possibilities for them to interact with the Han population (Benson, 2004: 190–202). An official survey conducted in 1986 showed that only 4.4% of the Uyghurs reported that they were fully communicative in Mandarin Chinese, with 90% reporting that they did not even have the basic communicative skills in the language (Zhongguo Shehui Kexueyuan, 1994). However, this situation is changing rapidly as an increasing number of Uyghur pupils in mixed communities or cities attend Chinese medium schools or Chinese-Uyghur mixed schools from childhood (Tsung & Cruickshank, 2009).

In 2001, there were 6221 primary schools in Xinjiang of which 56.37% (3507) were Uyghur language medium schools; there were 1457 lower secondary schools of which 39% (566) were Uyghur schools; at higher secondary school level, the proportion of Uyghur schools is under 34% (158) of a total of 472 schools (Zhao, 2004). According to Zhao (2004), the percentage of ethnic minority students receiving education in their native language medium schools represented somewhere between 65 and 70% of the total number, but in the south of Xinjiang where Uyghurs are dominant the percentage can be as high as 96% of the total. A recent survey confirms that the proportion of Uyghur university students who graduated from Uyghur language medium schools remained at over 90% (Cui, 2005). Those Uyghur students who had not attended Uyghur language medium schools went through a variety of other schooling where the medium of instruction is Mandarin Chinese. These include Mandarin Chinese language medium schools in Xinjiang, special classes set up for ethnic minorities outside Xinjiang (内地新疆班), specially set-up classes for ethnic minorities in Mandarin Chinese language medium schools in Han majority areas in Xinjiang (疆内民族班), mixed Uyghur-Han schools and experimental Mandarin Chinese language medium-based classes in Uyghur language medium schools.

Turning to foreign language teaching and learning, the first of two policy documents specifically mentioning foreign language education for minority nationalities in the region was issued in May 1950 by the then provincial government. The document entitled 'Directive on Reforming the Current Education System' required Mandarin Chinese language-medium schools to opt either for an ethnic minority language or Russian and the minority language medium schools to opt for Mandarin Chinese or Russian (Xinjiang Weiwuer Zizhiqu Difangzhi Bianzuan Weiyuanhui, 2000). Therefore, in the first couple of decades, the teaching of Russian as a foreign language was possible in principle, even for minority schools.

On 15 December 1977, another foreign language education policy document was formulated in Xinjiang and promulgated by the Xinjiang Uyghur Autonomous Region Education Bureau. The document entitled 'Curriculum Plan for Ten-year Full-time Primary and Secondary Schools in Xinjiang Uyghur Autonomous Region (draft plan)' stipulated that:

> ethnic minority schools provide Mandarin Chinese as the compulsory second language school subject from Year 3 of primary school until the end of secondary school education; no foreign language courses are to be provided. Han and Hui primary schools should generally teach an ethnic minority language as a school subject. At

the junior secondary school, two thirds of the Han and Hui schools should offer ethnic minority language courses and the other third should offer foreign language courses. At the senior secondary school level, all Han and Hui schools should offer foreign language curriculum; no ethnic minority language curriculum is to be offered. (Quoted in Xinjiang Weiwuer Zizhiqu Difangzhi Bianzuan Weiyuanhui, 2000: 275; authors' translation and emphasis)

This document has made explicit two subsystems and has left the vast majority of the Uyghur and other linguistic minority students studying at non-Mandarin Chinese medium schools out of the national foreign language education system.

Though a 'draft plan', the document seems to be the only official policy that has been practised for the past decades. Foreign language provision has been very limited for minority pupils. For example, a recent survey at six junior and senior secondary schools in the Kashgar Prefecture, which is dominated by Uyghurs, revealed that until the end of the 1990s, no Uyghur school (at primary, junior or senior secondary level) had offered any English or other foreign language classes (Li, 2005). English was not a required subject for the university entrance examination for Uyghur students. In the late 1990s, some junior and senior secondary schools in relatively developed areas in Xinjiang started teaching English to a selected group of 'talented' students in the so-called experimental classes. Due to resource constraints, most of them only offered English on a two-hour-per-week basis. Qualifications of English teachers in schools also looked gloomy (Li, 2005), with 20% of the teachers having received diploma level education, 30% having gone through only one-year intensive English language teacher training, 30% with high school level education and only 15% being university graduates, most of whom majored in a subject other than English.

Olan (2007) conducted a survey among 618 minority students at the most prestigious university in Xinjiang and found that, even there, 62% of them had had no English learning experience at all. For the remaining 38% of students surveyed, according to Olan, they had gained English learning experience through the following channels: by attending schools where Chinese is the medium of instruction; by taking private lessons from profit-making English language teaching (ELT) agencies; by virtue of living in socio-political and economic centres, such as Urumqi or the major city of a prefecture where educational opportunities are more accessible; and for the highly motivated, through self-study.

At the turn of the century, despite the promulgation of the New Curriculum Standards (see Cheng, this volume), which is specified to be applicable to schools all over the country, the official position in Xinjiang with regard to ethnic minorities learning English or other foreign languages has not changed, i.e. the document issued in 1977 still applies to Xinjiang. What has evidently changed in Xinjiang, however, is the fact that while the Chinese language has been strongly promoted and its curriculum enhanced in minority schools (Blachford, 2004), minority languages have gradually disappeared from the curricula in Han schools or for Han pupils in mixed schools and have been replaced by English (Tsung & Cruickshank, 2009). This has widened the gap between the two subsystems for the Han majority group and other ethnic minority groups and created further obstacles for pupils to integrate in the region.

While English provision for minority students, particularly those who live in remote areas and study in minority language medium schools, is limited, the demand for English in the region is clearly on the rise. Ever-growing tourism (see Tables 13.1 and 13.2) and the presence of

Table 13.1 Statistics of international tourist arrivals in Xinjiang (excluding overseas Chinese, Taiwanese, Hong Kong and Macao tourists)

Years	Xinjiang	National total
1997	157,067	7,428,000
1998	141,000	7,107,700
1999	190,151	8,432,300
2000	208,400	10,160,400
2001	218,600	11,226,400
2002	233,700	13,439,500
2003	149,916	11,402,900
2004	270,959	16,932,500
2005	290,140	20,255,100
2006	313,101	22,210,300
2007	402,700	26,109,700

Sources: Guojia Tongjiju [State Statistical Bureau] (1998–2007) *China Foreign Economic Statistical Yearbook*; Guojia Lüyouju [State Tourism Bureau] (1997–2007) *Yearbook of China Tourism Statistics*.

Table 13.2 Statistics on international tourist agencies and hotels in Xinjiang

Series/ year	International travel agencies	No. of employees	No. of international tourist hotels	No. of employees	Foreign exchange earnings from international tourism (unit: $1 million)
1997	26	1,260	103	10,541	71
1998	36	1,032	173	17,204	86
1999	38	1,111	176	19,948	86
2000	39	1,266	233		95
2001	38	1,292	173	20,567	99
2002	39	1,735	190	22,835	99
2004	39	27,307		30,117	92
2007	51		432		

Sources: Guojia Lüyouju [State Tourism Bureau] (1997–2007) Yearbook of China Tourism Statistics.

multinationals (see Table 13.3) are two indicators suggesting increasing opportunities for people with foreign language competence.

Some issues appear unequivocal in this context. First, while the demand for English-knowing personnel is high, as Table 13.1 and Table 13.2 show, few people of minority background are qualified for the market since they have no opportunity to study the language during compulsory education. Second, there is a clear discrepancy between the national policy and the regional policy in foreign language provision as the systems followed by the majority group and the minority groups differ. Third, many authors (e.g. Bastid-Bruguiere, 2001) argue that the current national drive for English language education is further empowering the already powerful majority Han group, leaving minority and indigenous peoples, like the Uyghurs and Tibetans, even further behind. As the Uyghur and other linguistic minority students are required to learn Mandarin Chinese as a priority, and because the majority of minority groups live in impoverished areas where few can afford private English lessons for themselves and/or their children, Beckett and MacPherson (2005) state that the expansion of English

Table 13.3 Number of foreign owned enterprises and their employees in Xinjiang (excluding Taiwan, Hong Kong and Macao owned)

Year	No. of companies	No. of employees
1997	76	6129
1998	80	6000
1999	65	5000
2000	58	5093
2001	72	5502
2002	64	6428
2003	342	No official figure
2004	331	Ditto
2005	345	Ditto
2006	421	Ditto

Sources: Guojia Tongjiju [State Statistical Bureau] (1997–2006) *China Labour Statistical Yearbook*; Guojia Tongjiju [State Statistical Bureau] (1998–2007). *China Foreign Economic Statistical Yearbook*.

language education is widening the gap and augmenting educational inequities that minority peoples already face in the traditional system.

The gloomy picture portrayed in the literature has often led to calls for making special policies on foreign language education for minority groups. However, the claims that the calls are based on are often inadequately researched empirically. For example, ethnic minority students are often represented as having low motivation to learn English and showing cognitive difficulties in learning it (see the following section). Is that really the case? Drawing from narratives and semi-structured interviews with Uyghur students attending English language and Chinese-English 'bilingual' classes, in this chapter, we will examine how the learning of English language and the English language medium education are perceived by Uyghur students. The analysis of the empirical data is done using Bourdieu's (1977) notions of cultural and linguistic capital and symbolic power within the context of power relations among different ethnic groups in Xinjiang. The need for such a focus will become obvious in the following section in which we critically review current discussions on English language education, or the lack of it, for these minority groups.

English Language Teaching for Minority Students: An Overview

The literature on foreign language provision for minority groups is relatively new because, traditionally, language education for minority groups primarily aimed for developing *Min-Han Jiantong*, minority language and Mandarin Chinese bilinguals (Feng, 2005). In recent years, owing to the various forces of globalisation and the promulgation of the new English Curriculum Standards (ECS), there is an increase in English language provision for minority groups in China and thus an increase in research and discussions. A number of researchers and scholars working inside and outside China (Adamson & Feng, 2009; Beckett & MacPherson, 2005; Chen, 2008; Feng, 2007; Feng & Sunuodula, 2009; Olan, 2007, Yang, 2005) have contributed to a literature that aims for an understanding of issues related to tensions between mother tongue, national language and English in policy formulation, the policy making and implementing cycle, and socio-cultural, economic and political factors that affect English language education, or the lack of it, in specific contexts. This new literature can be broadly divided into three categories.

The first category collects writings in English that give general accounts of English language provision or trilingual education for the 100 million strong minority groups living within the boundaries of the People's Republic of China. These writings aim to make this literature, primarily in Chinese, accessible to international readers. Feng's (2005) analysis of the parallel conceptions of bilingualism and Yang's (2005) account of English as a third language fall into this category. Some chapters in Feng (2007) also contribute to a general understanding of the ELT situation in minority regions in China. In Feng's (2005) discussion on the parallel conceptions of bilingualism in the country, namely, the Chinese-English bilingualism for the Han majority and minority language-Chinese bilingualism for the minority groups, he points out that the former inevitably impacts on the latter. What is urgently needed is research into the extent of the impact and into how this impact could possibly be addressed in the particular socio-political, cultural and economic context of each minority group. In many of the writings under this category, a shared concern is that ethnic minority students' ethnic identity, personality development and academic performance are undermined because many issues regarding policies, curricula and pedagogy remain unaddressed. Most of the authors agree on the need for empirical research into local responses to national policies and pedagogical issues in relation to cognitive and identity development as findings from such research would provide not only useful insights for practitioners in similar contexts, but also constructive feedback for policy making (Feng & Sunuodula, 2009; Wang & Gao, 2008).

Falling into the second category are those that focus on issues in English language provision for minority groups since the turn of the century, particularly since 2001 when the ECS was promulgated. These discussions are particularly on the rise inside China. While some (e.g. Jing, 2007; Wang, 2000) show optimism about trilingualism and trilingual education for minority pupils, many educators and commentators give dismal accounts of the situation by listing various difficulties and problems that minority students face in learning English, from lack of resources to cognitive, affective and socio-cultural hurdles that minority pupils experience in learning a third language (Ju, 2000; Li, 2003; Wu, 2002; Yang, 2005).

Yang (2005) makes the case for the diverse needs of ethnic minority education and argues for diversity of English language bilingual or trilingual education in China. In his analysis of the issues facing minority pupils, Yang lists four factors that negatively impact on ELT in ethnic minority regions: lack of resources, lack of motivation, the interference of existing bilingual policies and difficulty in learning a third language. Yang asserts that ethnic minorities appear to be interested in learning Han language and the opportunity to study in coastal cities. Here, he seems to adopt a point of view of financial gains in speculating that ethnic minorities in impoverished border areas pursue the powerful national language because that would bring them economic benefits. There is hardly any empirical evidence for such claims and no serious reflection on the complex socio-political, cultural and linguistic dimensions at play in language learning.

Beckett and MacPherson (2005), in analysing the impact of the spread of English on native languages, critique the trend of equating China and Chinese with the majority Han ethnic group without paying due attention to the diversity and contrasts that exist in the country. Through an analysis of the Uyghur and Tibetan cases, two of China's largest minority ethnic groups, they strongly argue for and demonstrate the existence of very different social, political, cultural and linguistic conditions and inequities in educational opportunities between the Han and other ethnic minority groups. Based on an examination of the conditions of the two groups and their relation with the Han nationality, the authors speculate that the promotion of bilingual English-Chinese education for the Han language speakers and making it a requirement for social, economic and political advancement for all citizens of China will further polarise and disadvantage the already marginal communities by creating additional obstacles: 'English is exacerbating the educational inequities facing minority and Indigenous peoples, who already face significant educational and literacy disadvantages' (Beckett & MacPherson, 2005: 305).

Out of the second category of the writings comes the argument for lowering expectations for minority students' English proficiency. Strong calls are often made by educators and scholars, such as Cao and Xiang (2006) and Zhang (2002) to formulate special policies for minority students at all levels. One key part of the special policies they argue for is to lower the 'standards' as specified in the English Curriculum Standards (ECS). These calls, however, are usually based on claims that are hardly supported with empirical evidence, or only supported with *ad hoc* observations, and the consequences of the special policies, if made, are rarely discussed.

More recently, several empirical studies have been conducted in different minority-dominated regions and these studies form the third category of literature on English provision for minority groups in China. They include Adamson and Feng (2009), Blachford and Jones (forthcoming), Feng and Sunuodula (2009), Huang (2007) and Jiang *et al.* (2007). Feng and Sunuodula (2009), for example, focus on the 'policy cycle' by providing empirical evidence of the formulation and implementation processes of national, regional and local policies with regard to English language provision for three minority groups, namely, Yi, Zhuang and Uyghur. With a theoretical framework developed on the basis of policy studies, they have carried out an analysis of English language education for the ethnic minority groups, taking into account the functions of all agents and stakeholders in the policy cycle. In this chapter, as mentioned before, we focus on two widely made claims, i.e. that minority students often attach little value to English learning and that the current national drive for English language education will inevitably further marginalise minority groups in China. Are they empirically true?

Theoretical Concepts

To analyse our data, we have chosen to use critically the notion of 'cultural capital' put forward by French sociologist Pierre Bourdieu to explain the power relations between Uyghur and Han language in the current situation. According to Bourdieu (1977), cultural capital consists of ideas and knowledge that people draw on as they participate in social life. Everything from rules of etiquette to being able to speak and write effectively can be considered cultural capital. Bourdieu is particularly interested in the unequal distribution of cultural capital in stratified societies and how such inequality disadvantages people. This is especially true in schools and other institutions where ignorance of what the dominant classes define as basic knowledge makes it difficult for those in marginal or subordinate groups to compete successfully (Johnson, 2000). Uyghur students, for example, do not do as well in many school subjects because they lack the cultural capital presumed by the education system in which knowledge is essentially defined by the dominant group. Bourdieu refers to this lack as cultural deprivation.

By identifying language as an area in which power relations are created and exercised, Bourdieu (1977: 648) shows that the act of speaking does not merely involve exchanging information: 'language is not only an instrument of communication or knowledge but an instrument of power'. Bourdieu argues that the value ascribed to speech cannot be understood apart from the person who speaks, and the person who speaks cannot be understood apart from larger networks of social relationships – many of which may be unequally structured. The acquisition of certain types of socially valued linguistic behaviour may then allow a person to access additional resources that can be translated into material wealth. The ability to speak a language and use it in certain ways, therefore, signifies a measure or subcategory of cultural capital, i.e. the linguistic capital a person possesses (Bourdieu & Passeron, 1990). Although the notion of linguistic capital is coined by them primarily to explain the 'hidden mediations through which the relationship (grasped by our tests) between social origin and scholastic achievement is set up' (Bourdieu & Passeron, 1990: 116) in a given society, many educators make use of the concept to explore power relationships in social interactions where a powerful language such as English is used and/or taught as a second/foreign language (e.g. Abdullah & Chan, 2003; Lin, 1996; Norton, 1997).

Norton (1997), for example, extends Bourdieu's (1977) social theory into second language learning by questioning how relations of power in the social world affect social interaction between second language learners and target language speakers and proposes a theory of social identity that assumes power relations play a crucial role in social interactions between language learners and target language speakers. She introduces the notion of investment instead of second language learning motivation. The notion of investment attempts to capture the relationship of the language learner to the changing social world. It conceives of the language learner as having a complex social identity and multiple desires. The notion presupposes that when language learners speak, they are not only exchanging information with target language speakers, but they are also constantly organising and reorganising a sense of who they are and how they relate to the social world. Thus, an investment in the target language is also an investment in a learner's own social identity, an identity that is constantly changing across time and space. If learners invest in a second language, Norton (1997) points out, they do so with the understanding that they will acquire a wider range of symbolic and material resources, which will, in turn, increase the value of their cultural capital. Learners will expect or hope to have a good return on that investment – a return that will give them access to hitherto unattainable resources.

Norton's definition of the term identity is also worth noting here. Norton (1997: 410) refers to identity as the process of 'how people understand their relationship to the world, how that relationship is constructed across time and space, and how people understand their possibilities for the future'. She also takes the position, following West (1992), that identity relates to desire – the desire for recognition, the desire for affiliation and the desire for security and safety. In this view, a person's identity will shift in accordance with changing social and economic relations.

Furthermore, relevant to our discussion is Vaish's (2005) argument about the groups who have historically been linguistically 'subalternised' and have only now gained more equitable access to linguistic capital due to the market forces of globalisation. His argument is based on the notion of 'subaltern', a term popularised by Antonio Gramsci (1971) to refer to depressed groups in society that suffer from the hegemony of the ruling class. Vaish proposes the 'peripherist' view of English language use in India, which disagrees with those sociolinguists who think that English endangers local languages and perpetuates inequality. He sees this as Orientalism disguised as liberal sociolinguistics that, in fact, reproduces the inequitable distribution of linguistic capital and fails to acknowledge the tenacity of indigenous cultures in being able to maintain their longevity (Vaish, 2005). The way English is taught adds a domain to the multilingual/multiliterate repertoire of subalterns, a workplace literacy domain that can help them break the constraints of class and caste (Vaish, 2005).

This chapter makes use of all these concepts, namely, cultural capital, identity that is related to desire, and linguistic capital, other than the factors directly or indirectly related to economic or material reward, which are believed to be at play in second or third language learning. In the case studies of Uyghur university students[1] that we present in this chapter, we will analyse the data focusing on evidence that shows these factors at play. We chose to conduct the case studies at tertiary level for the obvious reason that, unlike many other regions, as the context section shows, most Uyghur students do not start learning English till they go to university. Our primary focus is on their perceptions of the third language, English, in relation to their home language and Chinese, the second language, their willingness to invest in the third language and the process of social identity negotiation and transformation (Olsson & Larsson, 2008: 10–11).

Case Studies

Our research was conducted following ethnographic research principles developed for education research (Hammersley & Atkinson, 2007; Spradley & McCurdy, 1972). We adopted this methodology mainly for the purpose of identifying perceptions and attitudes of students about the role of English and about the new form of bilingual or trilingual education, without assuming any consequences as a result of it. Ten tertiary students were chosen for two rounds of ethnographic interviews that involved a first round of minimally structured interviews followed by a second round of semi-structured interviews with a focus on emergent themes from the first round. The interviews were conducted in Uyghur. The findings of our research in respect to English language learning can be categorised under the following five subheadings, which are interrelated.

English as linguistic capital

One of the general questions asked in the interviews was to elicit interviewees' perceptions of the English language. The following answers are representative:

> English is an important language. It is a world language. ... It is important to know English for learning new and cutting edge academic knowledge and scholarly exchange. Many Han scholars publish their work in English. English dominates the academic literature published. (S-6, Uyghur male, first year MA in humanities)

> English is now a popular language in China. A few years ago, knowing Chinese was sufficient for getting a job. Now everyone

knows Chinese, so learning English gives extra qualification to get better jobs. (S-2, Uyghur male, fifth yearin social sciences)

I wanted to learn English because when I went to see my sister in Beijing where she was studying I came across her speaking English with some of her friends. I think English is easier to learn than Chinese. But my sister is now a teacher in Kashgar region and her English is wasted. (S-4, Uyghur female, fourth year in humanities)

As an MA student, the Uyghur male who gave the first quote viewed the language as the access to 'cutting edge academic knowledge and scholarly exchange', that is, the linguistic capital he needs to acquire to be able to participate in his specialised field successfully. In the third quote, the word *wasted* reveals all; her sister had gained the linguistic capital but failed to translate it into a life chance that usually goes with it. In all quotes, the importance of the language is perceived and the motivation to acquire it is obvious.

Though Uyghur students usually start English learning at a later stage than their Han counterparts, many set up high goals for themselves, e.g. to pursue studies abroad and to achieve the competence to access information through English:

I am studying English because I have a desire to continue my studies in a European country. I also want to learn about the world through the medium of the English language, rather than the limited and filtered information I get through the Han language. Europe has been leading the world in cultural and technological terms for hundreds of years and many important inventions were discovered by Europeans, for example, trains, Newton, Shakespeare, Dante, Rousseau, Picasso, these are just a few. (S-3, Uyghur male, fifth year in journalism)

I would like to go abroad to study if I get the opportunity. English is also a very important tool to learn about what is happening around the world, rather than reading about it in Chinese translation or reinterpretation. Knowledge of English has also become important for finding employment and being able to use computers. Teachers in my hometown (in Kashgar region) are required to have the knowledge of English and being able to offer English language classes. (S-1, Uyghur female, fifth year in sociology)

In addition to their high expectations, it is also worth noting that both interviewees wish to learn what is happening around the world through the medium of English directly, not through their second language, Mandarin Chinese. This suggests that, to the interviewees, the meaning of obtaining the multilingual and multiliterate repertoire goes beyond economic benefits to include socio-political and cultural gains.

Willingness to invest

Norton's (1997) notion of investment has great relevancy to the interview data we collected. The investment can be either in the form of time, through self-learning, or in the form of financial resources, by paying to attend private English learning lessons available in the market.

> I started studying English because I wanted to progress to Masters level programme. I also wanted to explore the possibility of studying abroad. English is the language of international contact and exchange. I studied English by myself, but also attended some private tuition. I did not even know the English alphabet when I started. (S-5, Uyghur male, majoring in humanities)

> Learning Uyghur, Han and English languages will provide me with greater employment opportunity. I learned English by myself but stopped when it became too hard. I would like to go abroad for visits if get the chance. I feel confident about finding employment and my knowledge of English will be an asset for that. (S-4, Uyghur female, fourth year in humanities)

Despite the difficulties the Uyghur female student in humanities found herself in, she made the time investment with the understanding that the value of her cultural capital will be increased.

Some may have even started cashing in on the demand for the language with their hard-acquired competence.

> I started learning English in 2002. I heard of English being offered to experimental classes (selected class for top performing students) only while at high school. I am now privately coaching Uyghur primary school children in English at home. (S-3, Uyghur male, fifth year in journalism)

Perceptions of languages at play

As a language with a long history, Uyghur is spoken by about 10 million speakers in Xinjiang and other countries such as Kazakhstan. Its culture in terms of literature, medicine, arts and music is among the most sophisticated in the world. Not surprisingly, in the interview data there is clear evidence of confidence in maintaining the Uyghur language and culture.

> I am confident that Uyghur language will survive in future and my aim of learning other languages is to learn the valuable aspects of other cultures. (S-1, Uyghur female, fifth year in sociology)

> I do not worry about the threat to Uyghur language and culture. Uyghur culture and language are well advanced and deeply rooted among the Uyghurs. Uyghur culture has had many influences on the Han culture in things such as food, dress, respect for the elderly. ... Uyghurs possess a well developed tradition of commerce and trading. This is also very important for preserving the Uyghur identity. (S-3, Uyghur male, fifth year in journalism)

This could be seen as an illustration of what Vaish (2005) calls the tenacity of indigenous cultures. However, because of the rapid increase of the majority Han population and its growing economic and socio-political influence on the region, many interviewees also showed anxiety about the status of minority groups in society and about their own future for lacking Mandarin Chinese competence. The same male student in his fifth year in journalism had the following to say:

> I am more worried about the great influx of Han immigration into Uyghur areas. This trend will have greater impact than the language assimilation policy. (S-3, Uyghur male, fifth year in journalism)

> Mandarin Chinese is a difficult language to learn. I am required to write my thesis in Mandarin Chinese. There is little originality and creativity in it because I don't have deep enough knowledge of Mandarin Chinese to fully express myself. What is happening is language assimilation, not bilingual education. Most lectures are about politics, Han China's history and culture. I can't relate myself to what was taught about Qing history. (S-6, Uyghur male, first year MA in humanities)

> I am very concerned about the overwhelming influence and pressure to learn Mandarin Chinese. Uyghurs are least knowledgeable in Mandarin Chinese compared with most other minority nationalities in China. I am not sure if I will be able to progress to Masters degree course when I finish my BA. (S-2, Uyghur male, fifth year in social sciences)

Decades of rigorous, top-down promotion of Mandarin Chinese language education does not seem to bring about the desired outcomes. The data as a whole suggest that the strong influence of the majority culture and the 'concealed assimilation' policy (Feng, 2007: 271–272) cause anxiety and even resistance, which may well be the major hurdles for minority students to learn the Chinese language they wish to acquire.

Surprisingly, when they talked about English language learning, most interviewees demonstrated a keen interest and there seemed to be a consensus that Uyghur students can perhaps have a real chance to compete with the majority Han counterparts when it comes to English.

> Uyghur children perform better than their Han counterparts in learning English because they are genuinely interested and motivated to learn it, rather than only interested in passing exams. I have now passed the Level 4 English language test for university students. Han people also recognize the Uyghur students' ability to learn new languages. (S-3, Uyghur male, fifth year in journalism)

> If a lecture is delivered in English and other factors being equal, Uyghurs can compete with the Han students. In the oral English language classes that I have recently attended, most Uyghur students perform better than their Han counterparts attending the same class, despite the fact that the Hans would have studied English at least seven or eight years longer than the Uyghurs. (S-5, Uyghur male, majoring in humanities)

Most interviewees agreed that the motivation to learn English among Uyghurs is very strong and this 'genuine interest' is not the same as in learning Mandarin Chinese. The intrinsic motivation to learn English shown in many interviewees, such as the two above, seems to be derived both from the desire to show their competitiveness or capability of learning and from the fact that English is not a compulsory subject for minority students and thus they learn it out of real interest. When combined, these two factors, as the interview data suggest, have brought about desirable outcomes.

Mother tongue and learning

To develop competence in a third language, a practical question often raised in China is: which language should be adopted as Zhongjieyu, i.e. the language used to teach and learn English in the classroom and in compiling textbooks for minority students. Many educators and researchers involved in teaching and researching minority students, such as Xiao (2003) and Xu (2000), argue that Zhongjieyu should be the students' mother tongue. However, in practice, the Chinese language dominates the classroom and text material for English teaching and learning. This mismatch is also evident in our data. For Zhongjieyu, the view expressed by the female English major was representative:

> Yes, I think the use of mother tongue as the explanatory language in classrooms and textbooks will bring about better results. Students can use the mother tongue to learn grammar, to recite vocabulary, and this helps memorise things easily. (S-9, Uyghur female, majoring in English)

Quite a few interviewees also commented on the correlation between creative thinking and the use of the mother tongue. They seemed to agree unanimously that the use of the second language as Zhongjieyu inhibits the thinking and learning process rather than facilitating it. However, one interviewee pointed out that:

> There is a practical problem here. In exams, there is always a part that asks us to translate English into Chinese. This is where Uyghur students who are not good at Chinese lose points (marks). What can you do? (S-7 Uyghur male)

The issue of Zhongjieyu is certainly not trivial according to these interviewees as they believe that the majority Han students benefit from the linguistic capital, but the use of Zhongjieyu limits minority students' options of learning strategies and affects their learning outcome as measured by high-stake tests.

Desires for equality and recognition in identity negotiation

The most striking evidence shown in our data is the interviewees' strong desire to be recognised in society and get equal opportunities to access the linguistic capital, usually English in their perception. This is in correspondence to Norton's (1997) and West's (1992) conception of identity that relates to such desires. The following quotes are representative:

> Uyghur children perform better than their Han counterparts in learning English because they are genuinely interested and motivated to learn it, rather than only interested in passing exams. I have now passed the Level 4 English language test for university students.

Han people also recognize the Uyghur students' ability to learn new languages. (S-3, Uyghur male, fifth year in journalism)

I very much welcome the opportunity to study the subjects in English. This will provide both Han and Uyghurs with the same starting point and equal footing and the Han student will get the taste of how it is like to learn subject knowledge in a foreign language. I think Uyghurs are better in learning languages. (S-5, Uyghur male, majoring in humanity subject)

When I was at primary and secondary schools, there was no English offered to us. So at the university, I had to learn English all by myself. I found myself quite confident. Unfortunately, I had to drop the language because of other pressures... However, I feel that if Uyghur students are put on equal footing with Han students, we can compete with them. (S-8, Uyghur female, fourth year in history)

As the quotes show, most of the interviewees were conscious of their minority status, but at the same time, in Vaish's (2005) words, they seemed to sense that the national drive to English education may be the opportunity for equitable access to the linguistic capital that is valued in today's society.

Discussion

As shown in the literature review section, the majority of authors who have written about the effect of the national drive for English language education on the linguistic minorities, such as the Uyghurs, have taken the view that it would strengthen the hand of the already powerful majority Han group as this group sets the rules and has access to vastly superior cultural and economic resources in achieving that goal. This would, in turn, further marginalise the linguistic minorities. Our data show that the Uyghur students at the tertiary level perceived the importance of the English language and were highly motivated to learn it, although they faced more difficulties than their Han counterparts because of the lack of or limited English education they received in earlier schooling. The origin of this motivation commonly shown in the students we interviewed can be too complex to trace; however, their strong desire for recognition and for equal conditions in education and their willingness to invest signify that they were trying to acquire a wider range of symbolic and material resources, which would increase the value of their cultural capital. Consideration for economic and material gains in second or third language learning, as argued by several authors reviewed above and by some policy makers, is not the only factor influencing the second or third language learning by linguistic minorities. The three elements related to social identity as seen by Norton (1997) are all at play here: how students understand their relationship to the world, how that relationship is constructed across time and space and how they understand their possibilities for the future.

As social groups, Uyghur and Han students are unavoidably situated in a dynamic power relationship that has significant influences on how they invest in linguistic capital. While the Uyghur students face great difficulty adjusting to learning their university subjects in their second language, Mandarin Chinese, they are aware that this puts the Han students in an advantageous position because of their linguistic capital. English, which is a foreign language for both groups, may provide Uyghur students with a real chance to balance this power relationship. Our data show that Uyghur students were aware of this and many invested heavily in the third language. This may explain why Faruk Mardan, the winner of Most Energetic Speaker award at the CCTV Cup English Speaking Contest 2008, was quoted in the introduction as saying figuratively, 'English is really new and it is like new blood in their [the Uyghur youth in Xinjiang] body'.

A related issue we wish to discuss is the question of whether there should be 'special policies' to set up English standards lower than those required by the NCS. This is a call often found in the literature but seldom debated. Of many issues listed in the literature (e.g. Yang, 2005), financial issues such as inadequate resources and lack of funding cannot justify the call as these problems can be and should be addressed gradually by a country that is fast developing economically. If the need to lower the standards is based on the argument that minority students attach low value to foreign languages and/or they face more cognitive and affective barriers than their majority counterparts in English language learning, this argument is clearly refuted by the data presented in this chapter. On the contrary, those interviewed showed strong motivation to learn the third language and they saw their strengths in learning it. Thus, we wish to re-state an argument we made elsewhere (Feng, 2008; Feng & Sunuodula, 2009) that, if minority groups are expected to be structurally integrated into the mainstream society, which is a widely acknowledged political objective, it is then misguided to make calls for lowering the standards. Those policies, once made, would not benefit the minority groups in any way, but would segregate them further from the mainstream society and put them on an unequal footing for life opportunities. Having restated our view, we also make it explicit that we do not argue against special policies that have proved necessary both nationally and internationally for minority groups, such as 'preferential policies' or positive discrimination in education (see Feng & Sunuodula, 2009). In the case of English provision, we agree with many other authors that special policies to provide additional funding, resources and incentives for minority regions are not only necessary but crucial. These policies can help create 'equal conditions' (Feng, 2008) for minority people to engage with the nation and the world.

Last but not least, the data indicate that the issue of Zhongjieyu, the language used to teach and learn English in the classroom and in compiling textbooks for minority pupils, should be further researched and debated. Research has already shown that the use of the mother tongue as Zhongjieyu is more effective in helping minority students to acquire a third language (Xiao, 2003; Xu, 2000). With respect to the cognitive dimension of learning, our interviewees agreed unanimously that the use of the mother tongue rather than Mandarin Chinese facilitates the thinking and learning process. While there does not seem to be any regulation or policy against the use of the mother tongue in English classrooms where ethnic minority pupils dominate and which are taught by a minority teacher of English, our data show that the use of the mother tongue in high-stakes examinations is unusual and this, to us, is clearly an issue that needs addressing. For minority students such as the Uyghurs whose mother tongue is an official language in the region, it can be speculated that when their home language is used not only for classroom teaching and learning, but also in high-stakes examinations, they will be less disadvantaged linguistically and more significantly, socio-culturally, they may well feel confident in maintaining their own linguistic identity and become empowered through learning a third language. Without a system that fully honours their home language in both learning and examination, this remains speculative.

Conclusion

Having reflected on our findings in terms of social identity, linguistic capital, policies and Zhongjieyu, we feel in a position to argue that, although having to learn a third language is an enormous challenge for minority students given the usually unfavourable conditions they are in, the challenge may not necessarily further marginalise them as many predict. Instead, for minority students, this situation could be a blessing in disguise. The situation could trigger minority students' motivation to negotiate their identity by investing in the linguistic capital and lead to debates among educators, researchers and policy makers on key issues in minority education. There is already evidence in the literature of language provision for minority students that the key stakeholders, as mentioned above, do not look at English education solely from the point of view of third language acquisition, but they also reflect on the role of the first language in relation to second and third language learning and the sociopolitical, cultural and economic dimensions of language use and language education. This may lead to repositioning of languages in classroom use and restructuring of curriculums, and impact on language provision for minority groups, which, indeed, has long been dissatisfactory.

Note

1. The university degree programmes normally lasts for four years in China, but it is five years for most minority students who are not proficient enough in Mandarin Chinese. Those students spend their first year learning Mandarin Chinese before proceeding to the formal degree programmes.

References

Abdullah, A.N. and Chan S.H. (2003) Gaining linguistic capital through a bilingual language policy innovation. *South Asian Language Review* 13 (1 & 2), 100–117.

Adamson, B. and Feng, A. (2009) A comparison of trilingual education policies for ethnic minorities in China [Electronic Version]. *Compare: A Journal of Comparative and International Education* 39 (3), 321–333.

Bastid-Bruguiere, M. (2001) Educational diversity in China. *China Perspectives* 36, 17–26.

Beckett, G.H. and MacPherson, S. (2005) Researching the impact of English on minority, and indigenous languages in non-western contexts. *TESOL Quarterly* 39 (2), 299–307.

Benson, L. (2004) Education and social mobility among minority populations in Xinjiang. In S.F. Starr (ed.) *Xinjiang: China's Muslim Borderland* (pp. 190–215). Armonk, NY: M.E. Sharp.

Blachford, D.R. (2004) Language spread versus language maintenance: Policy making and implementation process. In M. Zhou (ed.) *Language Policy in the People's Republic of China: Theory and Practice since 1949* (pp. 99–122). Norwell, MA: Kluwer.

Bourdieu, P. (1977) Economics of linguistic exchanges. *Social Science Information Sur Les Sciences Sociales* 16 (6), 645–668.

Bourdieu, P. and J.C. Passeron (1990) *Reproduction in Education, Society, and Culture*. London; Newbury Park, CA: Sage.

Cao, Y.N. and Xiang, X.H. (2006) Needs analysis of Yi students learning English. *Xichang Xueyuan Xuebao* 18 (3), 118–121, 127. (In Chinese)

Chen, X. (2008) Strengthening the achievement of bilingual education in Xinjiang and explore English language teaching for ethnic minorities. *Kaoshi Zhoukan*, 31, 89–91. (In Chinese)

China Central Television (2008) CCTV Cup English Speaking Contest. Beijing: CCTV International. On WWW at http://www.youtube.com/watch?v=hzngnZlR1. Accessed 16.4.09.

Cui, J. (2005) A study on bilingual teaching given to ethnic minority students of colleges and universities in Xinjiang. Unpublished MA Dissertation, Xinjiang Normal University. (In Chinese)

Feng, A. (2005) Bilingualism for the minor or the major? An evaluative analysis of parallel conceptions in China. *International Journal of Bilingual Education and Bilingualism* 8 (6), 529–551.

Feng, A. (2007) *Bilingual Education in China: Practices, Policies, and Concepts*. Clevedon and Buffalo: Multilingual Matters.

Feng, A. (2008) Trilingualism or Bilingualism, or Else? Language Use and Provision for Ethnic Minorities in China. A key-note speech given at the Conference on 'Capacity Building in Ethnic Minority Language Education' held on 19th April at Hong Kong University.

Feng, A. and Sunuodula, M. (2009) Analysing language education policy for China's minority groups in its entirety. *International Journal of Bilingual Education and Bilingualism* 12 (6), 685–704.

Gramsci, A., Hoare, Q. and Nowell-Smith, G. (1971) *Selections from the Prison Notebooks of Antonio Gramsci*. London: Lawrence & Wishart.

Guojia Tongjiju [State Statistical Bureau] (1998–2007) *China Foreign Economic Statistical Yearbook*. Beijing: Zhongguo Tongji Chubanshe. (In Chinese)

Guojia Tongjiju [State Statistical Bureau] (1997–2006) *China Labour Statistical Yearbook*. Beijing: Zhongguo Tongji Chubanshe. (In Chinese)

Guojia Lüyouju [State Tourism Bureau] (1998–2007) *Yearbook of China Tourism Statistics*. Beijing: Zhongguo Tongji Chubanshe. (In Chinese)

Hammersley, M. and Atkinson, P. (2007) *Ethnography: Principles in Practice* (3rd edn). London: Routledge.

Huang, B.L. (2007) An empirical study of teachers' perceptions of bilingual teaching in Guangxi. In A. Feng (ed.) *Bilingual Education in China* (pp. 219–239). Clevedon: Multilingual Matters.

Jiang, Q.X., Liu, Q.G., Quan, X.H. and Ma, C.Q. (2007) EFL education in ethnic minority areas in Northwest China: An investigational study in Gansu Province. In A. Feng (ed.) *Bilingual Education in China* (pp. 240–258). Clevedon: Multilingual Matters.

Jing, C.X. (2007) Take language teaching as a starting point to comprehensively implement education for cultivating talents. *Zhongguo Minzu Jiaoyu* 2, 30–31. (In Chinese)

Johnson, A.G. (2000) *The Blackwell Dictionary of Sociology: A User's Guide to Sociological Language*. On WWW at http://www.credoreference.com/entry/723631. Accessed 16.4.09.

Ju, J.N. (2000) An examination of the problems encountered in teaching beginning minority students at college. *Qinghai Minzu Yanjiu* 11 (3), 76–77. (In Chinese)

Li, D. (2005, 20 April) Improve educational environment and elevate the level of English language education of Ethnic minorities. *Xinjiang Ribao*. (In Chinese)

Li, Y.L. (2003) An analysis of the special characteristics of minority students in learning English. *Xinan Minzu Daxue Xuebao* 24 (8), 334–336. (In Chinese)

Lin, A.M.Y. (1996) Bilingualism or linguistic segregation? Symbolic domination, resistance and code switching in Hong Kong schools. *Linguistics and Education* 8 (1), 49–84.
Norton, B. (1997) Language, identity, and the ownership of English. *Tesol Quarterly* 31 (3), 409–429.
Olan, M. (2007) An investigation of the status quo of minority college students learning English. *Xinjiang Daxue Xuebao* 35 (2), 156–160. (In Chinese)
Olsson, J. and Larsson, T. (2008) Attitudes towards English as a Foreign Language in a multicultural context – a study carried out from the perspectives of identity, social context and future use. On WWW at http://hdl.handle.net/2043/5746. Accessed 29.3.09.
Spradley, J.P. and McCurdy, D.W. (1972) *The Cultural Experience : Ethnography in Complex Society*. Chicago: Science Research Associates.
Tsung, L.T.H. and Cruickshank, K. (2009) Mother tongue and bilingual minority education in China. *International Journal of Bilingual Education and Bilingualism* 12 (5), 565–580.
Vaish, V. (2005) A peripherist view of English as a language of decolonization in post-colonial India. *Language Policy* 4 (2), 187–206.
Wang, W.Z. (2000) An analysis of positive transfer of Zhuang in English acquisition. *Zhongnan Minzu Xueyuan Xuebao* 20 (1), 122–124. (In Chinese)
Wang, W. and Gao, X. (2008) English language education in China: A review of selected research. *Journal of Multilingual and Multicultural Development* 29 (5), 380–399.
West, C. (1992) A Matter of life and death + the question of identity. *October* 61, 20–23.
Wu, Y.M. (2002) An analysis of the barriers to learning College English encountered by minority students in Yunnan. *Yunnan Caijing Xueyuan Xuebao* 18 (6), 116–120. (In Chinese)
Xiao, X. (2003) An investigation of Yi-English bilingual teaching at the Xichang School for Nationalities. *Minzu Jiaoyu Yanjiu* 14 (2), 58–65. (In Chinese)
Xinjiang Uyghur Autonomous Region Government (2009) Xinjiang gaikuang (An over view of Xinjiang). (In Chinese) On WWW at http://www.xinjiang.gov.cn/. Accessed 8.5.09.
Xinjiang Weiwuer Zizhiqu Difangzhi Bianzuan Weiyuanhui (2000) *Xinjiang tongzhi: di 76 juan: Yuyan wenzi zhi*. Urumchi: Xinjiang People's Publishing House. (In Chinese)
Xu, J. 2000. Obstacles of Zhuang students learning English and their solutions. *Minzu Jiaoyu Yanjiu* 2, 72–75. (In Chinese)
Yang, J. (2005) English as a third language among China's ethnic minorities. *International Journal of Bilingual Education and Bilingualism* 8 (6), 552–567.
Zhang, Z.D. (2002) Formulating special policies for the development of western regions. *Jichu Jiaoyu Waiyu Jiaoxue Yanjiu* 11, 22–24. (In Chinese)
Zhao, X.J. (2004) Current status of ethnic minority education in Xinjiang and analysis of difficult points. *Qiushi* 11, 272–273. (In Chinese)
Zhongguo Shehui Kexueyuan Minzu Yanjiusuo and China Guojia Minwei Wenhua Xuanchuansi (1994) *Zhongguo shaoshu minzu yuyan shiyong qingkuang [Language Use among the Ethnic Minorities in China]*. Beijing: Zhongguo Zangxue Chubanshe. (In Chinese)

Index

Adamson, B. 1, 8, 24, 26, 27, 28, 29, 40, 56, 73, 75, 102, 152, 153, 154, 155, 157, 160, 161, 163, 165, 212, 267, 269
Affective 138, 268, 279
Attitude 25, 38, 40, 56, 70, 74, 88, 136, 137, 138, 155, 162, 179, 195, 208, 218, 224, 230, 239, 253, 272

Beijing 27, 29, 32, 33, 35, 128, 135, 145, 153, 214, 228, 229, 231, 235, 252, 273
– Olympic Games (or Olympics) 29, 32, 35, 163, 212
Bilingual education (teaching or programme) 9, 12, 34, 38, 46, 48, 52, 53, 54, 55, 56, 57, 58, 59, 61, 62, 63, 65, 66, 86, 171, 214, 228, 229, 232, 234, 236, 261, 266, 268, 269, 272, 275
Bilingual policy 53, 60, 61, 62, 65, 116, 261, 268
Bilingualism 7, 10, 46, 47, 66, 143, 144, 228, 232, 267
– Additive 175, 184
– English-dominant 52, 58
– English-knowing (*see* English-knowing bilingualism)
– Subtractive 9, 63
Bourdieu, P. 14, 15, 63, 89, 248, 255, 266, 269, 270

Cantonese 95, 96, 97, 99, 100, 101, 102, 106, 107, 109, 110, 117, 121
China English (or Chinglish) xi, 24, 36, 37, 105
Chinese Communist Party (CCP) 28, 155, 232
Chinese language (Putonghua, Mandarin) xi, 2, 9, 16, 25, 59, 60, 61, 63, 75, 78, 87, 90, 96, 97, 101, 107, 110, 117, 121, 229, 232, 233, 234, 237, 239, 242, 245, 248, 249, 250, 252, 253, 255, 261, 262, 267, 276, 281
Cognitive development, advantage, factors, or theory 10, 136, 144, 145, 175, 178, 183, 208, 234, 266, 268, 279, 280
College English Test (CET) 34, 157, 192, 214, 221, 222, 226, 236
Communicative competence 63, 136, 137, 141, 160, 213, 225

Communicative Language Teaching (CLT) 136, 137, 141, 160, 161, 213
Compradores 24, 26, 152
Compulsory education 50, 79, 82, 98, 122, 134, 192, 196, 197, 208, 236, 265
Compulsory subject (English) 10, 53, 74, 122, 134, 163, 197, 208, 223, 236, 276
Confucianism (Confucius) 27, 153, 154
Cross-cultural awareness (knowledge) 9, 136, 137, 138, 139, 222
Cultural capital 14, 15, 88, 89, 231, 255, 266, 269, 270, 271, 274, 278
Cultural Revolution (China) 8, 28, 31, 40, 155, 161, 261

Dialect xi, 17, 26, 59, 60, 61, 63, 65, 117

English as a Foreign Language (EFL) 3, 7, 9, 10, 12, 14, 15, 80, 87, 89, 102, 103, 114, 115, 133, 135, 146, 148
English as a global/international language xi, 2, 3, 6, 11, 23, 85, 107, 119, 134, 146, 218, 222, 274
English as a Native Language (ENL) 2, 3, 9, 15, 114
English as a Second Language (ESL) 2, 3, 7, 10, 12, 14, 15, 86, 102, 103, 105, 106, 114, 148, 180, 185, 135
'English corners' 11, 16, 34, 214
English Curriculum Standards (ECS) 10, 11, 12, 13, 14, 133-149, 161, 162, 163, 165, 166, 170, 267, 268, 269
English-knowing (bilingualism) 4, 9, 11, 46, 52, 55, 58, 59, 65, 66, 127, 128, 213, 265
English Language Teaching (ELT) 71, 74, 79, 81, 83, 84, 86, 88, 109, 134, 136, 137, 139, 142, 148, 151, 152, 155, 156, 158, 160, 162, 164, 166, 171, 212, 213, 263, 267, 268
English syllabus 123, 124, 128, 139
Examination 39, 55, 87, 97, 98, 108, 123, 127, 128, 145, 148, 157, 159, 193, 198, 202, 205, 207, 223, 224, 225, 232, 238, 244, 248, 249, 263, 268, 280

Index

Examination-oriented approach (mentality) 11, 164, 165, 192, 225

Feng, A. xii, 1, 12, 13, 14, 40, 160, 232, 267, 268, 269, 276, 279, 280
(The) 'First Wave' 6
Functions of English 10, 25, 30, 33, 35, 38, 55, 106, 117, 119, 121

Globalisation 4, 6, 70, 85, 89, 105, 156, 162, 164, 228, 233, 267, 271
Greater China 1, 14, 73, 96, 97, 123, 128
Guangxi 8, 12, 13, 17, 151, 212-226

Hong Kong 1, 2, 3, 8, 9, 17, 53, 56, 95-110, 114, 116, 117, 118, 120, 127, 128, 151, 152, 162, 186, 264, 266
– 'Biliteracy and Trilingualism' policy 9, 96, 102, 107, 109
– Cantonese 95, 96, 97, 99, 100, 101, 102, 106, 107, 109, 110
– Chinese as the Medium of Instruction (CMI) 108, 110
– English as the Medium of Instruction (EMI) 107, 108, 110
– Hong Kong English 10, 103, 104, 105, 106
– Language Proficiency Assessment for Teachers' test (LPAT) 98, 102
– Medium of Instruction (MOI) 102, 103, 107, 108, 110
– Mixed code 103, 106
– Streaming policy 98, 107, 108, 110
– Typological differences 99, 101, 109
Human capital 235, 248, 255

Identity 14, 70, 256, 286, 271, 275, 277
– Cultural 14, 23, 228, 231
– Ethnic 64, 234, 267
– Linguistic 14, 17, 280
– National 47, 70, 75, 89
– Social 270, 271, 271, 279, 280
IELTS ((International English Language Testing System) 98, 99, 192, 193
Immersion (English) 11, 15, 16, 55, 82, 86, 169-186
Inequality 9, 11, 66, 88, 89, 165, 166, 208, 229, 235, 255, 270, 271
Internationalisation 8, 70, 78, 85, 160
Internet xi, 31, 32, 121, 223
– 'netizens' 32, 39

Japanese (language) 27, 35, 74, 75, 97

Kachru, B.B. 1, 2, 3, 5, 10, 17, 18, 25, 30, 33, 35, 72, 102, 103, 106, 115, 117, 119, 121

Language knowledge 138, 146, 164
Language skills 16, 29, 62, 73, 82, 87, 136, 138, 146, 147, 173, 190, 213
Learning strategy 136, 137, 138, 139, 142, 178, 196, 234, 277
Linguistic capital 14, 15, 16, 223, 266, 270, 271, 272, 273, 277, 278, 279, 280

Macao 1, 2, 8, 10, 25, 56, 103, 114-128, 151, 264, 266
– (The) Basic Law 116, 117
– Function of English 117, 118, 119, 120
– 'Gaming' 117, 118, 120
– Language policy 114, 115, 116, 128
– Macanese 117
– One Country, Two Systems 114, 116
– Portuguese 115, 116, 117, 118, 119, 120, 121, 122, 127
mainland China 1, 2, 7, 8, 15, 17, 23-41, 74, 89, 97, 114, 115, 118, 120, 133, 153, 168, 187, 215
Mandarin (*see* Chinese)
Minority
– Languages 17, 225, 232, 235, 237, 238, 262, 264, 267
– Regions or areas 13, 16, 40, 213, 224, 236, 267, 268, 280
– Schools 230, 262, 264
– Students or pupils 13, 14, 40, 228, 229, 230
Missionary schools (universities) 115, 153, 191
Modernisation 8, 28, 29, 37, 41, 75, 76, 78, 79, 90, 155, 157, 169, 170, 189, 212
Mother Tongue 2, 9, 13, 17, 46, 52, 53, 54, 56, 58, 59, 60, 61, 62, 63, 64, 65, 66, 75, 87, 90, 106, 107, 108, 109, 177, 225, 229, 237, 261, 267, 276, 277, 280
Multilingualism 3, 7, 17, 46, 53, 62, 144, 274

Native English speaker 12, 87, 117, 128, 158, 182, 206

(The) Pearl River (Zhujiang) Delta 8, 11, 95, 96, 114, 151, 165, 166
Perception 7, 11, 52, 73, 85, 191, 213, 223, 272, 274, 277
Popularity (of English) 4, 8, 9, 12, 28, 70, 76, 77, 87, 89, 154, 191, 192, 213, 215, 225
Private English schooling (kindergartens, schools, tutors, etc.) 7, 34, 52, 65, 81, 86, 87, 89, 90, 107, 121, 122, 123, 125, 127, 128, 155, 162, 194, 197, 214, 224, 228, 263, 265, 274

Proficiency (in English) 10, 29, 33, 52, 70, 71, 73, 75, 83, 84, 85, 86, 98, 99, 102, 107, 108, 109, 122, 123, 128, 145, 157, 175, 184, 185, 189, 194, 197, 198, 199, 200, 207, 208, 212, 213, 217, 22, 222, 226, 236, 238, 255, 269
Putonghua (*see* Chinese)

(The) Republican era 27, 152, 154, 155
Russian (language) 7, 8, 27, 28, 35, 155, 262

(The) 'Second Wave' 6, 151, 152, 155
Shanghai 8, 12, 15, 16, 27, 29, 33, 135, 153, 163, 189-209, 213, 214, 228, 231
– Inequality 208
– Social status 194, 195, 208, 209
– Socioeconomic status 194, 195, 196
– Suburban schools 204, 205
– Urban schools 204, 205, 207
– The World Expo (Shanghai) 29, 163
Shenzhen 151, 157, 158, 160
Singapore 1, 2, 3, 4, 7, 8, 15, 16, 17, 46-66, 72, 103, 106, 128, 171, 190, 217, 218, 219
– Bilingualism (English-knowing) 46, 52, 55, 56, 58, 59, 60, 65, 66
– Chinese (including 'dialects') 46, 52, 53, 55, 56, 57, 59, 60, 61, 63, 65
– English-medium school or education 52, 54, 56
– Indian 9, 46, 59, 60, 61, 64
– Malay 9, 46, 52, 53, 56, 57, 59, 60, 61, 62
– Multiculturalism 61, 62
– Singlish 15, 65
– Social stratification 64
– Streaming 48, 50, 53, 55
– Tamil 52, 53, 56, 57, 59, 60, 61, 62
Social class 59, 63, 64, 66, 194, 195, 208, 209
Social or ethnic divisiveness 16, 47, 52, 108, 109, 110
Socioeconomic status (factors) 63, 64, 65, 66, 76, 108, 194, 195, 196
South China (focusing on Guangdong) 11, 114, 151-166
– China Export Commodities Fair (Guangzhou) 11, 156
– China-ASEAN Exposition (Nanning) 12, 214, 215, 216, 217, 219, 220
Spread of English 1-18, 36, 86, 115, 121, 152, 156, 164, 166, 268

Taiwan 1, 2, 4, 8, 9, 15, 17, 56, 70-90, 102, 103, 107, 118, 264, 266
– American (influence) 75, 76, 77, 85, 88
– Bilingual English Programme (BEP) 86, 87, 88, 90
– Cram schools (Bu-xi-ban) 71, 82
– English Fever 70, 71, 73, 85
– General English Proficiency Test (GEPT) 77, 85, 86
– Language Training and Testing Centre (LTTC) 77, 86
Task-Based Approach (TBA), or Task-Based Language Teaching (TBLT) 16, 140, 147-148, 159, 160, 161, 162, 178
Teacher training 80, 83, 146, 158, 159, 160, 161, 165, 243, 245, 247, 263
Teaching resources 11, 83, 161, 162, 229, 230, 241, 242, 244, 249, 250
Textbook (English) 11, 40, 57, 83, 123, 134, 135, 140, 141, 142, 143, 159, 161, 162, 170, 174, 179, 180, 181, 182, 183, 198, 238, 240, 241, 244, 245, 246, 247, 249, 250, 276, 277, 280
(The) 'Third Wave' 4-7, 16-17, 152, 156
'Three (concentric) circles' 2-4, 12, 15, 106, 115
– Expanding circle 2, 3, 4, 5, 7, 25, 106, 115
– Inner circle 2, 3, 4, 7, 9, 36, 72, 73, 115
– Outer circle 2, 3, 4, 7, 9, 106, 115
TOEFL (Test of English as a Foreign Language) 192, 193
Tongwen Guan 27, 153, 166
Trilingual education 17, 224, 229, 233, 234, 235, 236, 237, 249, 255, 267, 268, 272
Trilingualism 9, 17, 96, 102, 107, 109, 229, 230, 232, 268

World Englishes 3, 10, 17, 103, 114
World Trade Organisation (WTO) 29, 136, 163, 212, 232

Xi'an 8, 11, 15, 171, 172-174, 184, 186
Xinjiang 8, 13, 17, 231, 260-281
– Uyghur 13, 14, 261-267

Yunnan 8, 13, 228-256
– Naxi 13, 229-231

Zhuang 12, 13, 17, 213, 224, 225, 226, 269

For Product Safety Concerns and Information please contact our EU Authorised Representative:

Easy Access System Europe

Mustamäe tee 50

10621 Tallinn

Estonia

gpsr.requests@easproject.com

www.ingramcontent.com/pod-product-compliance
Lightning Source LLC
Chambersburg PA
CBHW071158300426
44113CB00009B/1245